Irvine's

Writing about Music

Irvine's
Writing about Music

by Demar Irvine

THIRD EDITION

revised and enlarged by
Mark A. Radice

Reinhard G. Pauly, General Editor

AMADEUS PRESS
Portland, Oregon

Earlier versions of *Writing about Music* copyright 1956 by Demar Irvine;
second edition, revised and enlarged, copyright 1968 by the University of
Washington Press

ISBN 1-57467-049-2

Printed in Hong Kong

Amadeus Press
The Haseltine Building
133 S.W. Second Avenue, Suite 450
Portland, Oregon 97204, U.S.A.

Library of Congress Cataloging-in-Publication Data

Irvine, Demar.
    [Writing about music]
        Irvine's writing about music / by Demar Irvine. — 3rd ed. / revised
and enlarged by Mark A. Radice.
        p.   cm.
        Rev. ed. of: Writing about music.
        Includes bibliographical references (p.   ) and index.
        ISBN 1-57467-049-2
        1. Musicology. 2. Academic writing. 3. Report writing.
I. Radice, Mark A. II. Title. III. Title: Writing about music.
ML3797.I79   1999
808'.06678—dc21   98-45510
                                                          CIP
                                                           MN

Contents

PART THREE: COMBINING WORDS AND MUSIC

Reading maketh a full man,
conference a ready man,
and writing an exact man.
— FRANCIS BACON

Preface to the Third Edition

When we write about music, we are deeply obliged to communicate our enthusiasm for this great art. Though many of the composers and performers whose work we admire may be long dead, they are nevertheless a living and dynamic force in our lives. Their artistic visions rescue us from despair; their music, their expressions of sentiment, and their dedication to art illuminate our lives. To aspiring writers seeking to share their passion and knowledge with a wider public, Demar Irvine—an experienced musician, esteemed scholar, and beloved teacher—provided practical help and valuable insights in his manual *Writing about Music*.

Irvine earned his Ph.D. in music esthetics at Harvard University; in 1937 he joined the faculty of the University of Washington School of Music, where he became professor emeritus in 1978. He died in 1995, shortly after Amadeus Press published his monograph on Jules Massenet. Irvine had previously written *Methods of Research in Music* and, of course, the two editions of *Writing about Music*, in which he took up, among other topics, the mechanical details of scholarly writing: Where does the comma go, inside or outside of the quotation marks? Should I use the abbreviation "p." or "pp."? Irvine patiently answered these and hundreds of other questions in a lively and often humorous manner. It seemed to me a great pity to let his hard-hitting advice go by the wayside: Clearly a new generation of writers about music deserves ready access to the same sort of detailed guidance, and as a comparison of the 1968 edition and this new edition will show, much of Irvine's pithy prose remains unaltered.

In many ways, Irvine produced a document of historical musicology. Emily Anderson's translation of *The Letters of Beethoven*, for instance, which had just appeared in 1961 (at the time Irvine was preparing the second edition of *Writing about Music*) has since become the standard English-language version of those letters. Though this and other studies chosen by Irvine as models for the various formats of citation and documentation are now decades old, many have earned a place in the musicological hall of fame: They are classics of research, criticism, and interpretation—not to mention *writing*. I have retained many of these citations as well as supplying additional references to more recent sources. The music literature cited herein is, therefore, integral rather than coincidental. At the same time, I must stress that the present volume remains fundamentally a style manual, not an introduction to music research and bibliography.

In revising and updating Irvine's book, I generally took a conservative approach, giving special attention to recent developments that affect the way we write. Times have changed, and writing techniques at the dawn of a new millennium are not what they were in Irvine's day. The production, reproduction, and distribution of written materials, in particular, is drastically different; word processing, computer graphics, and desktop publishing were unknown at the time Irvine compiled his manual. Similarly, the formats of both recorded sound and recorded information are now astoundingly diverse—compact discs, videocassettes, and laser discs, Web sites, CD-ROMs, and other venues for the communication of ideas require somewhat different treatment from books and periodicals in notes and bibliographic entries.

Part Three of this book is entirely new. Irvine's manual was intended primarily for the development of a clear and effective prose style supported by concise and accurate documentation. When we write about music, however, we normally combine prose and music notation as though they were a single medium (creating this illusion is, at least, the intention of a skillful writer), and our language must be as precise as the musical notation that composers have set down in their scores. The writer who has acquired facility in applying the concepts explained in Part Three will progress beyond the tedious "bean counting" that so often debilitates scholarly prose to a style whose genuine substance engages the reader. Here too writers will find some guidelines for deciding whether to use a musical example or to describe the same musical structure or event in prose.

Scholarly writers often draw upon the research of others. It is often sufficient to acknowledge our indebtedness in a note; in certain instances, however, we incur both an ethical and a legal obligation to explain the extent to which our work is based upon the achievements of others. Every writer needs a basic understanding of the legal responsibilities of distributing information that has been fixed in some tangible form. Since copyright restrictions and limitations can significantly affect our writing and even our choice of topics, I have included as an appendix an overview of the copyright law of 1976 and its implications for writers. Chrysa Radice Lawson, Esq., very kindly read this "note" on copyright to ensure that it accurately reflected the law. Her numerous suggestions for legal interpretations and simplification of language in this new appendix will, I am certain, make it more useful to readers.

The students in graduate courses that I taught at Ithaca College actively participated in the proofreading, correcting, and updating of this revision of *Irvine's Writing about Music*. For their assistance, insights, and generous cooperation, through several rounds of drafts, I am deeply grateful.

Many colleagues on the faculty of the Ithaca College School of Music gave freely of their time and expertise. Though I cannot name each of these individuals here, I would note the particular assistance of Mary I. Arlin, Steve Brown, Merilee Nord, Timothy Nord, William Pelto, Marjorie Porterfield, and Dana Wilson for their diligence and meticulous attention to detail. I am grateful as well to Keith Eiten, of our library staff, for his help. Caroline E. Radice contributed the calligraphic illustrations, and I thank her for that fine work.

Murray Bradshaw (University of California, Los Angeles), Alfred Mann (Eastman School of Music), and Massimo Ossi (University of Rochester) read preliminary drafts of the sample paper in Appendix One. I appreciate their expert criticisms and have incorporated many of their suggestions into the present text.

To Reinhard G. Pauly and Eve Goodman of Amadeus Press I am grateful for many reasons: It was owing to their encouragement that I undertook the revision of this text in the first place. Furthermore, they made the necessary legal arrangements with the University of Washington and the estate of Demar Irvine to make my work on this project possible, and they scrutinized the text of my revision, not only with their usual care but also with that characteristic graciousness that has made my work with them over the years a genuine pleasure. A final round of improvements was made by Franni Bertolino Farrell, a third Amadeus editor. To her, I am deeply grateful.

A wise scholar once told me, "The only way to write clearly is to *think* clearly." Lucid writing is a sure indication of a perspicacious mind. We need not rely upon trial and error; the thoughtful application of carefully considered principles, as presented in this book, may frequently save us needless trials and help us to reach our goal—the expression of ideas—with rather few errors.

Mark A. Radice

Preface to the 1968 Edition

Writing about Music first appeared in 1956, without the luxury of a preface, and with 102 rules. For the present edition the material has undergone a thorough overhauling. Some attempt has been made to answer questions arising out of the use of the earlier edition. It is hoped that the present organization into major sections will make the book easier to use. In the new arrangement, Part One is devoted to details of style in the typescript, while Part Two (with much new material) attempts to provide helpful suggestions for the improvement of literary style.

Whoever becomes involved with music, whether as student, amateur, or professional, is bound sooner or later to want to discuss this fascinating art. Reading about composers, performers, and various musical subjects improves our knowledge, and certainly conversation with our friends offers a ready forum for exchanges of opinion. But for exactitude and permanence of expression there is nothing quite like *writing* about one's subject, as Francis Bacon so epigrammatically pointed out long ago.

This book is obviously intended primarily for students of music. There are no age limits restricting one's status as "student," nor does one ever really reach a saturation point where knowledge is concerned. The whole exciting paradox of life is that the more we know, the more new avenues are opened for further discovery. In the old days, when people kept extensive diaries and wrote long letters to one another, perhaps much more of each individual's personal development and intellectual growth got reduced to writing. Nowadays, we have to force ourselves just a little to take our pen in hand.

Students of music are typically too busy with *music* to do much writing about it. There is no reason, though, why we cannot learn to be bilingual: to speak directly music's own language, and also to express our thoughts and ideas in words. This latter activity brings its own special kind of satisfaction, a refreshing change of pace from always practicing, performing, composing, or for that matter just listening.

Where writing is concerned, it is often a question of overcoming inertia and *getting started.* We all have excellent ideas from time to time, but we tend to be, let us say, too lazy to put them down. With a little persistent concentration and effort it is surprising how soon one can begin to look upon one's literary products with a certain pride. The secret is to start with the techniques. It is the acquisition of technical skill that gives us a command over what we are doing. An analogy: for good progress in piano playing, is it not best to devote some attention to scales, exercises, and études? Does not the building up of technique open doors to accomplishment of broader goals, such as artistic performance?

To acquire technical skill, it is best to begin with a great many very short papers, on a variety of subjects. (Compare rule 231.) It is comforting if one can have a sympathetic critic looking over one's shoulder. As with any form of communication, we need an audience in order to judge how well we are getting across. Still, there is much that can be accomplished in quiet solitude, and it is here that the present manual is intended to be helpful.

The various "rules" (so called for convenience, not because they are inflexible laws) are consecutively numbered for ready reference and cross-reference. It is recommended that they be taken as one-a-day capsules—as a kind of supplement to your main diet, which ought to consist of the best books you can find and read on musical subjects that interest you. A gulp here, a gulp there, taken with reasonable frequency, is guaranteed to build up iron-poor literary blood.

Writing is never exactly *easy.* There is ample testimony to that by many of the best writers, who have been known to struggle for long hours over a single paragraph. In other words, there is always room for improvement. But the student who takes time to think consciously about principles, and to practice techniques, will learn to make his writing seem fluent and carry conviction.

Demar Irvine

PART ONE

Style in the Manuscript

Prelude to Part One

In the chapters that follow, we will be concerned mainly with issues of style. "Style" is a technical term used in the publications field to mean a consistent and acceptable manner of handling details of typography, spelling, punctuation, documentation, and the like, in books, periodicals, and other formats that rely upon printed text.

Any text that is intended to be typeset and printed is known as copy. Complete copy for a book or article, as provided by the author, is usually supplied to the publisher in two formats: as hard copy and on a computer-readable disk of some sort. Publishers refer to these documents as a manuscript, although technically speaking, the word is inappropriate since it combines two Latin words, *manus* ("hand") and *scribere* ("to write"); in the strictest sense, therefore, a manuscript is a handwritten document.

There are many different styles, and these styles, like fashions in general, tend to change over time. To assist authors in preparing manuscripts, publishers or individuals may provide manuals of style ranging in size from mere leaflets to respectable volumes.

An author preparing a document for publication in a specific periodical, or by a specific book publisher, should be guided in matters of style by the editor in charge of publication. It may save time and embarrassment to address a preliminary inquiry to the editor, who may provide an abridged style sheet or other helpful advice. For excellent general advice relevant to all disciplines, whether in the humanities or the sciences, *The Chicago Manual of Style* remains a most useful volume. It and several other interesting sources are described in the Bibliography at the end of this book.

The present style book is designed primarily as a guide for the final form of a typed or word-processed report, term paper, or thesis not being prepared for immediate publication. Such a document will be referred to hereafter as a manuscript. It is assumed that, in most instances, the manuscript will represent the ultimate and permanent shape of the paper. The rules here given will therefore serve the convenience of potential readers rather than the convenience of a typesetter.

The printed book, to which the reader is normally accustomed, serves as a general model for style in the manuscript; however, this manual suggests certain conventions that adapt book style to manuscripts. These are fully covered in the pages to come, and the beginner should conform closely to the specifications given. More experienced authors may find in printed books and articles many helpful hints on stylistic details that can be adapted to the manuscript. One must be careful, however, to avoid bringing together inconsistent procedures from different models, or adopting from older publications stylistic devices that are out of fashion.

The rules given here are not necessarily the only acceptable rules. For any given rule, one or more variants can usually be found. To avoid tempting the beginner into inconsistencies, this guide omits most of the variants. The most important rule is that, whatever the style adopted, the author must remain consistent.

This book covers most normal operations in preparing manuscript. If problems arise that are not discussed here, readers can follow the formal principles presented in the discussions of notes and bibliographic entries. If the problem remains unresolved, the writer may consult a more elaborate style manual, or seek the personal advice of someone experienced in these matters.

CHAPTER 1

The Draft

1   Draftsmanship

Very few writers, including professionals, attain the desired results in a
single writing. Almost any prose communication will go through several
revisions before it becomes presentable. Let your motto be this: Good writing means *re*writing! A common fault is to assume that the first version,
typed out in a burst of supposed inspiration, will represent the writer's
best effort, or that it will be read with any pleasure by anyone else.

2   The outline

Assuming that the research is completed, or at least well under way, select
a title, and work up in outline form a plan of presentation that is logical
and convincing. An effective outline is the key to successful organization
of a report. Professors will often refuse to supervise the writing of a thesis until the student has submitted an outline demonstrating a reasonable
grasp of the subject.

 The chief fault of an outline is that key words are mentioned as subjects, but usually without predicates. Hence it may not always be clear
what stand the writer intends to take.

3   The brief

As an alternative to the outline, the brief is recommended. A brief consists
of a series of positive statements, in sentence form, representing the main
flow of ideas to be presented in the report. Each sentence in a brief is
roughly equivalent to a topic sentence governing a whole paragraph or
section in the completed report. Writing the paper then becomes a matter
of amplifying, explaining, and illustrating the main ideas thus succinctly
stated. To control organization, adjust and rearrange the sequence of ideas
in the brief until everything falls neatly into place.

A brief is like an abstract save that the brief is formulated before the essay is written, whereas the abstract is condensed from the completed essay. If your report seems weak and unconvincing, begin by abstracting: Select the successive topic sentences or other governing statements, and place them in various sequences to determine the most coherent arrangement.

If this experiment fails to produce satisfactory results, it may be that the defective report has no skeleton to hold it together, or that the skeleton has no convincing shape. Start afresh with a crisply worded brief, and the revised report will be vastly improved.

4   Rough draft

The first attempt to expand the outline or brief into a full-fledged report will usually take the form of a rough draft. A rough draft is for the author's exclusive use: It should never be submitted to anyone else to read. As a private document, it may be as ragged or as neat as you like; however, never permit a rough draft to become so cluttered that you cannot readily make a clean and accurate copy from it.

5   Draft revisions

For most reports and term papers, the final manuscript is made directly from the rough draft. But if the writer has difficulty in controlling style—or better yet, if the proficient writer would achieve still greater proficiency—it is advisable to plan one or more clean drafts before arriving at the final manuscript.

Any draft that is to be seen by others must be fair copy—that is, typed or word-processed with double-spacing in the main text, clean and legible, and free from excessive written-in corrections. The print for a fair copy should be of high quality. Dot-matrix printers make a poor printout and should be avoided. Both ink-jet and laser printers produce attractive documents that are easy to read. Select a font, typeface, and size that are congenial to the eye.

For most typefaces, 12-point for the basic text is appropriate. Chapter headings may be in 14-point type. Remember that many college professors already wear glasses, and that your paper is probably one of about a hundred that he or she will read over a period of weeks. Your writing will have a much better chance of achieving its purpose if the reader does not have to struggle to decipher the text!

Avoid lightweight paper. Pre-trimmed pages, 8½ × 11 inches, are preferable to perforated continuous sheets. If you must use continuous sheets, be certain to trim and tear all the sheets neatly before submitting the report. Submission of untrimmed continuous sheets is an insult to your reader.

If two or three persons will be critiquing your work, be sure that all photocopies are complete and as neat as the original. In most cases, reviewers prefer unmarked copies so that they will not be influenced by the comments of some other reader. A thesis advisor, however, may wish to have all criticisms made on a single copy, which facilitates their incorporation into the final version. Allow ample margins on all sides for this purpose. Be certain, too, that the pages are clearly numbered.

6 Criticisms of the draft

Theses always, term papers sometimes, and reports occasionally, need to be submitted in draft form for criticism. Put the word "draft" prominently at the top of the first page, as an invitation to the reader-critic to mark up the copy freely. A conscientious critic may write corrections and insertions above the line or in the margin, with a caret to show the exact location; cross out or enclose in brackets, with a "delete" sign in the margin, material that should be removed; and query (?) in the margin those places where your wording does not communicate, or where the validity of a statement or the logic of an argument is debatable. Queries are an invitation to the writer to engage in self-analysis. A critic may put "not clear" where you fail to communicate, "No!" where your facts or reasoning are wrong, or an occasional "Good!" where praise is merited.

A reader-critic may also make marginal comments, or an extended commentary on a separate sheet. Remarks addressed to the writer may be circled or prefaced with such words as "Read:" or "Put:"—making it clear that what follows is a recommended rewording of the text. Extensive rewordings or insertions may be made on separate sheets—and the paper itself marked with such directions as "substitute A" or "insert B." Consider supplying blank sheets along with the report for these purposes. Otherwise the critic may simply write on the backs of your typed pages.

If for some reason your manuscript should not be marked up, make this clear to the reader-critic orally or in an attached note at the top of the first page. In this case, the conscientious critic will draw up a separate report for you. Items or passages commented upon may be identified in various ways: "p. 2, line 6"; "p. 5, lines 16–23"; "p. 8, 3d par." It is a courtesy to supply extra sheets of paper for this purpose.

7 Editorial symbols

Alterations and insertions, if they are brief, may be written legibly above the line involved. If more space is needed, use the margins. Put a caret (^) at the exact place in the text where an interpolation is to be made.

Pay close attention to the details of the following conventional editorial markings; some of the shorthand indications—such as the symbols for "incorrect spelling" and "spell out the word completely"—are quite similar:

9̸	delete what has been crossed out or bracketed
∧	insert marginal addition
stet	let it stand; material crossed out should be put back in
ital	underlining: italicize these letters or words
caps	double-underlining: capitalize these letters or words
sc	use small capitals
lc	use lowercase letters where capitals have been crossed out with a slanting stroke
(|)	add parentheses where indicated
ꞇ|ꞅ	delete parentheses where indicated
[|]	add brackets where indicated
ꞇ|ꞇ	delete brackets where indicated; some readers will put brackets around a passage in your text merely to define its limits and will then suggest an action in the margin, such as "delete" or "clarify"
¶	start a new paragraph
no ¶	do not start a new paragraph, but run in as a continuation of the preceding paragraph
⋕	leave proper space
⅃	faulty alignment: move to the right
⊏	faulty alignment: move to the left
⅃⊏	center
⌐¬	move up

⌞⌟	move down
⌒	less space
⌒	close up entirely; no space
∽	transpose letters or words into proper order; if words to be transposed are widely separated, numerals above the words indicate the proper order
〰〰	wavy underlining: use boldface type
〰〰	short marks through an underscore: do not underline (italicize)!
(?)	query author
sp	correct the spelling
(sp)	spell out abbreviations or numerals

Note the following marginal signs for inserting punctuation:

⋀,	comma
⌵	apostrophe
⌵	quotation mark
-⋏	hyphen
$\frac{1}{N}$	en dash
$\frac{1}{M}$	em dash
;⋏	semicolon
:⋏	colon
⊙	period
?⋏	interrogation point

8 Final draft

If you intend to type your own report, term paper, or thesis, you may proceed from any of the drafts previously described directly to the final manuscript. But if the final keying-in is to be entrusted to a professional typist, there should be a version identifiable as a final draft, representing as closely as possible an exact model of what is to appear in the finished manuscript. Typists are not mind readers: The neater the final draft, the fewer will be the typist's distractions, and hence the greater the probability of a perfect manuscript. A clean final draft will also expedite the typist's work and, consequently, reduce the fee for the completed work.

Regardless of how neat the final draft is, the author absolutely must proofread the finished manuscript. Although spell-check programs are helpful in spotting obvious errors (see rule 55), many less obvious errors will surface with careful proofreading.

CHAPTER 2

The Manuscript

9   The appearance of the page

The manuscript should make a positive impression on the reader. Spelling, grammar, syntax, and other constructive elements should be in good order; see Chapter 4 for most of the relevant rules of punctuation. Always read over the completed manuscript and correct any inadvertent errors.

The imperfect manuscript distracts the reader beyond all proportion. The imperfections will command the reader's attention, and the message of the text will be lost because of these irritants. The perfect manuscript, on the other hand, miraculously melts into the background: The reader no longer notices the mechanics, but concentrates instead on the content.

10   Paper

Type on one side only of good, white paper, 8½ × 11 inches. Never use textured or tinted paper. The variations in textured papers result in corresponding variations in print reproduction. Remember: The paper carries expository prose that is intended to communicate data and explain ideas. It is not wallpaper, selected for its aesthetic quality. Similarly, for as many readers who find salmon-pink paper attractive, an equal number will find it disconcerting. Classic matte white paper is always a safe selection.

When writing essays for academic institutions as part of a degree requirement, authors must be aware of regulations prescribing the quality and weight of paper, as well as the number of copies to be furnished. In some cases, the office of graduate studies will insist upon retaining the original printout rather than a photocopy. The reason for this demand is simple: Should other scholars need a copy of the document, photo reproductions made from the original will presumably have a higher resolution than second- or third-generation copies. Nevertheless, ink-jet print will run if liquid is spilled on it or if it is subjected to significant moisture; photocopies will not. Similarly, musical examples, illustrations, or other items pasted onto the original may become loose as the document ages and the glue dries and flakes. In practice, a high-quality photocopy is often more durable than the camera master.

11   Typing

The body of the text should be double-spaced throughout, except for blocked quotations, which may be single-spaced. Notes and bibliographic entries should be single-spaced. Term papers ordinarily do not include prefaces, introductions, abstracts, or other front matter, but when these optional elements are included in theses and dissertations, they should also be double-spaced.

12   Typefaces

Modern word-processing programs have put a vast array of type fonts, styles, and sizes at the writer's disposal. When you select a typeface, clarity and visual appeal should be your main considerations. Avoid eccentric or exotic typefaces.

The two basic type styles are serif and sans serif. Serifs are thin lines attached to the top and/or bottom of a letter. Absolute clarity and accuracy were required in the handwritten diplomatic documents of times past; serifs were the lines left by the nib of the ink pen as the scribe set it to the paper, applied a gentle pressure, and began to draw each line of a particular character of the alphabet. Modern technology—and here the word "modern" would even include a typewriter—has eliminated the need for serifs. All the same, these lines are generally horizontal and consequently impart to the type a visual flow comparable to that of an elegant cursive script.

Roman typefaces include serifs; Gothic styles are sans serif. For manuscripts and printed books, Roman type is preferred, but Gothic type may be used when a particular shape, such as a U-shaped corridor, is being identified in the discussion.

Most text should be in 12-point Roman type. Typefaces such as bold-face, small capitals, and italics have specialized applications in expository writing. The proper use of particular typefaces will be discussed later. The important point to make here is that these typefaces should not be used whimsically. Italic print may be appropriate for wedding invitations, but it creates a fussy, unprofessional appearance when used incorrectly in scholarly essays.

One final consideration in selecting a typeface has to do with word processing and word-processing programs. Certain fonts, such as Courier, Times Roman, or Helvetica, are installed on most programs. If you will be using different word processors or sending your disk to someone who may not have the same programs that you have, select a generic typeface. This consideration is particularly important if your hard copy is to be scanned and transferred to a disk. Character recognition is quite accurate when the scanning equipment is reading a simple font like Courier. That accuracy decreases significantly as the typeface becomes more elaborate.

13   Spacing, headings, subheadings

In a general way, the spacing in the manuscript serves as a substitute for different sizes of type. Double-space the main body of the text throughout. Single-space matter that would be set in smaller type in a book, such as notes, long direct quotations, and the like. Triple-space following the byline. Leave three spaces above a heading so that readers will easily spot the change in focus that takes place in the discussion. One space after the heading is sufficient; it is not necessary to leave additional space following a subhead. Likewise, no paragraph indentation is needed after a heading or subheading. Avoid the old-fashioned practice of inserting spaced, centered asterisks instead of headings and subheads.

Headings and subheads should be flush with the left margin. Do not center headings or subheads; such unnecessary details in layout could create problems if the document is printed on equipment other than that on which it was created.

Headings and subheads are essentially the guiding, topic words of an outline. When headings and subheads are transferred from an outline to the context of an essay, their hierarchical arrangement should be retained. Apply boldface to the basic font size for heads; use the basic font size in italics for subheads. If at all possible, avoid going beyond three levels of headings (see rule 208).

14   Marks of punctuation and other signs

,	comma
;	semicolon
:	colon
.	period
-	hyphen; for compound adjectives, names, and

	noninclusive numbers, such as serial numbers and account numbers
–	en dash; shows inclusive numbers, as in a range of years
—	em dash; indicates a disruption of sentence structure caused by an abrupt change in thought
——	two-em dash; with instruction <2M>, indicates missing letters in a word; often for vulgarities, such as the word "f——"
———	three-em dash; with instruction <3M>, indicates an entire word is missing
?	question mark
!	exclamation point
" "	quotation marks
' '	single quotation marks
*	asterisk
&	ampersand
/	virgule
		vertical episema
( )	parentheses
[ ]	brackets
¨	dieresis (English); umlaut (German); tréma (French)
´	acute accent
`	grave accent
^	circumflex
ç	c with cedilla (French, Portuguese)
ñ, ã	letters with tilde (Spanish); til (Portuguese)
. . .	ellipsis; three ellipsis points or dots, one space between each
...	suspension points; three unspaced dots

. . . .	leaders; used in tables (including table of contents), two spaces between each
_____	underline (underscore)
1 2 3	Arabic numerals
I II III	Roman numerals
i ii iii	small Roman numerals
^{1}	superscript (above the line)
$_1$	subscript (below the line)

Most word-processing programs include a variety of options for obtaining non-English characters as well as diacritical marks and special symbols. Modifier keys (such as the shift, option, and control keys on Macintosh programs and the alt and F keys on IBM programs) are pressed in prescribed combinations to create these characters. Some programs include a key caps function that displays all available options on the monitor.

15   Margins

Generous margins not only improve the appearance of the page but also provide room for written comments or revisions. All four margins should be at least one inch. Provide a larger left-hand margin if the document is to be bound.

Note: Margins must be maintained for *all* pages. Musical examples, charts, graphs, tables, or other illustrative materials may not spill over into the margin.

A right margin in perfect alignment (as in books) is called a justified margin. To obtain a justified margin, the spacing of words and letters is altered by the word-processing program. A ragged, or unjustified, margin, on the other hand, preserves the same point spacing for all characters and words. Most word-processing programs allow either a justified or a ragged format, but justified margins often create format errors when transferred to different computers. The ragged margin is more reliable.

16   Paragraph indentation

Indent the first sentence of each paragraph one-half of an inch. The paragraph indentation should be set as a tab to ensure that it will be consistent throughout the text. Note: Paragraphs following headings or subheads need not be indented. The practice of separating paragraphs by triple spacing, thereby avoiding indentation of the first line, is appropriate only for business letters and other brief documents. In texts of any length, these additional blank lines can add many unnecessary pages to the manuscript.

17   Recessed left margin for single-spaced matter

Type with single-spacing such matter as would normally appear, in a book, in reduced type: long direct quotations, including poetry, or other extended verbal matter introduced by way of illustration. Recess the left margin two spaces: The single-spaced matter should have a new margin two spaces wider than the normal margin. Allow an additional space for paragraph indentation.

18   Note format

Most word-processing programs offer the convenience of automated documentation. Upon command, the program will insert a note at the indicated point in the text.

You can treat the notes either as footnotes or endnotes. If your notes are generally quite brief, footnotes will be more convenient for the reader who wishes to identify the sources of information. In many cases, though, footnotes may run on for several sentences, paragraphs, or even pages. When lengthy notes are forced into a footer position at the bottom of the page, they begin to spill over into subsequent pages, thereby violating their status as *foot*notes. In such cases, it is better to place the notes at the conclusion of the manuscript.

A thesis, dissertation, or other extensive document will probably require many notes, some of which will be both complex and lengthy. In such cases, it will be more convenient to place the notes at the end of each chapter.

Regardless of the position of the notes, the format should be the same. See rule 73 for details.

19   Hanging indentation for bibliographic entries

In a hanging entry, the first line is flush, and all subsequent lines are indented. This format is standard for bibliographic entries, where the first line (usually beginning with the author's last name) is flush, and subsequent lines of the same entry are indented several spaces (see rule 117).

20   Page numbers

Never use punctuation or ornamentation of any kind with page numbers. Front matter, such as the table of contents, acknowledgments, and introduction, are customarily compiled after the main work numbered in consecutive Arabic numbers, in which case these pages may have an independent pagination, in lowercase Roman numerals.

Beginning with the first page of text, use Arabic numerals consecutively throughout the rest of the manuscript, including any appendixes, bibliography, and index. Numbers may appear either at the top or bottom of the page.

If you elect to place numbers at the top, then you may omit the page number on any page that bears a display title (first page of a report; first page of each new chapter in a thesis), thus leaving an unencumbered space above the title. Alternatively, you may place the number in the footer area at the bottom of the page.

If top placement is used and numbers are omitted, the page is nevertheless counted in the consecutive numbering. Such pages are called blind folios.

21   Title page

A thesis, which will be a bound, permanent record analogous to a book, should have a title page. A report, which is analogous to a periodical article, should omit the title page.

22   End pages

As a courtesy, include one or two blank pages at the end of the manuscript to receive the comments of the person who is to read and criticize it.

23   Cover

Reports of up to twenty or thirty pages are most easily handled without a cover. Simply clip the loose pages together with a paper clip. Do not staple them.

Longer reports and term papers may be bound in a flexible bindercover bearing the title and author's name, together with other suitable identification. Decorations of any sort on the cover give a juvenile, unprofessional appearance; avoid them. Do not use extraordinarily large print or a different typeface from that used elsewhere in the essay.

CHAPTER 3

Titles, Captions, Legends

For reports and term papers, a title page is not necessary. Put the main title and byline on the first page of text, with sinkage (extra space at the top of the page), as here described.

24   Main title

Put the main title, centered, using the standard procedure for capitalization. Like headings and subheadings, the main title should appear in the same font style as the body of the text, but it should be a slightly larger point size (14-point if the main text is in 12-point) and in boldface. Do not follow the title with terminal punctuation. Long titles may be laid out in two or more double-spaced lines, preferably of unequal length, with each line centered.

Never underline your main title for emphasis; however, foreign words or titles of published works appearing within your title should be italicized (underlined). Subtitles should be introduced with a colon, as in the following example:

Twelve-Tone Techniques in the Music of Stravinsky:
An Analysis of Agon and Threni

25   Byline

The byline follows the main title and is also centered. In old-style publications, the word "by" actually introduced the author's name on the following line of text. More recent practice, however, simply centers the author's name beneath the title, without any terminal punctuation. Use the same font style and point size that is used for the body of the text. Leave a triple-space between main title and byline, and between byline and first line of text.

26 Book review

The recommended principal heading (main title) is simply "Book Review." The byline should follow the principal heading with the standard byline spacing just described.

The book description is essentially a modified bibliographic entry (see rule 76). Note the following differences: author's name in normal order, first name first; double-spaced type; all lines flush with left margin. Drop a triple-space below the book description and begin your review, with normal paragraph indentation. At the end of the review, drop a triple-space below the last line and type your name flush with the right margin.

27 Captions

A caption is a brief explanatory heading or remark placed immediately *above* a musical example, table, chart, diagram, or other illustrative material. Captions should use normal sentence capitalization even though captions do not form grammatical sentences as such. Punctuation is used only to clarify the meaning of the caption; terminal punctuation is optional. Foreign words or titles appearing within a caption should follow appropriate conventions: Foreign words and distinctive titles of large works require italics (underlining), generic titles simply use initial capitals. A caption consisting of two or more lines should be single-spaced. If specialized information is included in a caption, it should appear in parentheses:

Plate 2b. Christopher Wren drawing showing the floor plan of a theater. (By permission of the Warden and Fellows of All Souls College, Oxford.)

28 Legends

A legend is similar to a caption; however, legends consist of complete sentences. Since legends tend to be longer than captions, they are placed *below* the illustrative item. Legends normally will run beyond a single line of text, and they should be single-spaced. The example of a caption just given would read thus recast as a legend:

Plate 2b. The drawing shown is by Christopher Wren. The layout is a plan for the interior of a theater, possibly that of the Theatre Royal at Drury Lane. Note that the seating on the parterre meets the front of the stage; hence, the design was not intended to accommodate musicians in an orchestra pit. (By permission of the Warden and Fellows of All Souls College, Oxford.)

CHAPTER 4

Punctuation

The main purpose of punctuation is to impart clarity; the finer points of punctuation are therefore a matter of personal preference. But where your meaning is not clear to the reader, be prepared to forgo personal preference in favor of clarity of expression.

29   Sentence construction

Effective punctuation depends upon an understanding of how sentences are constructed. Short, simple sentences that contain little more than a subject and predicate may require only a period at the end, but longer sentences that include introductory phrases, subordinate clauses, or similar enrichments will require some internal punctuation.

30   Apostrophe

Use 's to form all possessive forms of a singular person, entity, or idea. The terminal letter of the word—whether "s" or "z"—is of no consequence. For plural nouns ending in "s," follow the "s" with an apostrophe:

> The boys' and girls' repertoire consisted almost entirely of Tudor church music by John Farmer.

Use 's for plurals of single letters: p's and q's. Apostrophes may also indicate omitted letters in contractions. Note: Avoid contractions in scholarly writing.

31   Brackets

Square brackets serve three basic functions: enclosing interpolations in quoted matter; supplying missing data, especially in bibliographic references; or substituting for parentheses within parentheses.

32   Colon

The appearance of a colon calls attention to what follows: a quotation or an example, a series of items, or an epigrammatic summation of ideas. The colon can also introduce amplification or explanation of an idea. If the information following the colon is a sentence fragment, a couple of words, or just a single word, use a lowercase letter. If the explanation following the colon is a complete sentence, begin with an uppercase letter:

> Nineteenth-century composers devised new formal plans: The pairing of a slow *cavatina* and a fast *cabaletta* (as in Verdi's "Ah, fors'è lui che l'anima" and "Sempre libera" from *La traviata)* became the preferred design in early Romantic opera.

Beginning a full sentence with a capital is especially important when the colon introduces a blocked quotation.

33   Comma

Put a comma before the words *and, but, for, or, nor,* and *yet* when these conjunctions join independent clauses. If the clauses are very long and internally punctuated with commas, use a semicolon.

Nonrestrictive modifiers are words, phrases, or clauses that are not essential to understanding the meaning of the substantive they describe. Nonrestrictive modifiers should be set off with commas:

> Rossini, who was a wealthy man at the time of his death, is best known for his opera *Guillaume Tell* (1829).

Restrictive modifiers, on the other hand, are words, phrases, or clauses that specify the meaning of the word modified. Restrictive modifiers should not be set off with commas:

> To finance the construction of the Bayreuth Festspielhaus, Wagner required a patron who was a wealthy man.

See also rules 214 and 225.

An appositive is a word or group of words placed beside some substantive. The word or word grouping bears exactly the same meaning as the noun beside which it is placed:

> Beethoven's last symphony, the Ninth Symphony, was completed in 1824.

Since "last symphony" and "Ninth Symphony" designate the same piece, the appositive should be set off by commas. Remember that the term "appositive" comes from two Latin words, *ad* ("to," "at") and *ponere* ("to place"). An appositive is therefore a word *placed beside* another word that means the same thing. Appositives are very much like parenthetical explanations, clarifying a word or phrase that might be unfamiliar or unclear to the reader.

In enumerating a series of three or more items, put a comma (a serial comma) after each item, and also before the "and" or the "or" that precedes the last item. The final serial comma is especially important in clarifying accepted pairs or groupings. Imagine the confusion that might arise from a sentence like this:

> Some of the greatest creative artists for the lyric stage were
> Lerner and Loewe, Rodgers and Hammerstein and Sondheim.

The use of commas where several adjectives precede a noun must be considered carefully. Merely putting a comma after each adjective is often unnecessary:

> Berlioz's *Symphonie fantastique* is an early Romantic orchestral
> masterpiece.

Here the three adjectives in the series describe one another. The effect of the three adjectives upon the noun is therefore cumulative; commas are not needed.

When the adjectives preceding a noun modify the noun only—but not one another—use a comma to separate them:

> The interlude played by the shepherd boy in Act I of Wagner's
> *Tannhäuser* was written for a single, double-reed instrument.

The comma in this example makes it clear that there is only one instrument and that the instrument is a double-reed instrument. Another test: See if you can reverse the adjectives without altering the sense. If so, no comma need separate the adjectives.

34 Dash

The most common of the several types of dashes is an em dash, which separates a parenthetical remark or an aside from the rest of the sentence. Such an aside does not have to be a complete sentence. In many cases, the words set apart by the dash are grammatically and syntactically unrelated to the main sentence. Whenever possible, reserve the parenthetical remark until the end of the sentence so that only one dash is needed. A pair of em dashes may sequester a mid-sentence aside from the surrounding material. Each em dash should be closed up tight with the words it separates.

The purpose of an en dash is to show a range from one point to another—pages in a book, days in a month, years in a lifetime. If your word-processing system cannot create en and em dashes, use two hyphens to represent an en dash and three hyphens to represent an em dash. The following example should clarify the difference between en and em dashes:

> The life of Robert Schumann (1810–1856) effectively "ended" in 1854—when he was committed to a mental asylum in Endenich.

Two-em and three-em dashes are rarely used in expository prose; nevertheless, the skillful writer should understand their proper use. Both represent omissions: The two-em dash is used before or following a letter or several letters of a word that is left incomplete. The three-em dash is used when an entire word has been left out—presumably one that the reader will easily be able to supply.

35 Ellipses

Ellipses consist of three spaced ellipsis points (or dots) and are used to indicate the omission of material from a direct quotation. Leave one space before the first dot and another space after the last. If the omission occurs after what might stand as a complete sentence, the ellipsis follows the sentence period:

> An ellipsis . . . is used to indicate the omission of material. . . . Leave one space before the first dot and another space after the last.

Authors must exercise good judgment when using ellipses. Clearly, the intention is to preserve the content of the original passage, but to shorten it for the given context. It is not necessary to put an ellipsis at the end of a cited quotation. For more details, see rule 197.

36 Exclamation point

Exclamation points usually indicate an interjection or a statement in the imperative mood; if used sparingly, however, they can call attention to an ironic statement. A bracketed exclamation point can also substitute for the Latin term *sic* (see rule 195), indicating an error in the original source consulted:

> The premiere of Handel's *Rinaldo* in 1911 [!] was, according to the instructor, a watershed date that we all were expected to remember.

The effect of using *sic* or even the less-intrusive bracketed exclamation point to call attention to each error can become disconcerting. As an alternative—especially in general as opposed to scholarly writing—explain the error or, in some situations, simply correct it.

37 Hyphen

Hyphens are different from dashes—even though many writers confuse the two. Hyphens are used to *join* elements; dashes are used to *divide*.

A common use of the hyphen is for connecting surnames. Given names too, particularly in French usage, are frequently joined with a hyphen: François-Joseph Fétis, for example, is the full name of the influential Belgian theorist. The French style of hyphenation should be preserved even when initials are used: F.-J. Fétis.

Hyphens frequently connect two words, the second of which is a noun, to produce a compound word modifying another noun:

> Nineteenth-century operas seldom drew on Italy's literary heritage.

Compound numbers between twenty-one and ninety-nine require hyphenation.

Hyphens are useful with certain prefixes and suffixes, especially where ambiguity or awkward letter combinations would otherwise occur (*pre-existing; self-appointed; bell-like*).

Open compound words may first acquire a hyphen and later become one word (*cook book; cook-book; cookbook*). The status of any particular compound will vary according to accepted usage as well as the individual style of the author. Consult a good, current dictionary. Be consistent in the form used throughout each piece of writing.

Most word-processing programs automatically account for end-of-line hyphenation, but if you must indicate hyphenation manually, be sure to split words by syllables. Standard dictionaries indicate syllabification by placing a dot between the syllables.

38 Parentheses

Parenthetical remarks are similar to appositives, but they tend to be a bit longer. Parentheses may enclose a numerical or chronological range, single words, short phrases, clauses, or even full sentences. Parentheses momentarily suspend the discourse, permitting the writer to convey supplementary information (comments, explanations, or passing references) at the precise moment it is needed. This precise moment may be within a sentence, or it may be between sentences. If the parenthetical information appears between sentences, then each of the surrounding sentences should include a terminal period, and the statement within the parentheses should be a complete sentence—even if an elliptical one—punctuated with its own period.

The left, or open, parenthesis sign should never be preceded or followed by any other punctuation. The right, or closed, parenthesis sign may be followed by a comma (if the sense requires it), or by a period (as here). When the information contained within parentheses is a complete sentence, put the period inside the closed parenthesis sign.

Numbers or letters in parentheses may be used to establish clarity in enumerating a series of items, as (1) where the items are complex and perhaps internally punctuated; or (2) where the reader has been led to expect an exact number of items and will be grateful if you count them as you go along.

A foreign title, or a foreign-language passage, may be immediately followed by an English translation in parentheses, if this seems appropriate. Similarly, a passing reference for the reader's orientation may be put in parentheses if the formality of a footnote citation appears too cumbersome. Further uses of parentheses are discussed in Chapters 7, 8, and 9.

39   Period

Every sentence should conclude with a period. Be sure that your sentence is complete, with a subject and a verb. All notes must end with a period. A common fault is to omit the period when the note ends with a page number.

Use periods following most (but not all) abbreviations and after personal initials. Leave a space following a personal initial and period:

J. S. Bach was the *Kantor* of the Thomaskirche in Leipzig from 1723 until his death in 1750.

Omit the period after titles, headings, and subheads; after page numbers; and after any numeral enclosed in parentheses. When two consecutive periods would occur—for instance, with the abbreviation "p." at the end of a bibliographic entry for a book—the single period will function both as the period for the abbreviation and as the period marking the conclusion of the entry.

40   Quotation marks

Use quotation marks to enclose brief, direct quotations run on as part of your text, but omit quotation marks from single-spaced quotations separated from the text by blocking. Where quotation marks are called for, American usage requires double quotation marks ("   ")—except for quotations within quotations, which take single quotation marks ('   '). Avoid the British usage of enclosing quotations in single quotation marks.

Note: Commas and periods always go inside quotation marks; a colon or semicolon goes outside. A question mark (?) or exclamation point (!) goes inside quotation marks if that punctuation is in the original text being quoted. If you yourself are supplying the question mark or exclamation point, put it outside.

Titles of articles, short poems, paintings, songs, named movements of larger compositions, and the like, are enclosed in quotation marks. It is rarely necessary to use quotation marks and italics simultaneously in manuscript. If you quote a passage that is consistently in a foreign language, quotation marks suffice, and no italics are necessary. Similarly, if you refer to a section of a larger work and both the section and the larger entity are distinctive titles in a foreign language, use quotation marks for the subsection and italics for the main work:

> Ottorino Respighi originally published the music for "La fuga in Egitto" (The flight into Egypt) as an untitled piano prelude in 1922. He orchestrated it three years later and used it as the first movement of his four-movement orchestral symphony, *Vetrate di chiesa* (Church windows).

41   Semicolon

The semicolon is very useful for bringing together independent clauses into a single sentence. Connecting statements in this way may improve sentence rhythm by eliminating awkward full stops (periods).

The clause following a semicolon must always contain a verb. (If the words following the semicolon do not include a verb, the punctuation should be a colon or dash.)

Conjunctive adverbs (*consequently; however; nevertheless*) are weaker connectors than conjunctions. To clarify the relationship of two main clauses, place a semicolon before and a comma after the conjunctive adverb:

> In 1720 Bach applied for the post of organist at the Jakobikirche in Hamburg; however, the position was awarded

to Johann Joachim Heitmann because Bach was unable to make
a suitable cash gift to the church.

Contact clauses are independent clauses juxtaposed without any conjunction or conjunctive adverb. The previous example could be recast as
two contact clauses, yoked with a semicolon:

In 1720 Bach applied for the post of organist at the Jakobi-
kirche in Hamburg; the position was awarded to Johann
Joachim Heitmann because Bach was unable to make a suitable
cash gift to the church.

Put a semicolon before a coordinating conjunction joining two main
clauses if the clauses are long and involved.

Use semicolons to separate items in a series if the items themselves
require internal punctuation with commas.

42   Suspension points

Even experienced writers often confuse the ellipsis with suspension points,
but these two types of punctuation are very different. Three *spaced* dots
represent an ellipsis. Suspension points, on the other hand, consist of three
unspaced dots and are *never* followed by any punctuation. Suspension
points are an invitation to the reader to imagine the completion of the
statement that has been initiated:

Felix Mendelssohn (1809–1847) composed a wealth of
excellent music before his tragically early death. Had he lived
even one decade longer...

43   Underlining for italics

Underlining indicates that a character or series of characters should appear
in italics. Underlining and italics are basically interchangeable; nevertheless, simple underlining transfers from one word-processing program to
another more easily than italic fonts. Similarly, graphic recognition scanners will have a much higher rate of error when reading italics than when
reading simple underlined text. Regardless of whether you choose to represent your italicized text with italic type or with underlining, remember
that this typeface is appropriate only under special circumstances.

Most punctuation following words in italics should also be italicized.
The exceptions to this rule are multiple punctuation signs (such as quota-

tion marks following a period: place only the period in italics); the concluding parenthesis where the first was not italicized; and question marks and exclamation points that are germane to the sentence proper rather than to the italicized segment that precedes them.

Italics are used for *some* titles. Titles may be generic or distinctive. A generic title—such as when we refer to Beethoven's Fifth Symphony—gets capital initials but needs no italics. Distinctive titles are essentially pieces with names rather than mere indications of genre: Prokofiev's *Alexander Nevsky*, Vaughan Williams's *Sea Symphony*, and Orff's *Carmina Burana*. These examples of distinctive titles are associated with large works of many movements and significant duration. Note: Movements within large works may also have either generic or distinctive titles. The sixth movement of *Alexander Nevsky,* for example, is entitled "From the Field of the Dead." Here, the quotation marks show that this distinctive title refers to a segment of the larger work.

Titles of books and certain distinctive titles of musical compositions or art works require italics in the body of the essay as well as in notes and bibliographic citations. Do not underline your own main title, headings, captions, or legends.

When a distinctive title contains another distinctive title, the title within the title should be taken *out* of italics:

Wagner's Rienzi: A Reappraisal Based on a Study of the Sketches and Drafts

Foreign words within English text normally appear in italics as an assurance to the reader that there has been no error in reproducing the text. The German word *Komposition*, for example, means the same thing as the English cognate, but someone encountering the German spelling might suspect a typo if the word were to appear without italics.

When citing stage directions from a play, opera, or other theatrical work, retain the italics so that they will not be confused with the text of the drama.

Avoid italics merely for emphasis, but if you are sure that your material would be appropriate if set in italics in a book or article, then go ahead!

44   Vertical episema

The vertical episema is used for separating stanzas of poems that are run into text, with virgules separating the individual lines. It is also used to separate the rhyme schemes of multiple stanzas:

In *terza rima,* three-line stanzas have an interlocking rhyme scheme, such as *aba | bcb | cdc.*

45   Virgule

Use the virgule, or slash, when two or more lines of quoted poetry are run into your text, or when it is necessary to indicate the line layout of a text as it appeared in the original source. Allow one space before and one space after the virgule:

> For the third song of his Serenade for tenor, horn, and strings,
> Op. 31, Benjamin Britten used the text of Blake's "Elegy":
> O Rose, thou art sick; / The invisible worm / That flies in the
> night, / In the howling storm, / Has found out thy bed of
> crimson joy; / And his dark, secret love / Does thy life destroy.

The virgule also appears regularly in fractions (1/2) and time signatures (4/4 time). Although various combinations of super- and subscript can approximate fractions and time signatures, these modified typeface styles are often misread by scanners and jumbled when data is transferred from one program to another. You will be safe using numerals separated by a virgule and keyed in on the main type line.

Musicians have a special use for the virgule: to show hierarchical relationships of chords belonging to various tonalities. If, for example, a dominant chord in C major appears, it would be designated by the Roman numeral V. If the dominant of the dominant appeared, it would include the tone F-sharp, a pitch that is not contained in the C-major scale. To show that the secondary dominant—that is, the dominant of the dominant—is being described, the Roman numeral V (indicating the dominant chord) would be separated by a virgule from another V as follows: V/V. Note: In this case, no space precedes or follows the virgule.

The virgule has further applications within musical notation, particularly for writing jazz lead sheets and for showing chords appearing over a bass note that is not a chord tone. The sign F/G, for instance, would indicate an F-major triad appearing over a G in the bass. See rule 272 for more details on the use of successive virgules in jazz and pop music.

46   Words discussed

To direct attention to a nontechnical English word or expression, enclose it in quotation marks: the word "copyright"; the verb "to be"; the phrase "the present writer." When a series of such terms would result in an unwieldy accumulation of quotation marks, use underlining (italics) instead.

To direct attention to a term being discussed, italicize the term only at its first appearance in the discussion. This principle applies to both English and foreign terms.

Do not capitalize common nouns for emphasis.

CHAPTER 5

Numerals and Dates

47 Arabic, Roman, and small Roman numerals

The three types of numerals are conventional Arabic (0, 1, 2, 3, 4, 5, 6, 7, 8, and 9); Roman (such as I, V, X, and L); and small Roman (i, ii, iii, iv, v, etc.).

Never represent Arabic numeral 1 with a lowercase letter "l" or zero with an uppercase letter "O." All Roman numerals are typed using the letters of the alphabet.

Many Roman numerals clearly derive from gestures related to the human body, and in fact the word "digit" is derived from the Latin *digitum* ("finger"). The number one looks like a single finger; two is a pair of fingers; three is three fingers raised; the V for five is the shape of a hand held open.

The Roman manner of representing numbers is indeed cumbersome. In the Roman system, I = 1, V = 5, X = 10, L = 50, C = 100, D = 500, and M = 1,000 (there is no symbol for zero). Other numbers are formed by compounds of these symbols. When a symbol follows another of equal or greater value, its value is added to the one that preceded it: CC = 200; CL = 150. When a symbol precedes another of greater value, its value is subtracted from the one that follows: IX = 9. When a symbol appears between two other symbols, each of greater value, the value of the intervening symbol is subtracted from the symbol that follows: CXC = 190. A bar placed over a Roman numeral is a shorthand method of indicating multiplication by a thousand.

48 Numbers: When to spell out, when to use numerals

In the text of an essay, spell out a number if it is under a hundred, or a round number (thousand; million; billion). Always spell out a number that begins a sentence. If the number is so large that it would be awkward spelled out at the opening of a sentence, reconfigure the words of the sentence so that you can use numerals within the sentence. Hyphenate most fractions (one-half; two-thirds) and compound numbers between twenty-one and ninety-nine.

Times of day are usually spelled out in text ("four o'clock"; "half past three"); use numerals to stress a specific time or with abbreviations ("the 3:52 train"; "4:00 p.m."). Do not spell out addresses, dates, mathematical ratios, years, measure numbers in a musical score, precise monetary amounts, page numbers, and certain measurements. Always use numerals for such figures, regardless of their size:

> Since the length of a standard *quaree* court was 100 feet, the exterior of Lisle's Theatre must have measured approximately 75 feet in length and 30 feet in width.

If more than two or three words would be needed to spell out a number, use numerals instead: 55 1/2; 1256 or 1,256. To represent amounts of money, the signs $ or ¢ should be used in conjunction with numerals. Never use these signs with spelled amounts. For very large round numbers, a combination of cash signs, Arabic numerals, and words is permissible:

> The addition to Ithaca College's School of Music will cost approximately $11 million.

For numbers designating an individual item, either use a numeral after the item or spell out the ordinal number before the item: page 1, the first page; measure 8, the eighth measure. Avoid mixing these treatments in a single construction; refer to "page 1 of volume 2" *not* "the first page of volume 2."

Volume and page numbers often appear in tandem in notes and bibliographic entries. You may use Roman numerals to indicate the volume and Arabic numerals for the page. Separate the two numerals by a comma, followed by a space. If you prefer to avoid Roman numerals altogether, use an Arabic number with the abbreviation "vol." to avoid confusion: vol. 1, p. 221 (certainly *not* 1, 221).

49   Arabic numerals

Use Arabic numerals for musical examples, figures, and page numbers in your manuscript, except for preliminary matter. Use Arabic numbers for notes too. Footnotes are often numbered beginning with the number one for each new page. If you place the notes at the end of your essay, you will use consecutive numbers. Bibliographic entries should not be numbered.

In both notes and bibliographic entries, it is standard practice to combine Arabic numerals with letters to form ordinal numbers indicating editions (1st, 2d, 3d, 4th).

50   Roman numerals

Present-day writers tend to avoid Roman numerals. Nevertheless, they are sometimes unavoidable, and, if used sparingly, they can be quite useful. Use large Roman numerals for volumes, parts, chapters, tables, plates, and individuals in a series (Henry VIII). Where higher numbers are involved, however, consider using Arabic numerals throughout: plates 1–149 (*not* plates I–CXLIX).

Remember: You set the style for your essay. It is not necessary to reproduce Roman numerals merely because they happen to appear on the spine of some encyclopedia or on the title page of some journal.

Small Roman numerals may also be used for front matter, such as the table of contents, acknowledgments, and introduction.

Use large and small Roman numerals, respectively, for acts and scenes of a play or opera: *Nabucco,* Act I, scene ii; *Julius Caesar,* I, ii.

51   Inclusive numbers

Inclusive numbers, such as an author might use in a note to indicate the pages of a source being cited, may be shown in one of two ways: You may give the full number on both sides of the en dash (pp. 113–117); or you may show only the changed portion of the number (pp. 113–7). When the numbers are relatively small, complete numbers are preferable. In some cases, however, complete numbers would be unnecessarily cumbersome:

> The three Steinway Model M baby grand pianos with serial numbers 259179–81 were all manufactured in the year 1928.

52   Dates

The popular American style for dates is June 12, 1966, or June, 1966, with a comma both before and after the year. (At the end of a sentence, the second comma is replaced by a period.) In scholarly writing, European format is preferable; it not only progresses logically from smaller to larger divisions of chronology but also eliminates the comma: 12 June 1966; June 1966.

References to particular centuries should be spelled out using lower-case letters:

> Richard Wagner (1813–1883) has proved to be the single most important German opera composer of the nineteenth century.

Hyphenate when "century" is part of a compound modifier: "nineteenth-century forms."

Note the Italian designations for centuries: *trecento*—1300s (fourteenth century); *quattrocento*—1400s (fifteenth century); *cinquecento* —1500s (sixteenth century); *seicento*—1600s (seventeenth century); *settecento*—1700s (eighteenth century); *ottocento*—1800s (nineteenth century); *novecento*—1900s (twentieth century).

Decades usually appear as numbers rather than spelled words:

> Most of Liszt's orchestral tone poems were written during the 1840s and '50s.

Note: The apostrophe preceding the decade indication is necessary to show the omission of the first two numbers. Avoid the old convention of placing an apostrophe between the numeral zero and the letter "s."

53 Inclusive years

The simplest style is to give both years in full: 1781–1791; 1761–1809; 1858–1924. This is a necessity for years before the Christian era, which represent a diminishing series: 460–429 B.C.

Alternatively, give only the last two figures for the second year if it falls within the same century: 1723–50; 1756–91; 1906–75. In this system, do not repeat a zero in penultimate position: 1707–8; 1900–4; 1903–5. If the century changes, or if the first year ends in two zeros, write out both years in full: 1685–1750; 1899–1905; 2000–2001. The en dash should also appear with inclusive dates indicating the month, or the month and the day: 17 February–28 May 2004.

54 Numerals in musical analysis

Musicians often use numerals for musical analysis. Roman numerals show chords within a functional harmonic context: Capital Roman numerals indicate major chords; small Roman numerals show that a chord is minor.

Arabic numerals appearing in conjunction with a Roman numeral indicate the inversion of the particular chord. A dominant chord with a double suspension in the upper voices includes all the pitches of a tonic chord, but the fifth of the chord is in the bass; hence, it should be shown in the major mode as the Roman numeral I with Arabic super- and subscripts beside it as follows: I_4^6.

CHAPTER 6

Spelling, Foreign Words, Abbreviations

55 Spelling

Spelling should be correct and consistent in accordance with accepted American usage. Make a habit of using a dictionary. If you have serious trouble with spelling, procure a spelling dictionary that contains only an alphabetical listing of words with syllabification indicated. Some words have more than one correct spelling; the one that appears first in the dictionary is preferred, and in most cases, it is the one that should be used.

Most word-processing programs contain spell-check programs, but such programs, obviously, will be less useful for scholarly documents using languages other than English. Remember that foreign words, technical terms, names of individuals, and other specialized vocabulary will probably not be included in the spell-check program.

If certain foreign or technical terms appear throughout your essay, it might be wise to install these words in the user dictionary of your word-processing program. In most word-processing programs, it is possible to create multiple user dictionaries with distinctive names. Such dictionaries are particularly useful when specialized vocabulary is required in several different essays. Be sure to select dictionary names that you will immediately recognize and associate with the corresponding essay. Note: Specially created dictionaries must be reactivated each time you open your word-processing program.

56 Musical terms

An occasional lapse in the spelling of an unusual or even common English word is excusable, but the misspelling of musical terms is inexcusable. In your reading, pay attention to spelling. Many musical terms are found in standard general dictionaries, as well as in specialized music dictionaries.

Attention is called to the following—frequently misspelled—musical terms:

a cappella	mesuré
accelerando	obbligato
acciaccatura	ophicleide
accoppiare	ottava bassa
affettuoso	perpetuum mobile
affrettando	piuttosto
agréments	pizzicato
appoggiatura	quatuor
caccia	rhythm
caesura	soggetto cavato
capriccio	solfège
dal segno	solfegietto
détaché	sprezzatura
échappée	staccato
formes fixes	temperament
fugue (German, *Fuge*)	tessitura
gigue (Italian and Spanish, *giga*)	timpani
impresario	toccata
laisser	virtuosic

If your word-processing program has a user dictionary, you may want to consider installing these terms to ensure correct spellings.

Many of these terms normally appear in Roman type, others in italics, and some may appear in either Roman or italic type, depending on the topic of the essay and the frequency with which they are used. It is sometimes helpful to introduce a technical term in italics, but to use Roman for its subsequent appearances.

57   American *versus* British usage

In our research, many sources—beginning with the ubiquitous *New Grove Dictionary*—follow British usage or one of its variants. Note: The word "British" is intended here to mean both Great Britain and its present or former colonies, such as Australia, Canada, New Guinea, and New Zealand.

American usage differs from British usage in certain details. If you are citing a title or giving a direct quotation, it is, of course, necessary to preserve the spelling as it is in the original source. When you are summarizing the information in your own words, use American spellings unless you are submitting your work to an academic institution or scholarly journal that employs British style.

58 Verbs in *-ise* or *-ize*

To determine whether a verb ends in *-ise* or *-ize*, consult a dictionary. The following brief list is suggestive:

-ise	*-ize*
advertise	analyze
advise	authorize
arise	characterize
disguise	civilize
exercise	criticize
improvise	harmonize
revise	italicize
supervise	organize
	realize
	recognize
	summarize
	symbolize

Note: Verbs in *-ize* tend to have corresponding nouns ending in *-ization*. Some exceptions: analyze, analysis (*never* analyzation!); criticize, criticism; summarize, summary.

59 Adjectives in *-ible* or *-able*

Most such words end in *-able*, so that the problem is to remember which ones end in *-ible:*

accessible	responsible
audible	sensible
intelligible	visible
invertible	

Words ending in "e" usually drop the "e" when adding *-able:*

sale, salable	use, usable

But *-ce* or *-ge* at the end is retained:

change, changeable   notice, noticeable
manage, manageable   peace, peaceable

60 Special plurals

Some words adopted from foreign languages retain their original plurals:

alumna, alumnae (women)   genus, genera
alumnus, alumni (men)   intermedium, intermedia
cantus firmus, cantus firmi   memorandum, memoranda
crisis, crises   millennium, millennia
criterion, criteria   stratum, strata
datum, data   thesis, theses
erratum, errata

Some words retain their original plural forms or use alternative, English plurals:

appendix; appendices or   formula; formulae or formulas
    appendixes   index; indices or indexes
beau; beaux or beaus   persona; personae or personas
cherub; cherubim or cherubs   seraph; seraphim or seraphs
    (-im is a Hebrew plural)   tableau; tableaux or tableaus
focus; foci or focuses

61 Miscellaneous words

The following spellings are recommended. Where dictionaries give alternate spellings, the implication is that the first version presented is preferable.

acknowledgment   foreword (an introductory
advisor   statement)
aesthetic   forgo (relinquish)
cannot   forward (onward)
catalog   fulfill
descendant (noun)   further (in time, quantity, or
enroll   degree)
eurhythmics   gaiety
farther (in physical distance)   goodbye
focused   gray

judgment	skillful
labeled	stationary (stable, unmoving)
medieval	stationery (paper, writing supplies)
practice (noun and verb)	technique
principal (foremost)	toward
principle (rule)	

62   Foreign words in English context

Italicize foreign words appearing in an English context. Foreign words that have been absorbed into almost daily English speech need not be italicized:

alma mater	façade
apropos	genre
bona fide	hors d'oeuvres
bourgeoisie	laissez faire
cafe	matador
dilettante	naiveté
ersatz	status quo
ex officio	

Among musical terms, Italian words were among the first to become embedded in the English language:

aria	gamba
cantata	intermezzo
capriccio	maestro
concerto	opera
crescendo	opus
fantasia	sonata

From the French, we have the following words:

allemande	courante
amateur	détaché
ballade	étude
chanson	fauxbourdon
clavecin	nocturne

German terms are less readily absorbed, partly because of the German custom of capitalizing common nouns. If words of this sort appear in your essay, capitalize and italicize them only if they are used infrequently. If these terms constitute the standard vocabulary of your essay, captialize them only, thereby avoiding the constant shifting from Roman to italic type and back, which would be distracting to the reader.

Denkmäler	Ländler
Empfindsamkeit	Leitmotiv
Fortspinnung	Lied
Gebrauchsmusik	Minnesinger
Gesamtkunstwerk	Nebenstimme
Hauptstimme	Zeitmass

The possibility remains, however, of italicizing the word at its first appearance, either to introduce it as a technical concept or for the more subtle purpose of bringing out its foreign flavor. Use good judgment, and avoid cluttering up the page with too many italicized words.

Although it is customary to italicize foreign words when they are spelled out, common abbreviations of foreign words do not require italics: d.c., *da capo;* d.s., *dal segno;* v.s., *volti subito.* See rule 64 for others.

Italicize words that, in rapid reading, might not otherwise be understood immediately: *infra, passim, supra, vide.*

When presenting a passage that is entirely in a foreign language, you may elect either to italicize the entire passage, or, if it is clearly set apart from the main text by quotation marks or blocked single-spacing, simply to continue with Roman type.

In preparing copy for a typist or printer, include marginal instructions whenever there might be cause for confusion. Recall further that when your written work will constitute a portion of a larger document, the editor will have to formulate a volume style that may differ in some details from yours. In such cases, be guided by the recommendations of your editor.

63   Accents, diacritics

An accent mark, properly speaking, would show stress. Diacritical marks represent a broader category of signs that may be attached to either vowels or consonants to indicate a particular sound that differs from the sound of the unmarked letter. Copy all such marks faithfully.

64   English and Latin abbreviations

The following abbreviations are common in scholarly writing, and they may be freely used wherever abbreviations are in good taste, particularly in citations and parenthetical references. Capitalize where appropriate, such as at the beginning of a note, or where matter immediately preceding is closed with a period.

Abbreviations that are italicized here should appear thus in your manuscript. Italics in the explanatory column merely indicate Latin derivation. Such terms and their abbreviations may also be italicized in manuscript, if this seems essential for clarity.

Note carefully whether the abbreviation or term is or is not followed by a period. Quotation marks used here enclose a definition or call attention to a word or phrase: They should not appear in the manuscript.

anon.	anonymous
ante	"before"; previously mentioned
arr.	arranged, -ment
art., arts.	article(s)
b.	born
bibliog.	bibliography, -er, -ical
biog.	biography, -er, -ical
bk., bks.	book(s)
c	copyright; without period or space, to show copyright date (c1968); the sign © is also used
c., ca.	*circa*, "about"; used with approximate dates (ca. 1400); the form "ca." is preferable
CD	compact disc sound recording
cf.	confer, compare; do not use "cf." where "see" is intended
chap., chaps.	chapter(s)
col., cols.	column(s)
comp.	composer, -ed, -ition
d.	died

diss.	dissertation
ed., eds.	editor(s), edition(s); after a title, "ed." may stand for "edited by"
e.g.	*exempli gratia,* "for example"; preceded and followed by punctuation: , e.g., or ; e.g.,
enl.	enlarged, as in "rev. enl. ed." (revised and enlarged edition)
esp.	especially, as in "meas. 19–35, esp. 26"
et al.	*et alii, aliae, alia,* "and others"
etc.	*et cetera,* "and so forth"
et seq.	*et sequens,* "and the following" (see "f., ff.")
ex., exx.	example(s)
f., ff.	used after a numeral to mean "and the following page (f.) or pages (ff.)"
fac., facsim.	facsimile
fasc.	fascicle
fig., figs.	figure(s)
fl.	*floruit,* "flourished"; reached greatest development or influence
fol., fols.	folio(s)
front.	frontispiece; an illustrative plate that precedes the title page in a book
hist.	history, -ical, -ian
ibid.	*ibidem,* "in the same place"
idem	"the same person"
i.e.	*id est,* "that is"; preceded and followed by punctuation: , i.e., (i.e.,) or ; i.e.,
illus.	illustrated, -ion(s)
infra	"below"; later in the discussion (see *supra*)
intro., introd.	introduction

IPA	international phonetic alphabet
ips	inches per second (for reel-to-reel tapes)
loc. cit.	*loco citato*, "in the place cited"
LP	long-playing sound recording
meas.	measure(s); "mm." should not be used as it may easily be confused with the abbreviation "mm" for millimeter
MM	Maelzel's metronome (indicating tempo)
Ms., Mss.	manuscript(s)
n., nn.	note(s)
N.B.	*nota bene*, "note well"
n.d.	no date; used where no publication date is given, as "London: Novello, n.d."
No., Nos.	number(s), usually capitalized; avoid #
n.p.	no place; used where no place of publication is given
N.S.	New Series, New Style (cf. O.S.)
numb.	numbered
Op., Opp.	Opus, Opera, "work(s)"; capitalized before the number of a specific work, as "Op. 106"
op. cit.	*opere citato*, "in the work cited"
op. posth.	opus posthumous; a work published after the composer's death
O.S.	Old Style; used principally to indicate dates not in conformity with the Gregorian calendar
p., pp.	page(s); omit if volume number precedes, as "II, 356"; the plural form (pp.) is used only preceding a group of inclusive pages, as "pp. 15–90." In bibliographic entries giving the total number of pages, use only "p." For example, "236 p."
par., pars.	paragraph(s)
passim	"throughout the work"; used where it would be tedious to cite all pages where a given thing is mentioned or discussed

pf.	pianoforte
pl., pls.	plate(s); capitalize when referring to specific plates, as "Pl. 16." (Note the possible confusion with "place.")
post	"after," "later"; not recommended unless in a meaningful Latin phrase, as *post hoc* ("after this point")
posth.	posthumous; occurring after one's death
pref.	preface
pseud.	pseudonym
pt., pts.	part(s); capitalize when referring to a specific work or followed by a numeral (Pt. 1); lowercase when preceded by a number (2 pts.)
publ.	published, published by, publication(s)
q.v.	*quod vide,* "which see"; normally follows a term which the reader is expected to look up under that heading; may be put in parentheses or italicized: "Sonata" (q.v.) or "Sonata," *q.v.*
r	*recto,* "right"; right-hand page, written superscribed without period after a folio number, as "fol. 27^r" (see *verso*)
recte	"rightly"; used to signal a correction of spelling or fact
rectius	"more rightly"; a better version
reg.	registered
rev.	revised
rpm	revolutions per minute; used for 78- and 45-rpm sound recordings
sc.	scene
ser.	series
St., SS.	saint(s)
supra	"above"; earlier in the discussion
s.v.	*sub verbo,* "under the word" (to indicate a dictionary or encyclopedia heading)

trans.	translation, translated by
transcr.	transcribed, -iption
v	*verso,* "reverse"; left-hand page, written superscribed without period after a folio number to indicate the reverse side of that folio, as "fol. 27^v " (see *recto*)
vc.	violoncello
vide	"see"; followed by a reference which the reader may look up (see also "q.v.")
viz.	*videlicet,* "namely" (the "z" is a corruption of medieval Latin *-et*); appropriate for conveying the meaning "that is to say"; requires punctuation: , viz., or, viz.:
vl.	violin
vla.	viola
vol., vols.	volume(s); capitalize when followed by a numeral (Vol. 1); lowercase when preceded by a number (2 vols.); omitted when using Roman followed by an Arabic page reference (II, 356)
vs.	*versus,* "against"; loosely, "compared with"; also "verse," as in a poem or a song

Note: If you are writing for a wider, general readership, you should use only contemporary, English terminology. Many publishers suggest avoiding Latinisms, such as e.g., et al., etc., and i.e.

65   German and French abbreviations

The following list will serve to acquaint the student with some of the more common abbreviations encountered in German and French scholarly writings.

a.a.O.	*am angeführten Ort,* "in the work cited"; like "op. cit."
Anh.	*Anhang,* "appendix"
Anm.	*Anmerkung,* "note"; like "n."
Aufl.	*Auflage,* "edition"

Ausg.	*Ausgabe,* "edition"
Bd., Bde.	*Band, Bände,* "volume(s)"
Bearb.	*Bearbeiter, -ung,* "editor," "version"; lowercase *bearbeitet von,* "edited by"
Begl.	*Begleitung,* "accompaniment"
bzw.	*beziehungsweise,* "or, respectively"
Cie	*Compagnie,* "company"
das.	*daselbst,* "in the same place"; like "loc. cit."
dgl.	*der-, desgleichen,* "similarly"; *u. dgl., und desgleichen*
ebenda	"in the same place"; like "ibid."
evang.	*evangelisch,* "Protestant" or specifically "Lutheran"
evtl.	*eventuell,* "perhaps," "possibly"
Flg.	*Folge,* "series"
fr.	francs (monetary unit)
geb.	*geboren,* "born"
gen.	*genannt,* "called," "surnamed"
gest.	*gestorben,* "died"
G.m.b.H.	*Gesellschaft mit beschränkter Haftung,* "limited (liability) company"; loosely equivalent to "Co., Ltd."
h.	*heure,* "hour"; 10 h., "10 o'clock"
hrsg.	*herausgegeben,* "edited"
Hs., Hss.	*Handschrift(en),* "manuscript(s)"
Jh., Jhdt.	*Jahrhundert,* "century"
Jhrg.	*Jahrgang,* "volume"
K., Kap.	*Kapitel,* "chapter"
k.k.	*kaiserlich-königlich,* "imperial-royal" (Austria)
kais.	*kaiserlich,* "imperial"
kath.	*katholisch,* "Catholic"

kgl.	*königlich,* "royal"
kl.	*klein(e),* "small"
Lbd.	*Leinband,* "cloth binding"
M.	*Monsieur,* "Mr."; plural: MM. *(Messieurs, Mssrs.)*
Mlle	*Mademoiselle,* "Miss"; plural: Mlles
Mme	*Madame,* "Mrs."; plural: Mmes *(Mesdames)*
N.-D.	*Notre-Dame,* "Our Lady"
né, née	"born" (masc., fem.)
Nr.	*Nummer,* "number"; like "No."
o.J.	*ohne Jahr,* "without year"; like "n.d."
o.O.	*ohne Opuszahl,* "without opus number"
ouvr. cit.	*ouvrage cité,* "in the work cited"; like "op. cit."
resp.	*respektiv,* "respectively"; often with the force of "and, on the other hand"
S.	*Seite,* "page"; like "p."
s.	*siehe,* "see"
s.a.	*siehe auch,* "see also"
S.A.	*Son Altesse,* "His (Her) Highness"; S.A.R., *Son Altesse Royale*
S.M.	*Sa Majesté* (French), *Seine Majestät* (German), "His (Her) Majesty"
sog.	*sogenannt,* "so-called"
St, Ste	*Saint(e),* "Saint" (masc., fem.)
s.v.p.	*s'il vous plaît,* "if you please"
t.	*tome,* "volume"
u.	*und,* "and"
u.a.	*unter andern,* "among others"; *und andere,* "and others"
übers.	*übersetzt,* "translated"

u.s.w.	*und so weiter,* "and so forth"
v.	*von, vom,* "by," "from," "of"
verb.	*verbessert,* "revised," "improved"
Verf.	*Verfasser,* "author"
verm.	*vermehrt,* "enlarged," "increased"
vgl.	*vergleiche,* "compare"; like "cf."
voir	"see"
z.B.	*zum Beispiel,* "for example"
z.Z.	*zur Zeit,* "at the time," "at present"

66 Acronyms

Acronyms are a specialized type of abbreviation. Normally, the initial letter of each word in the name of some person, title, institution, or organization is given as a capital letter and combined to form a series of letters that may either be pronounced as a single word or spoken as individual letters. In writing, an article may or may not precede a particular acronym, according to custom.

An acronym should not be introduced until its constituent words have been spelled out in full. The first full statement of the words should be followed, in parentheses, by the acronym, in unspaced capital letters:

American Guild of Organists (AGO)
American Musicological Society (AMS)
American Society of Composers, Authors, and Publishers (ASCAP)
Bach Werke Verzeichnis (BWV)
Beatae Mariae Virginis (BMV or BVM)
Broadcast Music, Incorporated (BMI)
College Music Society (CMS)
International Musicological Society (IMS)
International Society for Contemporary Music (ISCM)
Music Library Association (MLA)
Musik in Geschichte und Gegenwart (MGG)
Neue Bach Ausgabe (NBA)
Neue Mozart Ausgabe (NMA)
Répertoire international de littérature musicale (RILM)
Répertoire international des sources musicales (RISM)
Society for Music Theory (SMT)

Even if more than the initial letter of each word is used to form the acronym, all letters remain uppercase: Society for Electro-Acoustical Music (SEAMUS).

Acronyms are not generally used to represent titles in notes or bibliographic entries. For certain types of studies, however, the use of acronyms for source identification offers many advantages. In such cases, a table of acronymic abbreviations should be included in the front matter.

CHAPTER 7

Documentation and Notes

67 Note logic

Notes customarily serve one of two purposes: They may refer the reader to sources of information; or, they may give explanatory comments or additional evidence that might obscure the focus of an essay if incorporated into the text. A carefully documented essay will consequently have two texts: the body of the essay and the accompanying notes. Be sure to keep the two texts separate at all times: The body of the text cannot rely upon previous note discussion or information.

In writing for the general public, keep notes to a minimum or avoid them entirely. Readers of the scholarly paper, on the other hand, will be both knowledgeable and critical and will want to know your sources of information: Who says that the facts are thus? Whose opinion are you stating? Notes anticipating these questions will usually give the name of an author, a title, and a page number. Brief notes of this sort are less distracting than explanatory notes, which can consist of several sentences, paragraphs, or even pages. Recall that a note diverts the reader's attention from the main issues of an essay. If the information in the note is really important, consider putting it into the body of the text.

68 Documentation of facts

Facts may be loosely grouped into three realms: common knowledge—things that are readily accessible in most standard reference works and hence generally known to anyone conversant with the subject; special knowledge—things noted by only one or a few persons, such as specialists or experts, and hence not generally known; and personal knowledge—things that the writer-investigator has observed firsthand, which may agree with, supplement, or even repudiate common knowledge and special knowledge.

Statements of fact from the realm of common knowledge are usually not documented. Facts drawn from someone else's fund of special knowledge must always be duly credited and documented. Information acquired from the writer's own personal knowledge and experience are usually incorporated into the body of the paper. When personal knowledge supplements or repudiates a widely held view, it is wise to explain where and how the observation was made.

Remember: If you do not give a citation, the reader will assume that your statement of fact is either common knowledge or else your own personal observation, for which you assume full responsibility.

69   Documentation of opinion

An opinion is a point of view that someone develops after amassing and evaluating factual information. Part of this process may involve drawing inferences and conclusions. Observe the rules of property: Some opinions are in the public domain; some are clearly the private property of individuals; some may be your own personal property.

An opinion that is without documentation is ostensibly the view of the writer whose byline appears at the head of the essay. If you have taken the trouble to formulate an opinion, your very manner of presenting the facts and arguments should make this sufficiently clear. Or you may merely share an opinion that is widely held, not particularly controversial, or so logical as to seem obvious, in which case no documentation need be given.

If you borrow an opinion that clearly belongs to another, you must credit the source. Then, if it turns out to be a bad opinion, you will already have attached the blame to its original author. If a good opinion, you and your source mutually substantiate each other, and you are in good company.

70   When to give credit

A common misconception is that only direct quotations require documentation. Actually, statements of fact and opinion are usually formulated as abstracts or paraphrases. Still, the logic of documentation is fully applicable.

71   Note format: Principles of organization

Notes put the reader in touch with a source of information that has been preserved in some fixed form. Use the following organizational principles whenever you need to improvise a note for which you can find no model.

Begin by identifying the creator of the information—whether this be an individual, a group of authors, or a committee or organization. Give the title, or an approximate title, for the document being cited. Provide details concerning the provenance of this document: Where was it put into fixed form? How might one obtain this document? When was this document made? Finally, give the location of the particular bit of information that you invoke for your argument. Progress from larger elements (such as the volume) to smaller elements (the page, the column, the note).

This general pattern of documentation will provide you with a secure basis of organization regardless of whether you are invoking the information contained within a book, periodical, dictionary, musical edition, recording, pseudoperiodical, personal interview, Web site, or any other tangible source.

72   Note numbers in text

In double-spaced matter, note numbers are typed as superscripts a half space above the line. Most word-processing programs will automatically place the note number for you, but if you must do this manually, use the superscript style option. Put the note number, without leaving a space, immediately after the terminal punctuation—including any quotation marks—of the sentence requiring documentation. In general, do not place the note number within a sentence (compound sentences are an exception); neither should you use several numbers within a single sentence. Granted, it may be necessary to refer to several sources in a given sentence, but these should all be cited in a single note.

In single-spaced matter, numbers typed as superscripts will run into the line above. In the interests of neatness, avoid notes until the end of the single-spaced matter, then leave a space and type the number on the line.

It is a usual courtesy to mention an author's name before presenting what he or she has to say in abstract, paraphrase, or direct quotation. If the wait would be too long between the name and the end of the statement, attach the footnote immediately to the author's name.

It is a rare occasion indeed when two note numbers must appear contiguously; should you encounter such a circumstance, separate the two superscript numbers by a comma.

Endnotes are numbered consecutively throughout an essay, article, or chapter. If the report is very brief—something under ten pages in length—footnotes may be numbered anew for each page.

73   Form of the note

If the note program you are using does not already set the note form, you may follow the guidelines given here. For each note, indent two spaces from the normal left margin and put the note number on the line. Leave two more spaces and begin the note. Overgenerous indentation wastes space.

Subsequent lines of the same note should be run out flush with the normal left margin. Hanging indentation, as used in the bibliography, is not appropriate in notes.

End each note with a period. A common fault is to omit the period after a page number concluding a note.

The use of asterisks and other signs (such as the dagger, the double dagger, and the section mark) should be avoided; however, in those circumstances where a superscript number might be confused with an exponent—as might happen in studies of acoustics, set theory, or scalings of musical instruments—they serve a valid purpose.

Thus far, our discussion has presumed double-spacing. In single-spaced text, however, typed superscript numerals (or signs) can be messy. A printer's superscripts are special small figures that do not ascend higher than the tallest letters in the line. By avoiding superscripts, it becomes unnecessary to leave space between notes.

74   Notes in a draft

Most word-processing programs can easily insert notes wherever you want them. Should you later decide to remove one, all subsequent notes will automatically—magically!—be renumbered. If you happen to have a less virtuosic program, some old-fashioned manual work may be necessary.

In the preliminary drafts of a paper, type a line, flush with the left margin, both before and after the note, to separate it from the main text. Such notes should be complete and in proper form. This format is used by commercial publishers in galley sheets, which are essentially working drafts that will be put into final form at some later point. In the final, fair copy of the essay, transfer the notes to their appropriate position as footnotes or endnotes.

The problem of renumbering notes often arises, because of additions or deletions or reorderings made in the process of revision. The form here recommended for the draft has the advantage that no numbers are needed: An asterisk (*) suffices, since the note is immediately at hand. When preparing the fully revised draft for final typing, go through and number the remaining notes consecutively.

75   Note style

We speak of note sentences, but they are not actually complete sentences. Even so, internal punctuation will maintain clarity and precision. One fundamental rule is that all notes must end with a period. Observe carefully the models given in the examples that follow.

Any note should give, as completely and accurately as possible, yet in the tersest possible form, all the information needed at that particular point. When a source of information is first cited, follow the rule for a first reference. Subsequent citations of a source that has already been thus fully described should follow the rule for a short reference.

76   Books: First reference

Give the author's full name in normal order. Insert a comma, then give the book title, in italics. Put the publication information in parentheses (Place, *colon:* Publisher, *comma,* date), *comma,* page reference, *period.* The page reference usually indicates one particular page containing the information; but if the statement or discussion cited involves more than one page, give the inclusive pages. Do not use "pp. 112f" to mean "p. 112 and the following page." In such a case, simply write "pp. 112–113."

If the book title comprises more than one volume, give the volume number and the page number. If the volumes of a publication appeared over a period of several years, either give the range of years from the first volume to the last, or place the publication date in parentheses after the volume number. To refer to a note on a given page, put the abbreviation "n." after the page number.

> 1 Harold C. Schonberg, <u>The Great Pianists</u> (New York: Simon and Schuster, 1963), p. 221.
>
> 2 Gilbert Chase, <u>America's Music from the Pilgrims to the Present</u> (New York: McGraw Hill, 1955), pp. 433–435.
>
> 3 F. T. Arnold, <u>The Art of Accompaniment from a Thorough-Bass, as Practiced in the Seventeenth and Eighteenth Centuries</u> (London: Oxford University Press, 1931), vol. 1, pp. 318–322.
>
> 4 Charles Burney, <u>A General History of Music</u> (London: published by the author, 1776–1789), vol. 4, p. 37.
>
> 5 James McCalla, <u>Twentieth-Century Chamber Music</u> (New York: Schirmer Books, 1996), p. 100 n. 3.

At times, a full citation of the source would clutter the note: Omit lengthy subtitles, include only what is necessary for clear identification of the source, and leave the full description to the bibliography.

77   Books: Short reference

After the first, full reference to a document, publication information and other details are omitted. Give only the author's last name, unless the first name is necessary to avoid confusion with some other author with the same surname. Use only as much of the title as needed to make it sound literate and readily identifiable, and proceed directly to the page reference:

> 6 Schonberg, The Great Pianists, p. 223.
> 7 Chase, America's Music, p. 439.
> 8 Arnold, Art of Accompaniment, vol. 1, pp. 172–202.

78   Articles in periodicals: First reference

Give the author's full name in normal order. Insert a *comma* before the title of article. Show the hierarchy of components by placing the smaller element (namely, the title of the article) in quotation marks. Place a *comma* inside the second quotation mark, then identify the larger element—the title of the journal or periodical—in italics *(no comma)* the volume number *(no comma)* month or season and year, in parentheses, *comma*, page reference, *period*. The abbreviations "p." for page or "pp." for plural pages are usually omitted in citations of journal articles, but they should be retained in citations of pseudoperiodicals, such as newspapers, bulletins, and concert programs.

If a volume number is missing or irrelevant, give the month and year, or season and year, or the exact date of publication. If authorship cannot be determined, begin with the title. If there is no proper title, describe the item in your own words without using quotation marks or title capitalization.

> 9 Gunther Schuller, "Conversation with Varèse," in Perspectives of New Music (spring–summer 1965), 32–37.
> 10 Bernard Holland, "Wagner's Legacy of Unease," in The New York Times, Thursday 27 March 1997, pp. C9, C14.
> 11 Specifications for the organ of Young United Church, Winnipeg, Manitoba, Orgues Létourneau Ltée. advertisement in The American Organist 31 (June 1997), 87.
> 12 Robert Pascall, "Ruminations on Brahms's Chamber Music," Musical Times 116 (August 1975), 699.

Note that the page citation for Bernard Holland's article includes an uppercase C before each page number. This letter refers to the layout of the *Times:* The pages cited here are from section C. Books, manuals, and other publications often have idiosyncratic pagination. Sometimes this involves division into sections; in other instances, pagination may begin anew in each chapter, with a prefatory numeral to show the particular chapter in which the page appears; in still other circumstances, each page may contain two or more numbered columns. Be sure to preserve such details: They may not be immediately comprehensible to readers, but when they see the source, the significance of these details will become clear.

79   Articles in periodicals: Short reference

Give only the author's last name, the title of the article, and the page reference. You may shorten the title, being sure to select the words that will be most helpful to the reader. In the case of Robert Pascall's article, the first word is of little help in determining the topic at hand. The real issue is Brahms's chamber music, so choose those words. There is no need to use an ellipsis to indicate that words have been dropped from the title.

Even though authors' names will enable the reader to differentiate among several studies of Brahms's chamber music, it will be helpful if you find some distinguishing feature of each title so that your shortened titles are not confusing:

13 Pascall, "Brahms's Chamber Music," 698.
14 Holland, "Wagner's Legacy," p. C9.

80   Articles in dictionaries and encyclopedias: First reference

Signed articles should be attributed to the author whose name or initials are given, usually at the end of the article. If initials only are given, attempt to discover the full name. Very often the front matter of a reference book will include a list of contributors. There, the initials appear in alphabetical order, followed by the person's full name.

Notes for dictionary and encyclopedia articles require a format that combines elements of book and periodical article formats. State the author's full name in regular order, *comma,* the title of the smaller article in quotation marks, *comma,* the title of the larger dictionary or encyclopedia in which the article appears, publication information in parentheses, and the page reference (with abbreviations "p." or "pp." as necessary) followed by a period. Remember that multivolume publications should include the volume number as well as the page or column number.

15 Walter Blankenburg, "Historia," Musik in Geschichte und Gegenwart, vol. 6 (Kassel: Bärenreiter, 1957), cols. 465–489.

Note: The publication information appears *after* the volume number because this seventeen-volume encyclopedia was published from 1949 to 1986. Here, the date of publication applies only to this particular volume. Note, too, that the format divides the page into columns; hence, the abbreviations "p." or "pp." would not be appropriate in this case.

A common mistake in citing articles from dictionaries and encyclopedias is to give the editor's name where the author's should appear. Remember: Editors are primarily responsible for ensuring consistent format and style throughout a publication; although they may write *some* of the articles included in the source, they generally are not responsible for all. You should be crediting the specialist who wrote the article, not the editor who supervised the project.

Sometimes—for instance, when the article is very brief, or the publication dates from 1950 or earlier—it is impossible to identify the author of a particular article. You may then attribute it to the editor:

16 Don M. Randel, ed., "Germany," The New Harvard Dictionary of Music (Cambridge, Massachusetts: Belknap Press of Harvard University Press, 1986), pp. 336–339.

81 Articles in dictionaries and encyclopedias: Short reference

Give as much information as necessary to make it clear that you are again referring to a source already cited:

17 Randel, "Germany," New Harvard, p. 337.

82 Sections in symposia and other collections: First reference

If it seems desirable to call attention to a particular section or chapter in a book, treat the title as a combination of article and book, just as we have done with articles appearing within dictionaries. Where several authors have contributed to a symposium, collection, or miscellany, identify the whole book as well as the individual essay. If the citation becomes complicated, some of the information may be put in parentheses.

18 Paul Griffiths, "Shostakovich and the Multiple Quartet," Part 4 section 3 in The String Quartet (New York: Thames and Hudson, 1983), pp. 210–217.

19 Charles Hamm, "Dvořák, Stephen Foster, and American National Song," in Dvořák in America: 1892–1895, ed. John C. Tibbetts (Portland, Oregon: Amadeus Press, 1993), pp. 149–156.

83 Sections in symposia and other collections: Short reference

Enough information should be given to make it clear that you are referring once more to a source already described. Usually the author's last name and the section title will suffice:

20 Hamm, "American National Song," p. 152.

84 Volume in a series or multivolume publication

It is usually easier to indicate the series title in the bibliography at the end of the essay rather than in a note. On some occasions, though, it is helpful for the reader to have this information. Since volumes in a series are generally not published simultaneously, accuracy demands that publication information be provided immediately after the volume number:

21 Anthony Lewis and Nigel Fortune, eds., Opera and Church Music: 1630–1750, Vol. 5 (New York: Oxford University Press, 1975), in New Oxford History of Music, p. 313.

Note: The series name, though it may comprise many titles, is not itself a title and should therefore be given in Roman type.

If all volumes in a multivolume publication were issued concurrently, publication information should be given in the conventional place:

22 Corliss Richard Arnold, Organ Literature: A Comprehensive Survey; 2d ed. Vol. 1, Historical Survey (Metuchen, New Jersey: Scarecrow Press, 1984), pp. 54–61.

Note: Edition numbers, volume numbers, and other generic elements of the title are not placed in italics, but they should be capitalized—whether spelled out or abbreviated—since they refer to specific volumes.

85 Reviews: First reference

Reviews of books, music, and recordings are useful sources of information and opinion. These citations are invariably cumbersome: They include a title, but the title is for the item being reviewed; and, they include the names of at least two people, that of the creator(s) of the item under consideration, and that of the reviewer. Similarly, publication information is doubled since one set of data refers to the principal item whereas the other set of data is for the review:

23 James Aikman, review of Elliot Schwartz and Daniel Godfrey, <u>Music since 1945: Issues, Materials, and Literature</u> (New York: Schirmer Books, 1993) in <u>College Music Symposium: The Journal of the College Music Society</u> 35 (1995), 145–147.

86 Reviews: Short reference

Give the last name of the reviewer, *comma*, the words "review of" followed by the last name(s) of the author(s) of the principal item, a shortened title, *comma*, followed by the word "in," and a shortened title of the source accompanied by a page reference:

24 Aikman, review of Schwartz and Godfrey, <u>Music since 1945,</u> in <u>Symposium,</u> 146.

Notes that cite reviews of symposia, collections of essays, or multiauthor works may begin to look like the Manhattan white pages. On the one hand, clarity is essential. On the other hand, brevity is important. Use your own good judgment: Give no more—and no less—data than necessary!

87 Plural references

If more than one reference is given in one sentence of a note, separate the references with semicolons. Such a plural reference eliminates the need for more than one note number at the same place in the text. In introducing the reader to a subject, it may be convenient to cumulate a selection of required reading in one note. While most notes are terse and telegraphic, the selected-readings note often exhibits a more leisurely, discursive tone (see Chapter 8). The following note is an excellent example. Notice how a reference to an article after its full citation simply gives the author's last name and the page citation set apart by commas:

25 Two discussions of realism as it ultimately relates to <u>verismo</u> are to be found in Dona De Sanctis, "Literary Realism and <u>Verismo</u> Opera," (Ph.D. dissertation, The City University of New York, 1983); and David Kimbell, "Italian Opera," in <u>National Traditions of Opera,</u> ed. John Warrack (Cambridge University Press, 1991), p. 625. Kimbell, p. 623, notes additionally that "veristic" works were less political than the corresponding works in France, since the newly unified Italy was to its intellectuals still more a source of pride than discontent.

88   Imprint information: Place, publisher, date

Librarians generally refer to details of publication (the place of publication, the name of the publisher, and the date of publication) as the imprint. It is generally advisable to give complete imprint information in your first citation of a published document. If it is necessary to save space in the first reference, give place *or* publisher (whichever is more recognizable), followed by a comma and the date: (London, 1853); (Oxford University Press, 1963).

A shortened imprint is often used for reprinted publications. In 1899, shortly after its original, German publication, Philipp Spitta's monumental biography of Bach was translated into English and published by Novello. As a standard resource in Bach scholarship, it has been reprinted on various occasions. To avoid misleading the novice, who might think that the work is fairly recent, the following sort of note is useful:

> 26 Philipp Spitta, <u>Johann Sebastian Bach: His Work and Influence on the Music of Germany, 1685–1750;</u> trans. Clara Bell and J. A. Fuller-Maitland (Novello, 1899; New York: Dover, 1951), vol. 1, p. 257.

Omit *Co., Inc., Ltd., Publications, The,* and similar qualifiers when they are not needed to complete the sense, as in Boston Music Co. First names or initials of publishers may be omitted, unless they are necessary to avoid confusion, as with E. C. Schirmer and G. Schirmer.

89   Joint authorship: First reference

Where two authors are jointly responsible for a work cited, give both names. If three or more authors are involved, give only the name of the first, followed by "and others."

> 27 James A. W. Heffernan and John E. Lincoln, <u>Writing: A College Handbook;</u> 2d ed. (New York: Norton, 1986), pp. 641–644.
> 28 Christoph Wolff and others, <u>The New Grove Bach Family</u> (New York: Norton, 1983), p. 44.

90   Joint authorship: Short reference

When two authors have collaborated, give both author's last names followed by the shortened title and page citation. For works by multiple authors, simply give the last name of the lead author:

29 Heffernan and Lincoln, <u>Writing,</u> p. 643.
30 Wolff, <u>New Grove Bach,</u> p. 44.

91   Editor or annotator: First reference

Where a responsible author can be found for a work, put the author's name first, and the abbreviation for "edited by" after the title. If original authorship is sufficiently clear in the title, begin with the title. The editor of a miscellaneous collection may be mentioned first.

31 Charles Burney, <u>A General History of Music</u> (London, 1776–89); ed. Frank Mercer (New York: Harcourt Brace, 1935), vol. 2, p. 16.
32 <u>The Letters of Richard Wagner: The Burrell Collection,</u> ed. John N. Burk (New York: Macmillan, 1950), p. 372.
33 Oliver Strunk, ed., <u>Source Readings in Music History</u> (New York: Norton, 1950), p. 707.

Note that the range of years during which Burney published his history is indicated immediately after the title. If the original imprint information appeared after the name of Frank Mercer, the novice historian might take him for an eighteenth-century editor!

Historical documents of extraordinary importance are regularly reprinted, often in facsimile editions. A true facsimile reproduces every detail of the original as faithfully as possible: page size, binding style, type-face, and even colors of ink or pencil. Although its purpose is legitimate, a topnotch facsimile has, in fact, the character of a forgery.

Facsimile reproductions are free from editorial interference. They are useful to experienced scholars, but sometimes an edited reprint will be more valuable for the scholar investigating an unfamiliar topic. An edited reprint usually includes conveniences that were not part of the original document. Tables of contents, lists of illustrations, prefatory essays, tables of errata, indexes, and perhaps even notes inserted throughout the body of the text—all facilitate the location and evaluation of information.

The usefulness of edited reprints is undeniable; nevertheless, the nature of the reproduction and the precise material being used should be clear from the note:

34 G. B. Harrison, ed., Introduction to Thomas Campion, <u>Observations in the Art of English Poesie</u> (London, 1602; corrected reprint, London, 1922; reprint of 1922 ed., New York: Barnes and Noble, 1966), p. vii.

A comparable situation arises in the citation of scores or recordings accompanied by annotations. If you are referring to the musical composition, then put the composer's name in lead position; if you are quoting from someone's annotations to a particular score or recording, lead off with that person's name:

> 35 Robert King, Preface to recording of Henry Purcell, <u>The Complete Anthems and Services,</u> vol. 3. (London: Hyperion CDA66623, 1993), p. 5.

92   Editor or annotator: Short reference

Cite either the author's or editor's name first, depending on the information that you use. If you give the editor or annotator first, mention the principal author's name before the main title.

> 36 Burney, <u>History,</u> vol. 2, p. 25.
> 37 Burk, <u>Letters of Richard Wagner,</u> p. 376.
> 38 Harrison, ed., Preface to Campion, <u>Observations,</u> p. v.

93   Translator: First reference

Give the original author, *comma*, the title as it appears in translation, *semicolon*, the abbreviation "trans." *(no comma)*, and the full name of the translator. Proceed with the usual note information depending on the format (book, journal article, etc.) of the item.

> 39 Johann J. Quantz, <u>On Playing the Flute;</u> trans. Edward R. Reilly (New York: Free Press of Glencoe, 1966), p. 46.
> 40 Hans T. David, "Deceptive Performance Traditions"; trans. Alfred Mann, <u>Bach: Journal of the Riemenschneider Bach Institute</u> 25 (fall–winter 1994), 36–53.

94   Translator: Short reference

Indicate only as much information as is required to avoid confusion. Usually the original author's last name, *comma*, the shortened translated title, and a page reference will suffice:

> 41 Quantz, <u>On Playing the Flute,</u> p. 118.
> 42 David, "Performance Traditions," 39.

95   Editions

Statements of fact or opinion may vary in different editions of the same work. Identify the edition used, and verify the date at which the particular passage cited appeared in print. A reissue or reprint may bear a later date on the title page; check the *verso* of the title page for the date of the edition—this is what carries weight in the timing of the author's statement or comment. Consider this example:

> 43 Cecil Forsyth, <u>Orchestration;</u> 2d ed. (New York: Macmillan, 1935), p. 115.

The copy consulted was reprinted in 1946; however, a reprint is not a new edition. Normally this designation simply means that the publisher—having sold their entire stock of a given title—printed additional copies, without any changes in content. The statement appearing in the second edition *may* have been made in the first edition (1914). Forsyth died in 1941. In any case, he believed in this statement as of 1935.

Scholarly literature reflects its time: A new edition will not only correct errors of earlier editions but will also take into account recent scholarship and adjust the focus and presentation to accord with current critical thinking. Unless there is a particular reason for using an old edition, writers should ordinarily consult the most recent edition of a source:

> 44 Rey M. Longyear, <u>Nineteenth-Century Romanticism in Music;</u> 3d ed. (Englewood Cliffs, New Jersey: Prentice Hall, 1988), pp. 54–56.

96   Musical editions

Always cite the edition used when referring to a passage in a musical score. Follow accepted procedure in citing titles: Italicize distinctive titles of substantial works; place distinctive titles of movements within double quotation marks; use capitals for generic titles of large scores; and capitalize tempo words for subsections of generic works. In some cases, you may prefer to designate movements with ordinal numbers.

Since publication dates are seldom given for music, consider using the copyright date with the sign © or the lowercase letter "c" followed immediately by the year, without a period or space between. Sometimes the preface may be dated. If a date is associated with the edition but does not appear in its customary location on the *verso* of the title page, enclose the date in brackets to make it clear to the reader that this is the best information you have been able to find. You may verify publication dates by checking the publisher's catalog for the year in question; consider, as well, the possibility of confirming the date by consulting a library catalog or union catalog. Where relevant to the discussion, mention the editor. If the volume used is part of a series, give the series title as well.

> 45 Franz Joseph Haydn, Sonata in C major, Hob. XVI/50 in Vol. 3 of <u>Haydn: Sämtliche Klaviersonaten;</u> ed. Christa Landon (Vienna: Universal, [1964]), pp. 79–94.
>
> 46 Olivier Messiaen, <u>La Nativité du Seigneur: Neuf méditations pour orgue</u> (Paris: Leduc, ©1936).

Notes for musical editions require the same protocol as those for conventional text sources: If you are using a reprint edition, make that clear in the note. Either of the following formats would be suitable:

> 47 Franz Peter Schubert, "Im Dorfe" from <u>Winterreise</u> (Leipzig: Breitkopf und Härtel, 1895; reprint New York: Dover, 1970), pp. 110–113.
>
> 48 Franz Peter Schubert, "Im Dorfe" from <u>Winterreise</u> (Leipzig, 1895; New York: Dover, 1970), pp. 110–113.

If you refer to a movement within a larger work and both have distinctive titles, give the movement title in quotation marks first, then cite the main title in italics:

> 49 Daniel Pinkham, "The Miracle on the Lake," <u>Miracles for Flute and Organ</u> (Boston, Massachusetts: E. C. Schirmer, c1978), pp. 10–16.

Do not be dismayed when rules come into conflict: Foreign words normally appear in italic print; however, if you are showing a foreign-language title of a subsection within a larger work, use Roman type for the subsection title, enclose it in quotation marks, and give the main title in italics:

> 50 Charles Ives, "Qu'il m'irait bien," in <u>114 Songs</u> (Charles Ives, 1922; New York: Peer International, 1954), pp. 168–170.

97 Musical editions: Measure numbers, rehearsal letters, entry points

If possible, use an edition that includes measure numbers, rehearsal numbers, rehearsal letters, or some type of entry point system. Remember: Rehearsal numbers are not the same as measure numbers!

If an edition with printed entry points is unavailable, count measures consecutively through an entire movement, beginning with the first *complete* measure as measure 1. Do not count an incomplete opening measure. For first and second endings, designate the first with the uppercase letter "A" beside the number, and identify the second with the same number followed by the uppercase letter "B."

If the score you are using employs rehearsal letters or rehearsal numbers rather than measure numbers, identify a particular measure in the following way: Give the nearest designated entry point followed by a plus or minus sign and an Arabic numeral, showing how many measures before or after the entry point a particular measure is. In the following example, for instance, the measure at issue is two measures *before* rehearsal number 97:

> A difficult bit of vocal writing appears at 97-2 in the Wedding Feast tableau, where Stravinsky requires the solo bass to sing a portamento through the interval of a descending diminished octave.

In some cases, the most expeditious procedure will be to indicate the page number, the system on the page, and the particular measure(s) in the system. To avoid confusion, an explanatory note may be helpful when you make your first reference to a score. Since publishers use a wide variety of score formats, it is unlikely that you will be able to use the same system throughout your entire essay; nevertheless, references to any particular score should be consistent in style.

> 51 Arnold Schoenberg, String Quartet, Op. 30 (Vienna: Universal, 1927), first movement, meas. 130–139.
> 52 Maurice Ravel, String Quartet in F major (New York: International Music Co., n.d.), first movement, L+1–L+6.
> 53 Charles Ives, String Quartet No. 1 (New York: Peer International, ©1961), first movement, p. 5, system 2, meas. 4.

The preceding discussion has obviously presumed conventional, present-day notation. But there were no bar lines in most music written before the seventeenth century, and likewise in contemporary music, the identification of particular moments in the score will often be problematic; it is well known, for instance, that Ives did not use bar lines in all his works. Rely on your own good judgment in calling your reader's attention to some particular musical event. Notation is discussed further in Chapter 21.

98   Recordings

At a minimum, give the composer, title of the composition, record company, and issue number. Provide any further information that would be pertinent to the discussion or useful to the reader. Contemporary technology provides us with myriad formats for recordings. It may be helpful to note the recording medium in your documentation, whether long-playing record, audio cassette, videocassette, compact disc, laser disc, or some other venue.

Entry points in long-playing records are usually reckoned in terms of disc, side, and band. On modern compact discs, numbers enclosed in boxes serve the same purpose. In citing a recorded performance, provide all necessary information according to the standard format, and, where a page reference might be given for a book, simply note the appropriate disc and box:

> 54   Richard Strauss, "Di rigori armato il seno," from <u>Der Rosenkavalier;</u> cond. by Bernard Haitink (EMI Records CDS 7 54259 1/2, ©1991), CD 2, box 13.

If necessary, you may improvise note formats according to the general principles outlined earlier.

99   Record jackets

Information provided by annotators of recordings should be treated in the same manner as data provided by editors. For details, see rules 91 and 92.

100   Manuscripts

Reference to early manuscripts, composers' autographs, and the like, presupposes sufficient research experience for the student to make proper citations. Make clear in your discussion of the source and in the bibliography what exactly you have consulted, whether the original or a photocopy. Published facsimiles should be described as such. See rule 144.

101   Theses, dissertations

Titles of master's theses and doctoral dissertations are usually put in quotation marks in Roman type. Specify either thesis or dissertation, cite the sponsoring institution and its location (if that is not apparent), and give the date:

55 Susan Elyse Unmack, "Traditional German Music as a Propagandistic Device in the Third Reich" (Master's thesis, San Francisco State University, 1984), pp. 146–148.

56 Marie Ann Heiberg Vos, "The Liturgical Choral Works of Johann Christian Bach" (Ph.D. dissertation, Washington University, St. Louis, Missouri, 1969), vol. 1, p. 280.

102   Letters and other original sources

Even when citing published letters, lectures, master classes, interviews, diaries, or other items of a potentially personal nature, observe good taste: The fact that something appears in print does not necessarily mean that the person responsible for the statement intended it for the general public. If you use a published source, follow the customary procedures.

Substantiation of unpublished materials is somewhat more complex; nevertheless, the principles of documentation still apply. Identify the person responsible for the statements, the interviewer (if any), and the date and circumstances under which the statement was made. When the information is recorded in some document, such as a letter, give the location of the document. A note for an unpublished letter might look like this:

57 Aaron Copland, letter of 19 December 1978 to Mark A. Radice in response to an inquiry concerning the status of the original 1939 version of the incidental music for Irwin Shaw's play "Quiet City." Copland indicated that the work now known as "Quiet City" was written after the incidental music for the play, and that it is in effect a separate concert piece. The original incidental music exists only in manuscript and is not available. Letter in the present writer's collection.

When the person responsible for unpublished information is still living, it is both prudent and courteous to obtain corroboration of the statement and permission to use it. Correspondence between the writer and the person making the statement—in the form of signed, hard copy—is a sure way to avoid embarrassment or potential legal problems. Furthermore, such documentation will verify the authenticity of the information cited even in the event of the subject's death.

103   Web sites

Web sites are an ephemeral form of publication and should therefore be used sparingly. In a note, give the responsible person and/or organization, the indication "Web site" enclosed in brackets, *comma*, the title of the item and/or entry-point link in quotation marks, the date when the page was last modified enclosed in parentheses, *comma*, the words "Site address," *colon*, and the pertinent data. Do not add a period at the end of the site address! For example:

> 58 Mary I. Arlin, Music Theory Society of New York State [Web site], "Call for Papers for 1998 Meeting" (14 April 1997), Site address: http://www.ithaca.edu/music/music3/mtsnys

104 Iconography

You may sometimes wish to mention or describe visual objects in your writing. These images may be artistic (paintings, sculpture, architecture) or documentary (photographs, maps, drawings). If the image is readily available—a map of the United States, or da Vinci's *Mona Lisa,* for instance—you may not even need to refer your reader to a source. For more esoteric items, you can simplify your work by referring the reader to a published source:

> 59 Two shawms with slide trumpet as depicted in Brussels, Bibliothèque royale, Ms. 14967, in Keith Polk, <u>German Instrumental Music of the Late Middle Ages: Players, Patrons, and Performance Practice</u> (New York: Cambridge University Press, 1992), p. 65.

Any images included in your essay should be clearly identified with a caption or legend, indicating the source of the illustration. If illustrations are numerous, it may be helpful to provide a table of illustrations. Titles of artistic works should be italicized.

105 Latin terms for documentation: Op. cit., loc. cit., *idem,* ibid.

The abbreviations "op. cit." and "loc. cit." are cumbersome antiques. They should not be used in contemporary writing, and the reader encountering such potentially confusing directives in older sources should be cautious; nevertheless, a good researcher or writer should understand how these abbreviations are supposed to work.

Op. cit. (*opere citato,* "in the work [reference] cited") replaces a title only, and typically appears with an author's name and page reference. The assumption is that only a single work by the author named has been cited.

Loc. cit. (*loco citato*, "in the place [passage] cited") is always used in conjunction with an author's name. In such a context, the assumption is—as with op. cit.—that only a single work by the author has been cited. Loc. cit. has the effect of restating that title and referring the reader to the page location most recently cited from that source.

Idem ("the same person [author]") is not an abbreviation and hence requires no period, but it should be italicized. It refers to the author of the immediately preceding note; a different title by that author must follow, and a page reference must be included.

Of the Latin terms for documentation, only ibid. (*ibidem*, "in the same place [reference]") is still in current use. It refers to the author and title given in the preceding note. To avoid confusion, include a page reference whenever you use ibid., even if you are citing the same page as the previous note.

In closely documented papers, ibid. may be used in series (analogous to ditto marks in a vertical column). A note that refers to a different source will break the chain.

Note: When ibid. is the first word of a note or sentence, it should be capitalized. Do not capitalize the term if it appears within a sentence. Regardless of its position, ibid. should always be followed by a period. Italics are not necessary.

CHAPTER 8

Discursive Notes

106 Rationale

Besides serving the important function of documentation, notes may contain commentary or discussion that would be inappropriate in the main text of a paper or thesis.

107 Directives

An otherwise standard note citation may be introduced with one of the following directives:

see	refers the reader to the source cited for full details; implies that you have presented only the main gist of an extended argument or complex series of facts
see also	refers to still another source (besides any already mentioned) which corroborates your arguments or gives further details; implies that there is no room to deal with this additional item in the body of your text
but see	refers to a source that differs with your own argument on minor or major points; in order not to tease the reader, explain briefly the points of difference
compare	challenges the reader to look up the reference cited and compare it with your own argument; tends to suggest a blend of "see," "see also," and "but see"

108 Running comment

Writers can condense a great deal of information by incorporating commentary into notes, which, though discursive, should be written in a dry style. Although punctuation is used in such notes, it is not always within the context of complete or elegant sentences:

> 1 Richard Crawford, "Edward MacDowell: Musical Nationalism and an American Tone Poet," <u>Journal of the American Musicological Society</u> 49 (fall 1996), 528–560, argues that late nineteenth-century New York provided MacDowell with a conspicuous milieu for his career. Further, that Columbia University's first professorship of music gave him a prestigious forum, yet detracted from his creative energy. Lawrence Gilman's <u>Edward MacDowell</u> (1906; first monograph on an American composer) attempted to confirm MacDowell as evidence of American musical maturity.

109 Supplementary discussion, with citation

If you get involved with a side issue that has no place in the main text, refer the reader to essential information in a note. You may indicate your sources of information at the end of such a note.

110 Parenthetical citation

Where a short reference will do, a convenient form is to put the citation in parentheses at the end:

> 2 The Prelude to <u>Tristan</u> was performed at the Paris concert of 25 January 1860. (Barzun, <u>Berlioz and His Century,</u> p. 355.)

111 Addenda

When the meeting is over, the discussion is continued in the halls! Any information, illustrations, polemics, and so on, that cannot be gracefully incorporated into the main text may be placed in the notes—provided one does not abuse the privilege.

CHAPTER 9

Bibliography

112 Placement

In an essay, article, thesis, or any other document that does not have an index, the bibliography always comes last. The Arabic page numbers of the manuscript are continued consecutively through the bibliography (and also through the index, if present). For a long paper or thesis, begin the bibliography on a new page with the heading "Bibliography," treated in the same manner as a chapter title. For a shorter paper where the main text occupies only part of the last page, by all means drop two double-spaces below the end of the text, put the bibliography heading, and use the available space.

113 Purpose

The bibliography serves two purposes: the ethical function of notifying the reader concerning the sources of the writer's information and the practical purpose of providing interested readers with material for further study. As a consequence of the dual function, several philosophical approaches may be taken.

114 Philosophies of bibliography

Before assembling the bibliography, a writer must first determine which philosophical approach to follow. Is the primary purpose of the bibliography the documentation of the present essay? Or rather does this article have the character of a preliminary study? Is it likely that I—or some other scholar—will continue this research at some later point?

If your bibliography exists primarily or exclusively for the present essay, then use a selected bibliography. If on the other hand you are involved with a preliminary study, you might opt for a complete bibliography.

In a selected bibliography, it is customary to include only those sources that were consulted, and that contributed directly or indirectly to the study. In a complete bibliography, however, the writer attempts to give an exhaustive list of the sources relevant to the subject. Complete bibliographies often include items the author has not seen, which circumstance should be mentioned in an explanatory note or in annotations accompanying the entry for a particular item. Ordinarily the inclusion of such sources presumes that they are of paramount importance to the topic, but that they simply could not be obtained. Rare items held in private collections, fragile documents that cannot be photocopied, dissertations in progress, or even books forthcoming from a publisher often account for entries of this sort. In a complete bibliography, it is perfectly legitimate to include items not actually used, since the bibliography is intended as much to facilitate future research as it is to document the present effort.

Complete bibliographies are usually appropriate for research proposals (such as a formal proposal for a master's thesis or doctoral dissertation), grant proposals, or publication proposals. In such cases, the point to be made is twofold: First, that the research to date proves the topic is viable; and, second, that further investigation is necessary before closure on an issue can be reached.

115   Types of bibliographies

A unified bibliography brings together all items into one alphabetical listing. Unified bibliographies are practical for short articles that use relatively few sources.

As you read this chapter, you will notice that it has been divided into five main sections: books; periodicals; encyclopedias, dictionaries, and collections; music; and other sources, such as reviews, dissertations, iconography, and Web sites. This grouping of sources into generic types is a convenience for the writer, since the details of a bibliographic entry will vary depending on the item being described. A bibliography divided in this manner is called a classified bibliography. Additional classifications, such as videocassettes or CD-ROMs, may also be useful. The classifications that you use will depend upon your topic, the format of the related sources, and the number of sources of each type. As a general rule, if a particular classification has just several sources, it is better to subsume those entries under some other appropriate heading.

116 Explanatory matter

Any special circumstances connected with the bibliography may be explained in a short single-spaced paragraph just below the heading. Typical matters requiring explanation include symbols or abbreviations used in the entries; unavailability of important sources not listed, or listed but not seen; omission of obvious available sources; and general commentary on the whole bibliography, or on selected items within it.

117 Content, form

Bibliographic entries contain much of the same information as notes, but within the context of a bibliography, some data that was coincidental in a note assumes an integral place. Collect the data and organize it within the entry as follows: creator, creation, imprint, and collation.

The creator may be an author, composer, sculptor, computer programmer, or even a task-force or corporation. The creation might range from more traditional forms (a biography, a poem, a musical composition, a painting) to more recent formats—a computer program, videotape, radio or television broadcast, or any other manifestation now or soon to be made possible, as a result of technological developments.

The imprint refers to the duplication and distribution of the creation. In the case of a conventional book, the imprint will tell the city of the publisher, the publisher's name, and the year in which the item was published.

The physical features of the item or document are collectively subsumed under the concept of collation: Books will include pages and, perhaps, volumes of a particular size; recordings will involve either LPs, compact discs, cassettes, or some other medium.

The form of bibliographic entries is important. Use hanging indentation for each item listed. Begin the first line flush with the left margin. All subsequent lines of the same entry should be indented. Set a tab so that all indented lines have the same left-hand indentation. In manuscript, the material is all single-spaced. In short bibliographies, a blank space may be left between entries if desired. For a thesis, dissertation, or other document that may have hundreds of items, the blank spaces add up quickly: For the sake of economy, leave them out.

118 Style

Whereas notes employ commas, colons, semicolons, periods, and other sentence punctuation quite liberally, a bibliographic entry has mostly periods. The models presented here are dogmatic only in the interests of consistency. In practice, styles vary widely, relative both to layout and to completeness and accuracy of content.

Another fundamental difference between notes and bibliographic entries is that bibliographies are ordered alphabetically, making numbering superfluous, whereas notes should always be numbered.

119   Annotations

An annotation is a brief comment on the content or quality of a bibliographic entry. Such a commentary may be directed toward the work as a whole or only toward those portions that are relevant; it may be either in the writer's own words or an edited version of matter taken from the work being annotated, such as the table of contents or preface.

> McClary, Susan. Feminine Endings. Minneapolis: University of Minnesota Press, 1991. 220 p. Essays in feminist music criticism dealing with gender and sexuality in music ranging from the early seventeenth century to the present. Pages 148–168 explore the role of women as composers in pop culture.

Books

120   Standard entry

Consult the title page and the reverse (verso) of the title page for the information needed. In its simplest form, the entry should contain author's last name, comma, given name(s), period. Full title, underlined, period. Place, colon: publisher, comma, date, period. Number of pages, period.

> Yudkin, Jeremy. Music in Medieval Europe. Englewood Cliffs, New Jersey: Prentice Hall, 1989. 612 p.

121   Author's name

The author's name as given on the title page is usually the correct form, but if the title page omits names or initials normally associated with the author, or required to establish identity, supply them from some other reliable source.

In strictest bibliographic form, such emendations are enclosed in brackets:

Asafiev, B[oris] V[ladimirovich], [pseud. Igor Glebov]. <u>Russian
Music from the Beginning of the Nineteenth Century.</u>
Trans. Alfred J. Swan. Ann Arbor, Michigan: J. W. Edwards,
1953.

Glebov, Igor [recte Boris Vladimirovich Asafiev]. <u>Russian Music
from the Beginning of the Nineteenth Century.</u> Trans.
Alfred J. Swan. Ann Arbor, Michigan: J. W. Edwards, 1953.

122   Joint authorship

Only the first author's name need be alphabetized. It is unnecessary to
give associate authors' names in reverse order:

Dart, Thurston, Walter Emery, and Christopher Morris. <u>Editing
Early Music: Notes on the Preparation of Printer's Copy.</u>
Fair Lawn, New Jersey: Oxford University Press, 1963.
22 p.

Occasionally, where several authors are involved, the entry may be sim-
plified by putting only the most important name(s), followed by "and others." The additional names may be given later in the entry, or in an annotation.

Nichols, Roger, and others. <u>The New Grove Twentieth-Century
French Masters.</u> New York: Norton, 1986. 291 p.

123   Corporate authorship

Some documents are produced by organizations rather than individuals.
When citing sources of this type, the organization is considered the creator
or author. When organizational subcommittees are involved, indicate the
formal designation of these subcommittees:

College Music Society Study Group on the Content of the
Undergraduate Music Curriculum. <u>Music in the
Undergraduate Curriculum: A Reassessment.</u> CMS Report
Number 7. Boulder, Colorado: College Music Society, 1989.
65 p.

124   Same author

When listing two or more titles by the same author, do not repeat the
name, but put seven hyphens, followed by a period.

Cone, Edward T. The Composer's Voice. Berkeley and Los
Angeles: University of California Press, 1974. 184 p.
-------. Music: A View from Delft. Ed. Robert P. Morgan.
University of Chicago Press, 1989. 334 p.

125   No author

A few works may be said to have no author, properly speaking. The title
itself is run out to the left margin, alphabetized along with the other
entries. With some standard reference works, the original editor's name
has now become a part of the accepted title.

Baker's Biographical Dictionary of Musicians; 8th ed. Rev.
Nicolas Slonimsky New York: Schirmer Books, 1990.
2,115 p.
The New Harvard Dictionary of Music. Ed. Don M. Randel.
Cambridge, Massachusetts: Belknap Press of Harvard
University Press, 1986. 942 p.
Prentice-Hall Author's Guide. Englewood Cliffs, New Jersey:
Prentice Hall, 1978.

Note: *The New Harvard Dictionary of Music* is alphabetized using "new"
(not "the") as the first word.

126   Titles

Most books have two title pages, one called a bastard-title page and the
other a full-title page. The bastard-title page acquired its unlovely name
because no responsible author is identified on that page. If the full title
includes a subtitle, the subtitle is also omitted from the bastard-title page;
consequently, this page is sometimes called a half-title page, but technically, the term is inaccurate when no subtitle is involved.

For the bibliographic entries, copy the exact wording from the full-
title page. You might need to add some punctuation as you transcribe the
display type; add a colon to separate the main title from a subtitle and a
period at the end.

Titles are often followed by supplemental data indicating such information as the number of volumes in the set, the edition, and the translator. Such details are not part of the title: They should not be treated as
titles when questions of italicization and capitalization are considered.

127 Title capitalization

Capitalize the first word of the title and subtitle (if any), and all principal words, including nouns, pronouns, adjectives, verbs, and adverbs. Do not capitalize articles, prepositions, or conjunctions unless they are the first word of the title or subtitle. Note: When used in an infinitive, "to" is part of a verb—*not* a preposition: It must be capitalized. Italicized words in the printed title are put in Roman type in the manuscript, and vice versa:

> Warrack, John. Richard Wagner: Die Meistersinger von
>   Nürnberg. New York: Cambridge University Press, 1994.
>   175 p.

128 Foreign titles

Give foreign titles in the original language. In German, capitalize the first word and all nouns, but not the adjectives or other parts of speech. In Latin, French, Italian, Spanish, Portuguese, and most other Western European languages, capitalize the first word and proper nouns only.

> Neumann, Friedrich-Heinrich. Die Ästhetik des Rezitativs: Zur
>   Theorie des Rezitativs im 17. und 18. Jahrhundert. Baden-
>   Baden: Verlag Heitz, 1962. 112 p.

If you wish, put an English translation of the title, in parentheses and in Roman type, after the foreign title. Do not use title capitalization for the English translation of foreign titles:

> Schering, Arnold. Geschichte des Instrumentalkonzerts bis auf
>   die Gegenwart (History of the instrumental concerto to the
>   present). Reprint of the 1927 ed. Hildesheim: Olms;
>   Wiesbaden: Breitkopf und Härtel, 1965. 235 p.

Information other than the title *(herausgegeben; zweite Auflage; nouvelle édition; augmentée)* should be given in English; but if you are in doubt about the meaning of these terms, leave them in the original languages.

129 Volumes

If the title as given covers more than one volume, give the number of volumes in Arabic numerals after the title, followed by the abbreviation "vols."

If the volumes all appeared within a few years, give the inclusive years of the first and last volumes as the publication date for the entire series:

Lockspeiser, Edward. <u>Debussy: His Life and Mind.</u> 2 vols. New
York: Macmillan, 1962–1965.

When a source includes many volumes that were published over a considerable period of time, indicate the publication dates for each volume:

Burney, Charles. <u>A General History of Music.</u> 4 vols. London:
published by the author. Vol. 1, 1776; vol. 2, 1782; vols. 3
and 4, 1789.

130   Editions

Information concerning the edition used normally follows the title. A typical note might take the following form:

Duckles, Vincent H., and Ida Reed. <u>Music Reference and
Research Materials: An Annotated Bibliography.</u> 5th ed.
New York: Schirmer Books, 1997. 812 p.

Accuracy is of primary importance in bibliographic entries, but to be accurate, one must understand some fundamental concepts about documents. For one thing, a reissue or reprinting is not the same thing as a new edition. An edition "published with new material" in 1967, reissued in 1985, and reprinted in 1986 and 1987, still belongs under 1967 from the standpoint of content. A new edition means that significant changes have been made in the content or organization of the original. Publishers generally assume that at least twenty percent of the information will be new when they write a contract with an author for a new edition. In many cases, the changes are so far-reaching that the connection between the new edition and the original becomes tentative at best.

Whenever you use a source, be certain that you are looking at the most recent edition. Use an old edition only when that particular edition has some special information or organizational feature that is crucial to your topic.

In your bibliographic entries, be sure that the edition is properly designated. Examine the *verso* of the title page and give the date of the edition used. A typical entry might look like this:

Wingell, Richard J. <u>Writing about Music: An Introductory
Guide.</u> 2d ed. Englewood Cliffs, New Jersey: Prentice Hall,
1997. 160 p.

If the copy happens to be a reprint, you should make that clear for several reasons: for the sake of accuracy, for the purpose of informing the reader of the most recent printing of the item, and for alerting the user to possible differences that may appear. Even though the content of a reprint may mirror the earlier version, publishers often modify the collation when issuing reprints. Some cases become extraordinarily complex, as new editions, supplemental volumes, translations, revised translations, reprints, changes in collation, and other features become involved. Consider the following examples:

> Fétis, François-Joseph. Biographie universelle des musiciens et bibliographie générale de la musique. Paris, 1835–1844; 2d ed., Paris: Didot, 1866–1870. 2-vol. supplement ed. Arthur Pougin, Paris, 1878–1880. Reprint of the 2d ed. with supplements. 10 vols. Brussels: Editions Culture et Civilisation, 1963.
>
> Hawkins, John. General History of the Science and Practice of Music. London, 1776. 5 vols. New ed., with the author's posthumous notes. 3 vols. London: Novello, 1853; reprinted 1875. Unabridged reprint of the 1853 ed. with an introduction by Charles Cudworth. 2 vols. New York: Dover, 1963.

131   Translator

Give original author's name, the exact title of the translation, the abbreviation "trans.," and the translator's name. The language from which the translation was made may be indicated, but in most cases, the original language will be obvious from the imprint information. If, for instance, the imprint of the original was given as Berlin 1906, most readers would assume that the original language was German. Admittedly, these assumptions are not always valid; however, it is better to call attention to the exceptions than to state what is obvious.

If desired, title and publication information for the original version may be given in an annotation. If the translated version contains material not included in the original—supplements, errata sheets, indexes, and so on—call attention to these features.

> Bach, Carl Philipp Emanuel. Essay on the True Art of Playing Keyboard Instruments. Trans. William J. Mitchell. New York: Norton, 1949. 449 p. Originally published Berlin, 1753.

132   Series

If the volume used is part of a series, include the series title (and number, if any) in the entry. The name of the series should follow the title of the individual volume. The series name, though it may comprise many titles, is not itself a title and should therefore be given in Roman type:

> Ringer, Alexander, ed. <u>The Early Romantic Era: Between the Revolutions, 1789–1848.</u> Music and Society. Englewood Cliffs, New Jersey: Prentice Hall, 1991. 325 p.

133   Imprint data

The imprint indicates where, by whom, and when a particular document was published. In almost every case, it is better to give abundant information rather than to have gaps that lead to confusion or inconvenience in locating source materials.

When citing first publications, always give the city, *colon,* the publisher, *comma,* and the year, *period.* A simple citation might look like this:

> Watanabe, Ruth T. <u>Introduction to Music Research.</u> Englewood Cliffs, New Jersey: Prentice Hall, 1967. 237 p.

For reprints, select either the city or publisher of the original—whichever is better known—followed by a *comma,* the year of the original publication, *semicolon;* then give the city, publisher, and date of the reprint edition:

> Daniel, Samuel. <u>A Defence of Ryme: Against a Pamphlet Entituled</u> Observations in the Art of English Poesie. London, 1603; New York: Barnes and Noble, 1966. [46 p.]

134   Place of publication

Sometimes several place names appear on the title page. When deciding which to name as the place of publication, keep in mind what would be most convenient and expedient for your reader. You may either cite the publisher's headquarters; cite the place from which you or your intended reader would probably try to obtain a copy; or cite the place from which the copy in hand originated. Consider the following example:

> Benestad, Finn, and Dag Schjelderup-Ebbe. <u>Edvard Grieg: Chamber Music.</u> New York: Oxford University Press, 1993.

In fact, this monograph on Grieg's chamber music is published in Oslo by the Scandinavian University Press. To obtain copies from abroad, however, would involve much time and expense, and probably some frustration. An author writing in the United States should simply direct the reader to the local representative, who can supply the item in question simply, easily, and quickly.

Where a work is issued separately or jointly by agreement between two or more publishers, give more details for the copy actually used and only the basics of the original publication. If you have seen both versions, include them in your entry. An alternate version not seen may be mentioned in an annotation.

> Burden, Michael. <u>Purcell Remembered.</u> London: Faber and
> Faber; Portland, Oregon: Amadeus Press, 1995. 188 p.

If the publisher's name is unknown, give the place and date, separated by a comma. This may be taken as a confession that you have not seen the book. Explain!

> Avison, Charles. <u>Essay on Musical Expression.</u> London, 1752.
> Not available for the present study.

If careful inspection reveals no publisher, give a warning in brackets: [no publisher given].

In cases where the author has personally published the work (French: *Auteur;* German: *Selbstverlag*), simply state, "published by the author."

If no place is given, use the abbreviation "n.p."

135 Date of publication

Check both the full-title page and its *verso* before settling on the publication date. If there is no date, use the abbreviation "n.d." Through your own detective efforts, you might find the date in a reliable bibliographic reference work; provide an exact date [1997] or approximate date [ca. 1997] in brackets.

136 Pages

Give total number of pages in the work, normally the last Arabic page number (which may be on the last page of an appendix, bibliography, or index). If introductory matter is important or extensive, indicate the number of pages involved (usually in small Roman numerals):

Hopkinson, Cecil. A Bibliography of the Musical and Literary
Works of Hector Berlioz. With Histories of the French
Music Publishers Concerned. Printed for the Edinburgh
Bibliographical Society, 1951. xix, 205 p. Introduction, pp.
ix–xix, has illuminating commentary on the bibliographer's
problems.

The annotation might be expanded by mentioning illustrations, plates, musical examples, and facsimiles. Account for significant or extensive bound-in or accompanying matter that is separately paged or unpaged:

Collaer, Paul. A History of Modern Music. Trans. Sally Abeles.
Cleveland: World Publishing, 1961. 414 p.; 48 p.
(unnumbered) musical examples bound-in between
pp. 400 and 401.

For very accurate bibliographic description, bracket blind folios (pages that are counted, even though unnumbered): Introduction, pp. [v]–viii; errata p. [36].

Be sure to note that a source consists of more than a single volume, if that is the case. You can use a combination of Roman and Arabic numerals separated by a comma to show the number of pages in each volume; or, if you prefer, use the abbreviation for "volume" followed by an Arabic number, *comma*, and then give the number of pages (or run of pages) in each volume. The individual volumes and their pagination should be separated by a *semicolon:*

Arnold, Denis, ed. New Oxford Companion to Music. New
York: Oxford University Press, 1983. Vol. 1, pp. 1–1,007;
vol. 2, pp. [1,008]–2,017.

Note: In this example, the pages of the two volumes are numbered consecutively. Because the second volume begins with an unnumbered page, its number must be deduced by counting backward from the first numbered page. Rigorous documentation requires the placement of the editorially supplied page number in brackets.

Where each volume has a title of its own, supply the individual volume titles for each. If the volumes were issued over a period of years, you may either give the range of publication years for the entire set of volumes, or place the publication date of each volume beside it in parentheses.

Westernhagen, Curt von. Wagner: A Biography. 2 vols. Trans.
Mary Whittall. New York: Cambridge University Press,

1978. Vol. 1, <u>Wagner: 1813–1864,</u> 327 p.; vol. 2, <u>Wagner: 1864–1883,</u> pp. 329–654.

137   Editors, annotators

In addition to the principal author or authors, bibliographies often contain information or even separate entries for editors, annotators, and the like.

Where a responsible author can be found, list the entry by author, and put the abbreviation for "edited by" after the title. When the editor is mainly responsible for a work, or when it would be unwieldy to cite individual authors, begin the entry with the editor's name:

> Forbes, Elliot, ed. <u>Thayer's Life of Beethoven.</u> Princeton, New
>   Jersey: Princeton University Press, 1967. 1141 p.
> Samson, Jim, ed. <u>The Late Romantic Era: From the Mid-</u>
>   <u>Nineteenth Century to World War I.</u> Englewood Cliffs, New
>   Jersey: Prentice Hall, 1991. 463 p.

The first of these two examples involves a complex sequence of events: Elliot Forbes revised Henry E. Krehbiel's 1921 translation of Alexander Wheelock Thayer's biography of Beethoven. Thayer, though born in Massachusetts, studied in Germany; the three volumes of his biography were published in German between 1866 and 1879. By that time, he had chronicled Beethoven's life and works up until the year 1816. Other scholars used Thayer's notes to supply the remaining two volumes of what was a five-volume work when the last volume appeared in 1908. Depending on the nature of the essay, an author may choose either to pass over these details in silence, or to provide some of this background information.

The second example shows a simple case where a volume has been compiled from related essay topics. The authors are too numerous to mention specifically, and the editor's name stands as the creator.

Periodicals

138   Standard entry

In its simplest form, the entry should contain the author's last name, *comma,* given names, *period.* The title of the article appears in quotation marks, *period inside the closing double quotes,* followed by the title of the periodical, italicized and with proper title capitalization *(no comma)* the volume number in Arabic numerals *(no comma)* year in parentheses, *comma*, inclusive pages, *period*.

> Hindley, Clifford. "Why Does Miles Die? A Study of Britten's The Turn of the Screw." Musical Quarterly 74 (1990), 1–17.

Some periodicals are published with both volume numbers and issue numbers (Vol. 4, No. 3). The issue number should be omitted for periodicals that are ordinarily bound in consecutively paged annual volumes. For issues that are not consecutively paged throughout a year, or that offer other complications, include the issue number and any other helpful clarifications.

Articles are sometimes too lengthy to be published complete in a single issue of a periodical. In such cases, the journal editor may decide to print the article in installments over several issues. If all installments appear within a single volume—usually consisting of all issues printed within a calendar year—simply give the pagination within each issue with a semicolon separating the page groups. When the installments appear in several volumes of a periodical, be sure to indicate the volume and imprint information, along with the collation:

> Radice, Mark A. "Purcell's Contributions to The Gentleman's Journal." Bach: The Quarterly Journal of the Riemenschneider-Bach Institute 9 (October 1978), 25–30; 10 (January 1979), 26–31.

Note: In this and the previous example, titles within article titles are italicized and subject to the conventional rules of capitalization.

139 Author unknown

Many news items in periodicals lack indication of authorship. Where this is the case, begin the entry with the article title. Do not use the indication "anonymous."

> "Here and There: William Albright Commissioned." The Diapason 88 (June 1997), 2–3.

Encyclopedias, Dictionaries, Collections

140   Standard entry

Where the author of the specific article is known, give the author's name (*not* the name of the general editor!) *period*, the article title enclosed in quotation marks, *period*, the title of the main publication, imprint information, *period*, and the volume and page references:

> Griffiths, Paul. "Fires of London." Thames and Hudson Encyclopedia of Twentieth-Century Music. New York: Thames and Hudson, 1986. P. 75.
> Pryer, Anthony. "Notation." The New Oxford Companion to Music. New York: Oxford University Press, 1983. Vol. 2, pp. 1247–1268.

Note the inclusion of "vol." and "p." or "pp.," with capitalization appropriate to the situation. If the layout of the source uses columns rather than pages, use the abbreviation "col.(s)" as necessary.

Essays in a collection are similar to articles in a journal in that they are titled documents that appear within a larger work with its own title. For this reason, the titles both of essays in collections and articles in journals should be enclosed in quotation marks. The two differ in that collected essays are published only once, whereas journals are ongoing publications. As a consequence, the imprint information for essays in a collection observes the same form as that for a book:

> Morgan, Robert P. "Coda as Culmination: The First Movement of the Eroica Symphony." Music Theory and the Exploration of the Past. Ed. Christopher Hatch and David W. Bernstein. Chicago and London: University of Chicago Press, 1993. Pp. 357–376.

It is not necessary to write the word "in" between the article title and the principal title.

141   Author unknown

When authorship for a particular article cannot be determined, begin with the name of the general editor of the volume. Some publications—such as *The New Harvard Dictionary of Music*—give only the initials of the author at the conclusion of an article. In such situations, determine the author's full name by consulting the list of contributors, which is usually located in the front matter of a book. If the source is a multivolume publication, it may be necessary to go to the front matter of the first volume for the list of contributors.

Music

142   Scores

If you cite a composition published separately, italicize it, as you would a book title. If you cite one composition within a collection, treat it as you would an article: title of work (in quotation marks), volume title (italicized). When your study involves all or most of a volume, give only the volume title (italicized). For a volume that is part of a series, put the series title in parentheses.

If an editor is involved, state that person's name after the title. Observe the procedures for giving imprint information for books, but remember that a great deal of published music lacks a date of publication. If no publication date is given, use the copyright date. In exacting studies, plate numbers should be included.

Use annotations freely to record pertinent information about the edition.

143   Types of musical editions

Musical editions vary considerably. The character of a particular edition depends upon whether it is a critical edition, an Urtext edition, or a practical edition.

A critical edition is for scholarly use. Such an edition is often the result of archival studies, in which all available sources of the work are examined, differences noted, and detailed commentary about variants provided. Normally the editor will make corrections where the musical text seems to have been corrupted. Sometimes it is also necessary to transcribe the music into modern notation. Additions to the score (key signatures, meter signatures, sharps and flats at particular points, bar lines) are clearly indicated as such.

Urtext is German for "original text." The intention behind an Urtext edition is to give the music exactly as it is in the chosen source. Presumably, the editor has chosen the best, single source for a composition. This text is then given without recourse to emendations borrowed from alternate readings, transpositions to a new key, or any additions to the score.

A practical edition is intended for use by a performer. Ideally, such an edition begins with a responsible presentation of the music. The editor's job in this case is to facilitate performance. Details of fingering, bowing, phrasing, tempo, and dynamics may be added. For vocal music, a translation may be provided. The layout of the score will also be considered. Awkward page turns, uncooperative bindings, and other physical features of the score may present impediments to performance. In such editions, it often happens that a page is left blank to eliminate an undesirable page turn.

Most scholarly essays rely mainly upon critical editions; however, some studies—such as those relating to pedagogy or performance practice—focus on practical editions. When citing musical scores in bibliographical entries, indicate the type of edition whenever this information might be appropriate.

The following examples show citations of single compositions, published separately:

> Ravel, Maurice. <u>Pavane pour une infante défunte.</u> Paris: Max Eschig, n.d. 4 p. [original version for piano solo].
> Schütz, Heinrich. "Wie lieblich sind deine Wohnungen," SWV 29. Ed. Günther Graulich and Paul Horn. Stuttgart: Hänssler, © 1968. [No. 8 of the <u>Psalmen Davids,</u> Op. 2 (1619)].

In the first example, the explanatory note is essential: The Ravel Pavane—one of his best-known compositions—is often performed in Ravel's own orchestration.

The Schütz selection was originally part of Schütz's Opus 2, though it is available as a separately published composition (as cited here). It would be misleading, therefore, to give the entry as follows:

> Schütz, Heinrich. "Wie lieblich sind deine Wohnungen," SWV 29. <u>Psalmen Davids,</u> Op. 2. Ed. Günther Graulich and Paul Horn. Stuttgart: Hänssler, © 1968.

Confronted with this bibliographic citation, a reader would conclude that the edition under consideration included *all* the psalms of Opus 2.

Cite one composition within a volume thus:

> Bach, Johann Sebastian. Sinfonia No. 9, in F minor, BWV 795. <u>Inventionen und Sinfonien.</u> Ed. Erwin Ratz; fingering by Oswald Jonas. Vienna: Wiener Urtext Edition. 1973. Pp. 60–61.

Grieg, Edvard. "Springdans" from Lyriske Stykker, Op. 47, No. 6. Music in the Romantic Period. Ed. F. E. Kirby. New York: Schirmer Books, 1986. Pp. 819–820.
Statham, Heathcote. "Drop down, Ye Heavens." Oxford Easy Anthem Book: A Collection of Fifty Anthems. London: Oxford University Press, 1957. Pp. 172–174.

In the case of practical editions, feel free to identify the individual(s) responsible for the performance suggestions. This information may be given within the note if it can be done expeditiously. Lengthy discussions should appear instead as annotations to the entry.

The following examples show citations of an entire volume:

Boublil, Alain, and Claude-Michel Schönberg. Les misérables. Milwaukee, Wisconsin: Hal Leonard Publishing, ©1991. 80 p. [14 selections in piano-vocal arrangement].
Schubert, Franz Peter. Impromptus [Opp. 90, 142], Moments musicaux [Op. 94]. Ed. Walter Gieseking, 1948; Op. 142 rev. and corrected by Paul Badura-Skoda. Munich: Henle, 1976. 95 p.

Depending on the nature of the discussion, it may be necessary to include an annotation listing precise items, as, for instance, the titles of the fourteen selections from Les misérables.

A composition within a volume in a series is cited thus:

Bach, Johann Sebastian. "Christe eleison." Mass in B minor, BWV 232. Ed. Friedrich Smend. (Johann Sebastian Bach: Neue Ausgabe sämtlicher Werke, series 2, vol. 1) Kassel: Bärenreiter, 1954. Pp. 26–30.

Here, as with periodical articles, songs within larger song cycles, and other distinctively named subsections of larger works, quotation marks enclose the smaller units. The convention of italicizing foreign text is not observed in these circumstances, so that the relationship of component parts remains clear at all times. Again, series titles are placed in Roman type, in parentheses.

The following examples show citations of an entire volume in a series:

Bach, Johann Sebastian. Organ Works, vol. 4. Third Part of the Clavier Übung. Ed. Manfred Tessmer. Kassel: Bärenreiter, 1983. [Separate, paperback edition taken from Neue Ausgabe sämtlicher Werke, series 4, vol. 4].

-------. <u>Sechs brandenburgische Konzerte.</u> (Neue Ausgabe
sämtlicher Werke, series 7, vol. 2) Ed. Heinrich Besseler.
Kassel: Bärenreiter, 1956. 243 p., 4 facsims. See
Commentary <u>(Kritischer Bericht)</u> by Heinrich Besseler, in
separate volume. Bärenreiter, 1956. 170 p.
Froberger, Johann Jakob. <u>Clavierwerke</u> (Keyboard works), vol.
2. (Denkmäler der Tonkunst in Österreich, vol. 6, pt. 2)
Vienna: Artaria, 1899. 84 p. [Contains 28 suites].

144   Manuscripts, autographs, facsimiles

When many composers are represented in a single manuscript, or in early
sources that fail to identify a composer, begin with the location and name
of the manuscript. Make it clear that you have used a microfilm or photocopy, if this is the case. Identify published facsimiles as such, and enclose
unpublished titles in quotation marks. If the item has no formal title, or if
some distinctive features of the item may not be immediately apparent,
give pertinent details in a description. A straightforward entry might look
like this:

Oxford, Bodleian Library, Canonici misc. 213. [ca. 1420–1440].
146 leaves. [More than 300 works of the Italian and
Flemish repertoires. Principal composers include Guillaume
Dufay and Giles Binchois. Ballades, virelais and ballate,
rondeaux, Mass movements, and motets.]

Note: The designation of the manuscript is not treated as a formal title; no
quotation marks or italicizing is required.

Sources frequently have complex histories and peculiar characteristics.
By all means, clarify these features if it can be done concisely. Some
sources require extensive annotation in order for the entry to be at all
meaningful. Consider the following example:

Bach, Johann Sebastian. Paris, Bibliothèque Nationale, Mus.
Ms. 17669: <u>Goldberg Variations.</u> Nuremberg: Balthasar
Schmid [1741].

This entry is confusing. Is it a manuscript? If so, why are imprint data
included as though for a published work?

In fact, this score *is* a published edition: the first edition (authorized by
Bach) of the *Goldberg Variations*. It is described as a manuscript because
this was Bach's personal copy of the publication. In it, he wrote fourteen
canons inside the back cover. He also noted, in his own hand, many cor-

rections, as well as additions and alterations to the text as printed by Schmid.

For critical editions, it is customary to consult multiple sources for a particular work. Bibliographic citations should reflect this:

> Bach, Johann Christian. <u>Confitebor</u> [Psalm 110. Vespers].
> Hamburg, Ms. ND. 540, No. 8 [Autograph: "1759"].
> Munich, Mus. Ms. 4240/1 [Score. Copied at Einsiedeln and
> dated 18 Sept. 1875].

Since Hamburg is listed first, and since it is described as an autograph (a document signed by the creator or in the creator's hand), the entry suggests that in contentious readings, the editor will defer to the text as it appears in this score. Exceptions to this tacit agreement should be noted.

The following examples show citations of modern reproductions of important manuscript sources:

> Angles, Higinio, ed. <u>La musica de las cantigas de Santa Maria</u>
> <u>del Rey Alfonso el Sabio.</u> Vol. 1. Facsimile of Codex j.b.2 of
> the Escorial. Barcelona: Biblioteca Central, 1964. xvi, 12,
> 361 plates, large folio.
> Bellini, Vincenzo. <u>Norma.</u> Facsimile of the autograph full score.
> 2 vols. Rome: Reale Accademia d'Italia, 1935. 147; 103
> leaves, oblong folio.
> Debussy, Claude. <u>Prélude a l'après-midi d'un faune.</u> Facsimile
> of the autograph particelle. Washington, D.C.: Lehman
> Foundation, 1963. 6 sheets, large folio.

145   Recordings: Audio, video, audiovisual

The many changes that have taken place in recording technology during the past decade have resulted in a great variety of source formats. Recordings may be either audio recordings, video recordings, or audiovisual recordings.

Audio recordings—such as LPs, CDs, cassettes, or reel-to-reel tapes—fix only the sound in some tangible form. Commercial recording companies update the formats of their sound recording archives to keep pace with consumer demand; hence, LP recordings are commonly reissued in CD format. Bibliographic citations should point out any such modifications or alterations in format.

Strictly speaking, video recordings fix only the visual element in some tangible form. The silent motion pictures made between about 1900 and 1925 are important examples of video recordings. Audiovisual recordings—commonly known as videos—are usually in the format of cassette tapes or laser discs.

Whatever the form, edit the information given on the recording to suit bibliographic style. Be selective. Is the discussion focused on a composer? Is the particular piece or performance the real issue? Perhaps an individual performer claims our attention in a certain case. Use good judgment as you decide what to include, but remember: Certain basics must be present if the interested reader is to obtain the recording without undue inconvenience.

Normally, begin with the composer and title. When appropriate, identify the principal performers. Imprint information will minimally include the issuing company, the format, and a serial number, as well as a copyright year or publication year. Whenever possible, give the running time of the complete recording or the segment of the recording under consideration. Use the word "Time" followed by Arabic numerals separated by a colon to indicate minutes and seconds. If the playing time is for an individual movement or selection on a recording, indicate the playing time in parentheses, immediately after the name of the excerpt.

Entry points—cue numbers for tapes; sides and bands for LPs; disc and box numbers for CDs—are always useful. Recording techniques, such as analog or digital recording, may also be specified. In short, include any details that are pertinent to the discussion or that would be helpful to the reader in following your essay.

> Menken, Alan, composer, with Howard Ashman and Tim Rice, lyrics. <u>Aladdin.</u> Walt Disney Home Video. VHS 1662. Time: 90 minutes. [1992; soundtrack available from Walt Disney Records. Audio cassette 60846-0. (Time: 50:02)].
> Messiaen, Olivier. "Jardin du sommeil d'amour," 6th move. (Time: 12:39) <u>Turangalîla-Symphonie.</u> Orch. of the Opéra de Paris-Bastille, Myung-Whun Chung, cond. Yvonne Loriod, piano; Jeanne Loriod, ondes martenot. Deutsche Grammophon, CD 1991. [Recorded in the presence of the composer, 1990].
> Munrow, David. <u>Early Musical Instruments.</u> 6 vols. Early Music Consort of London, cond. by David Munrow. Princeton, New Jersey: Films for Humanities. 1976. Audiovisual cassette. Time: 3 hours, each 30:00. [Vol. 1, Reed Instruments; 2, Flutes and Whistles; 3, Plucked Instruments; 4, Bowed Instruments; 5, Keyboard and Percussion; 6, Brass Instruments].

> Takemitsu, Toru. In an Autumn Garden [for gagaku orchestra].
> Tokyo Gakuso Orchestra. Tokyo: Victor Musical Industries,
> 1980. CD issued in the United States by Varèse Sarabande
> Records. Time: 43:45.

For outdated recording media, such as Edison cylinders, 78-rpm discs, 45-rpm discs, and reel-to-reel tapes, provide standard bibliographic data as well as a general indication of facilities that will be needed to utilize the item.

Let us take the case of reel-to-reel tapes. For published tape recordings, italicize titles. For unpublished phonotapes, put the identifying title in quotation marks, and describe the source sufficiently to establish its physical existence and location. For more careful library classification, the collation would include number of reels; reel size (diameter); speed in ips (inches per second); playing time; tape width (if other than standard quarter-inch); and, where applicable, stereo and number of tracks.

> Henze, Hans Werner. Five Symphonies. Berlin Philharmonic
> Orchestra conducted by Hans Werner Henze. Four-track
> 7 1/2 ips stereo tape, two reels. Ampex/Deutsche
> Grammophon S-9204.
> "Thirty-Seven Traditional Songs of Caithness and the Orkney
> Islands." Sung by John Gow and George Stewart. Collected
> by John McLeod, August, 1967. Two reels. In the private
> collection of John McLeod.

Other Sources

146   Reviews

The ideal place to enter a review is as an annotation under the book, music, or recording reviewed:

> Handel, George Frideric. Agrippina. Nicholas McGegan, cond.
> Harmonia Mundi CDs 907063–65. ©1992. This recording
> of the 1991 Göttingen Festival production reviewed by
> Mark A. Radice in The Opera Quarterly 10 (winter 1993/
> 94), [177]–181.

If you wish to call special attention to a review, however, you may enter it under its author's name with a cross-reference to the item reviewed:

> Harris, Ellen T. "Georg Friedrich Händel, <u>Kantaten mit Instrumenten, I–II</u>" (Review). <u>Notes: Quarterly Journal of the Music Library Association</u> 53 (March 1997), 978–981.

In such cases, where the review is given as the principal entry, details concerning the item reviewed—the editor, publisher, or series (for books and scores); the performers, recording company, and format (for recordings)—are omitted. Presumably, the information in the review is of greater importance than the item being reviewed. As in all documentation, use good judgment: Make critical points in the most expeditious way possible. Give essential information; forgo extraneous details.

147 Theses, dissertations

Titles of unpublished theses and dissertations are put in quotation marks. Mention the academic degree involved, the degree-granting institution, and the year in which the degree was conferred. Whenever possible, information that will help the reader to obtain the document should be included; indicate, for instance, whether a thesis is available through a photocopy service.

> Baxter, Jeffrey William. "A Descriptive Analysis of the Yevtushenko Settings of Dmitri Shostakovich." Ph.D. dissertation. University of Cincinnati, 1988. 115 p. [Available from University Microfilms Incorporated. Order No. 8903610].
> Vos, Marie Ann Heiberg. "The Liturgical Choral Works of Johann Christian Bach." Ph.D. dissertation. St. Louis, Missouri, Washington University, 1969. Vol. 1, 293 p.; vol. 2, 263 p. [Available from University Microfilms Incorporated. Order No. 69-22,565].

148 Letters and other original sources

Where original sources such as letters, lectures, master classes, interviews, and diaries are important for a particular study, they may be described in the bibliography, usually under a special heading.

> Hanson, Howard. Letter of 19 June 1978 to Mark A. Radice. [Hanson explains the origin of his Concerto for Organ, its various rescorings, and its connection with his earlier score of <u>North and West</u> for full orchestra and chorus. Letter in the collection of the present writer].

For published documents, it is simplest to list the entire publication and give needed details in an annotation:

> Beethoven, Ludwig van. The Letters of Beethoven. Collected, translated, and edited with an introduction, appendixes, notes, and indexes by Emily Anderson. 3 vols. London: Macmillan; New York: St. Martin's Press, 1961. iii, 484; xxxvii, 487–984; xxxiii, 987–1090 p. Letter to Archduke Rudolph, dated Vienna, December 31, 1817, vol. 2, p. 724, with facsimile, 2 p., facing pp. 720–21.
>
> Elgar, Sir Edward. Edward Elgar: Letters of a Lifetime. [Selected by] Jerrold Northrop Moore. New York: Oxford University Press, 1990. 524 p. [This volume complements earlier collections pub. by OUP beginning in 1974, including Elgar on Record (correspondence with His Master's Voice); Elgar and His Publishers (2 vols.); Letters of a Creative Life (1987); and Windflower Letters: Correspondence with Alice Caroline Stuart Wortley and Her Family (1989). The text includes selected letters written by Elgar in addition to significant letters written to him by such figures as Alfred Rodewal, Lord Northhampton, George Moore, and Henry James.]
>
> Strauss, Richard, and Stefan Zweig. A Confidential Matter: The Letters of Richard Strauss and Stefan Zweig, 1931–1935. Trans. Max Knight. Foreword by Edward E. Lowinsky. Berkeley and Los Angeles: University of California Press, 1977. 122 p. [Trans. from Richard Strauss/Stefan Zweig: Briefwechsel. Ed. Willi Schuh. Frankfurt am Main: S. Fischer, 1957].

For incidental use, a shorter form of citation might be appropriate:

> Beethoven, Ludwig van. Letter to Archduke Rudolph, dated Vienna, 31 December 1817. In The Letters of Beethoven. Trans. Emily Anderson. New York: St. Martin's Press, 1961. Vol. 2, p. 724, and facsimile facing pp. 720–721.

149   Web sites

Web sites are ephemeral and must be used with caution. To verify your citation, as well as to consult the document at some future time, print out the critical elements of the Web pages used, including the responsible person or organization, the title of the Web site and its address, and the information that you used.

If the citation appears within a classified bibliography, the designation "Web site" need not be stated with each item. *Do not* add any punctuation at the conclusion of a site address! The citation of a Web site is the single exception to the rule that all notes and bibliographic entries must conclude with a period. A bibliographic entry for a Web site within a unified bibliography might look like this:

> G. Schirmer and Associated Music Publishers: Schirmer News
> June 1997. [Web site] "News this Month: Late-Breaking
> May and June Premieres." ©1997. [Announcement of 22
> May 1997 premiere of John Corigliano, Dodecaphonia.
> Joan Morris, mezzo-soprano; William Bolcom, piano. New
> York City.] Site address: http://www.schirmer.com/

150   Iconography

Paintings, photographs, or other visual materials discussed in the text should be included in the bibliography. Identify the artist and the title (usually italicized) of the work. When the item is part of a larger set, italicize the larger work and use Roman type and quotation marks for the smaller units. Specify the year, the dimensions (or other appropriate physical features), the medium, and the current location of the item.

If you mention several iconographic sources, consider using a classified bibliography.

> Rouault, Georges. "This Will Be the Last, Little Father." Etching
> from portfolios of Miserere et Guerre. 1927. 28 1/2" ×
> 16 7/8". Museum of Modern Art, New York.

When the references to art works are incidental rather than integral to the essay, and if the art works are published reproductions in books, it may be simpler to give a conventional citation with an explanation of the iconographic matters in an annotation.

> Blanton, Joseph Edwin. The Organ in Church Design. Albany,
> Texas: Venture Press, 1957. 492 p. [Elaborate photographic
> documentation in 550 illustrations].
> Bory, Robert. Ludwig van Beethoven: His Life and His Work in
> Pictures. Trans. Winifred Glass and Hans Rosenwald. New
> York: Atlantis, 1964. 228 p. [Illus., facsims., large 4to].

CHAPTER 10

References in the Text

151 Mention of an author

Where the arrangement of ideas in a passage of text is primarily your own, it is sufficient to confine credits to note citations; but where you are consciously abstracting, paraphrasing, or quoting, be courteous and acknowledge the source of the idea right in your text.

The rule of academic familiarity favors the use of the last name only since the full name will appear in your first note reference and the corresponding bibliographic citation anyway. For the convenience of the reader, however, it is best to give the author's full name (in normal order) with the first in-text reference. Unless several authors share the same surname, subsequent references to the same author should be by last name only. Titles of address (*Count; Rev.; Sir; Dr.; Prof.*) are unnecessary.

Repeat the author's name as often as necessary to make certain that ideas are attributed to the right person. Once the name is mentioned, you may also refer back to "the author" or "this writer." Avoid referring to yourself in these terms.

If "the author" seems stilted, try using the word "this" and an intervening adjective (*noted; perceptive; discredited,* for example) in combination with a noun (*analyst; biographer; critic*).

152 Mention of self

In general, do not refer to yourself directly. The focus should be on the topic and the relevant data, *not* on your persona.

When you make positive statements reporting your observations, opinions, and conclusions, readers assume that you are personally responsible for these statements unless you have specifically attributed them to someone else. The proper control of sentence construction, emphasis, flow of ideas, and citation of sources will make your own contributions clear to the reader.

"The present writer" is the best way to refer to yourself. By convention, it means *you*, the writer, and should never be used to refer to anyone else. The word "author" applies to the writer of a published work; therefore, avoid referring to yourself in a manuscript as "the author."

On rare occasions, the pronoun "I" may be used frankly and openly. In passages where the writer and the reader are following an argument in close cooperation, it is proper to use "we," meaning you (the reader) and I (the writer) collectively.

The best way to avoid references to oneself is to reconstruct the sentence so that the topic under consideration appears first. This arrangement focuses the reader's attention on the critical issue rather than on the speaker's experience. Another approach is to shift the verb to the passive voice; however, active-voice constructions tend to be clearer, more interesting, and more engaging. Compare:

The present writer *found* many instances of irregularly resolved suspensions in the later works. [active voice]

Many instances of irregularly resolved suspensions *are found* (or *can be found*) in the later works. [passive voice]

Irregularly resolved suspensions *appear* frequently in the later works. [active voice]

153   Mention of a composer

Give the composer's full name the first time it is mentioned in your text and the last name only in subsequent references. If you are writing for knowledgeable readers, supplying birth and death dates for Bach, Beethoven, and Brahms is unnecessary; however, when the discussion deals with less-well-known figures, it is a courtesy to give the composer's dates in parentheses after the first mention of the name: Alexander Glazunov (1865–1936). Depending on the amount of detail that you want the reader to keep in mind, dates may even appear in a note:

1 Alexander Konstantinovich Glazunov (Glazunoff). Born St. Petersburg, 10 August 1865; died Paris, 21 March 1936.

154   Mention of titles

When you mention titles in text, the following guidelines should be helpful, though they are not absolute.

Italicize titles of books; large musical compositions with distinctive titles (but not opus numbers or thematic catalog numbers); operas; plays; films; long poems; paintings; sculpture; ships; periodicals; pamphlets; newspapers; and journals.

Quote (and do not italicize, even if a foreign language) titles of articles; parts, sections, or chapters of books; short musical compositions with distinctive titles; essays (if less than book length); and unpublished matter.

Note: Titles of vocal compositions are sometimes italicized since they are musical compositions, and they may be works of considerable duration. Schubert's *Der Hirt auf dem Felsen,* for example, should be italicized. On the other hand, titles of arias or songs being discussed as parts of a longer work, such as an opera, oratorio, cantata, or song cycle, may be quoted, highlighting the relationship between the smaller excerpt and the larger work.

Use conventional title capitalization (neither italics nor quotes) for titles of generic designations of movements of an instrumental composition (Introduction, Adagio, Scherzo); instrumental works in general (Beethoven's Sixth Symphony, Haydn's Second Cello Concerto); books of the Bible; and institutions (Paris Conservatoire; Gesellschaft der Musikfreunde).

Note: Generic titles assume significance (and, consequently, title capitalization) only when they appear in conjunction with the composer's name. For instance, Bruckner, Mahler, Tchaikovsky, and Vaughan Williams all wrote sixth symphonies, but none of these is Beethoven's Sixth Symphony.

155   References to measures

Musical compositions often appear in several editions; it is useless to the reader, therefore, to refer to page numbers without also referring to a specific edition. Always specify which edition you are citing.

Rule 97 offered guidelines for citing measures. The same guidelines apply to references in the text; however, since the discussion may proceed at a more leisurely pace in the body of an essay, the terse style of a note may be abandoned. It may, for instance, be convenient to give landmarks in the score that are not labeled entry points: "at the *molto crescendo* (p. 5)"; or, "on page 7, two measures after the instruction *sempre diminuendo.*"

156   Internal references

Use "above" and "below" in preference to the Latin *supra* and *infra*—but only with very good reason. Internal references to other portions of the manuscript should be avoided if at all possible. Every such cross-reference teases the reader to turn back or ahead, which can be distracting. Moreover, from the first draft to the final fair copy, the pagination of most essays changes many times. With each change, it may be necessary to reword or renumber precisely and accurately each and every internal reference.

Instead of an internal reference, give a brief résumé of the point previously made, or to be made later. Such a re-summation (or pre-summation) of key ideas often helps to draw the reader's attention to the discussion's broader organizational considerations. In a thesis, dissertation, or book, this principle works well with chapter references:

> Melodic and rhythmic idiosyncrasies are examined in the second chapter.

> A table for conversion into metric measurements appears as Appendix B.

Note: Both examples will remain valid regardless of the final copy's pagination.

CHAPTER 11

Illustrative Material

157 Verbal matter

Occasionally verbal matter illustrating or exemplifying some point in the discussion constitutes data rather than genuine text. Such matter may be set off from the main text in a variety of ways, such as single-spacing or columnar, interlinear, or sublinear format. Texts that might be subject to this treatment include

a series of definitions;
a long series of items that would be tiresome or out of place in
    double-spaced text;
a lengthy abstract;   ·
a model of verbal procedure;
the complete text of a vocal composition, whether poetry or prose;
two or more texts placed in parallel columns for comparison;
and stage directions.

Such verbal data may be given a subheading to make clear its purpose and to avoid its being mistaken for a long direct quotation. Leave a triple-space above such a heading, and a double-space between the heading and the single-spaced matter. Do not use the formal identification "Example" or "Table" in such headings.

158 Poetry

For brief quotations, the prevailing format may be used with virgules showing the original poetic layout of the text (see example at rule 45). Four or more lines of poetry are best set off from the text as single-spaced verbal data, approximately centered on the page.

Determining the beginning of each new line of verse may be difficult if the words have been taken directly from a musical score. If possible, consult a source that shows the poem printed as poetry.

Literal translations of vocal texts are most useful when given in an interlinear format (either above or below the main line). Singing translations, which mimic the poetic structure of the original so the English words "fit" the music, may be placed in a column parallel to the original language.

Sometimes such issues can become quite involved: The Roman Catholic plainchant "Veni Creator Spiritus" became the German Lutheran contrafactum "Komm, Gott, Schöpfer, heiliger Geist." To show the original Latin text, Luther's German translation of it, and a modern-day English translation, one might use three parallel columns, or the Latin text on the base line with the German above and the English below. Choose columns if your aim is to supply only the general gist of the text; interlinear format is a better choice for highlighting the precise meaning of each word, so that nuances of meaning and musical gesture will be apparent.

159 Lengthy titles

Unusually long titles, particularly of old books or musical editions, are sometimes given because of their documentary interest. These too may be set off from the text and treated as verbal data. Lay out the title and all its typographic characteristics to conform as closely as possible with the original in typeface, size, and distribution of lines. Of course, it is appropriate to eschew conventional title underlining, and to italicize only words that are in italics in the original title.

Alternatively, give the title in a blocked quotation, with virgules to indicate the separation of lines in the original. In this format, economy is generally the guiding principle, and the layout may dispense with print size, typeface, and other details of the original:

> Vermehrter und nun zum zweytenmal in Druck beförderter / kurzer jedoch gründlicher / Wegweiser / Vermittelst welches man nicht nur allein aus dem Grund / die Kunst die Orgel recht zu schlagen / sowohl was den General-Bass, als auch was zu dem Gregorianischen Choral-Gesang / erfordert wird erlernen und durch fleissiges Üben zur Vollkommenheit bringen: / Sondern auch / Weiland Herrn Giaccomo Carissimi / Sing= Kunst und leichte Grund=Regeln / Vermittelst welcher man die Jugend ohne grosse Mühe in der Music / perfectioniren kann zu singen seyn.

> (Expanded and now for the second time offered in print / a short yet comprehensive / guide / by means of which one may

learn not only / the art of playing the organ properly / but also thorough bass, a necessity for the accompaniment of Gregorian plainchant, / and through diligent practice bring these to perfection / but also / the late Mr. Giaccomo Carissimi's / easy fundamentals for the art of singing / by means of which youth, without much difficulty, in the study of music / may be brought to perfection.)

160   Musical examples

Musical examples should be of a quality compatible with the text portion of the paper. It will not do to have exquisite laser-printed pages degraded with sloppy examples. Producing elegant calligraphy is too time-consuming and/or expensive to be practical for most writers; as an alternative, consider either photocopying the musical examples needed or producing them with a music-notation program, such as Finale, Overture, Encore, Nightingale, Mosaic, or Professional Composer.

If you elect to photocopy the musical examples, the assumption is that the work in question is in the public domain. Even then, you must be certain either to use examples from editions that are no longer under copyright or to secure permission to reproduce the examples. Note: Examples produced by hand or with the assistance of a computer may still be subject to copyright restrictions. See Appendix Two for details concerning copyright, exclusive rights, and fair use.

Provide captions or legends for all musical examples, and observe the same margins as those that you have set for the text. Number the musical examples consecutively throughout the paper or essay. In larger works that include several chapters, it is more prudent to have a dual numbering system, with the first number indicating the chapter and the second number specifying the number of the example within that chapter. Numerals indicating chapter and example number may be Roman and Arabic, or exclusively Arabic. They may be separated by a point (a period), a hyphen, or a virgule, as you prefer. Be sure to refer to each and every example at some place in your text!

When an example is mentioned in your discussion, the reference may be part of the prose:

Example X shows an unusual instance of parallel fifths.

Or it may be enclosed within parentheses:

The recapitulation is marked by an unusual instance of parallel fifths (Example X).

Avoid unnecessary punctuation. The first period is superfluous in the following example:

> The recapitulation is marked by an unusual instance of parallel fifths (Example X.).

If the parentheses contain a complete sentence, however, use a period:

> (See the parallel fifths given in Example X.)

Consider the location of the example carefully. It is quite proper to finish the sentence or paragraph containing the cue before inserting the example. Do not insert examples too soon; the reader expects to encounter the cue before the musical example, which should appear later on the same page, or else on the page immediately following.

If it is impossible to insert the example in its ideal location, be certain to direct the reader to it. Remember: It is more natural to turn ahead one or more pages than to turn back. If, however, the reference is to an example that has already been given, do not waste space by reproducing the same example.

161   Format of musical examples

The current emphasis on original versions has fostered, understandably, a sense of insecurity among scholars: Will critics discredit my work if I don't use original clefs? Original key signatures? Original scoring? The reproduction of original score notation can consume a great deal of space —not to mention time, effort, and expense.

Writers will be safe if they ask themselves this: How does the appearance of the music on the page relate to the point of the discussion? A fully diminished chord can be shown just as accurately when reduced to two staffs (or even a single staff) as when demonstrated in its original instrumentation for an orchestra of a hundred players with sixteen solo voices.

Remember: Even in reduced scoring, distinctive features of orchestration and instrumentation can be shown by labeling the voices. If the principal melody is to be played by the flute, simply specify that instrumentation beside the top voice. The instrumentation of a bass line for bass trombone, euphonium, and tuba can be shown just as easily.

All musical examples should serve only to illustrate your verbal discussion, *which must be complete and satisfying in itself.* Do not think that you can turn your readers loose on the examples and expect them to do the work of analysis and criticism for you.

When citing extracts from music, identify each item clearly and concisely in the caption. Assign a number to each example, and provide a brief identification bearing the name of the composer, the title of the composition, an indication of the movement from which the example is taken (for multi-movement works), and the entry point (measure numbers, in conventional scores).

Nothing is simple—especially not issues to which people devote hundreds of hours of research, writing, contemplation, and rewriting! Certain musical examples will require an explanation in addition to the data given in the caption; in such cases, a legend may be appropriate. Point out distinctive features of the example. If from a symphony of six movements you have selected three measures for an excerpt, there must be something very special about those measures. Do not assume that the reader will know what drew you to them: Explain their significance!

Certain instances become so complex as to defy reasonable explanation in the caption or the legend. (The case of Mahler's Tenth Symphony, the first performing version by Deryck Cooke, its subsequent recording on Columbia Masterworks, the second Cooke performing version, and its recording on Philips by Wynne Morris leaps to mind!) In such cases, use a note to accompany the musical example, just as you would use a note to explain a controversial bit of prose. Refer the reader to other editions, important performances of the piece, alternate versions, source materials, and any other contentious issues that are important but that cannot be addressed in the text.

Where desirable, signs or symbols (letters, numbers, brackets, graphic markings) may be inserted into the musical example as precise points of reference for features deserving attention. Such cues will normally be explained along with the verbal discussion in the body of your text. Alternatively, provide a single-spaced explanation of symbols directly beneath the example.

A large number of examples or extended individual examples may be collected onto a single page (numbered consecutively along with the rest of the manuscript) or placed together at the conclusion of the document. Such a page of examples makes the most powerful impression when it is close to the related discussion. Margins must be observed, as usual.

Some examples—especially of early organ, harpsichord, or guitar music notated in tablature—customarily appear in oblong format. Such scores require more than six (and occasionally up to nine) inches of width and may be placed broadside. The top of a broadside, with liberal space above, should face toward the normal left margin; the page and its example are then turned clockwise for inspection.

162 Figures

A figure is a diagram, drawing, or pictorial representation included in the text for illustrative purposes. In a report on the history of instruments, for example, the illustrative material might consist largely of figures. Figures should be numbered consecutively within an essay, article, or other brief document; a compound numbering system is more practical for book-length works. Include a caption or legend—or both—for each figure.

163 Plates

A plate is a page of illustrative material that is printed on paper that differs in quality from that used for the text. Typically, a plate will consist of a photostatic reproduction, a photographic print, or an elaborate hand-drawn illustration. Occasionally several figures may be laid out together, filling a page of this special paper. In books, plates often appear between two pages bearing consecutive Arabic numerals, but the plate pages themselves are not numbered; a special type of plate, the frontispiece, faces the title page.

For all plates, including the frontispiece (which in a manuscript immediately precedes the first page of text), provide a number and an explanatory caption or legend. You may use either Roman numerals or Arabic numerals, as you prefer. Several images appearing on the same plate should be given individual numbers and legends, for ready identification.

Each plate should be listed, perhaps with some shortened designation, along with its number in a table of illustrations after the table of contents at the beginning of the manuscript.

Plates may be positioned in broadside format if this accords better with the shape of the image being shown.

Note: The numbers assigned to illustrative plates should not be confused with plate numbers, which are numbers used by music publishers to identify a particular publication. Plate numbers of musical scores, the same throughout an entire score, are centered at the bottom of each page.

164 Tables

A table is an arrangement in condensed form of data, statistics, and the like, often in parallel columns. Tables are typically included to provide detailed evidence to support or illustrate matters discussed in the main text. A table should bear a caption, be centered on the page, and be set off from the main text with suitable space above and below. If your manuscript contains several tables, begin each caption with a table number. You may use Arabic or Roman numerals, as you prefer. For clarity, it may be helpful to use a larger type size—perhaps 14-point—or boldface for the caption and table number.

Simple tables may be either single- or double-spaced; choose whichever appears neatest and most readily legible. For a more complex table, good layout is essential. Vertical and horizontal spacing and alignment; ruled lines to set off various columns and divisions; leaders to represent the flow of data; and special typographical features, possibly including various symbols—all will add up to a powerful and more effective table. A page that is entirely taken up by a table should still be numbered consecutively with the rest of the manuscript. Place tables requiring extra width in broadside position, with the top of the table toward the normal left margin.

CHAPTER 12

Printing

Letterpress, engraving, and lithography are the three fundamental printing methods. One widely used adaptation of lithography is known as offset printing. In all these methods, the master copy will be the mirror image of what will eventually appear on the page; hence, these classic printing techniques—especially engraving—offer left-handed people one of the few circumstances in our culture where their tendency to write "backward" is a natural advantage! At the same time, the student examining scores of early music should be wary of apparent errors: If you flip the figure around and read it "backward," you may discover that the musical aberration vanishes and the proper reading of the passage is revealed.

165   Letterpress

Letterpress involves a raised typeface to which ink is applied and from which it is transferred to paper. The exact method has varied considerably over the ages, and the various techniques often exhibit distinctive features on a printed page. These distinctive characteristics may seem at first inconsequential, but, in fact, such features are extraordinarily useful to the music historian attempting to determine the approximate publication date of a particular score.

The earliest sort of letterpress, the block press, used carved blocks. These blocks were made of wood, soapstone, or some other surface that could easily be carved. The desired figure was left as the basic surface, and the surrounding areas were carved away from it. The surface was then inked, and the inked figure was transferred to paper.

A page from a complex document might pass through the press several times before all the necessary signs and symbols were imprinted upon it (see Figure 1). The earliest printed music came from the press of the Italian publisher Ottaviano dei Petrucci (1466–1539). His first major publication, the *Harmonice musices odhecaton* (1501), used a triple-impres-

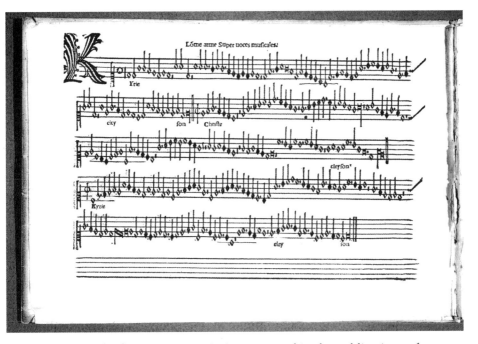

Figure 1. Multiple-impression printing was used in the publications of Ottaviano dei Petrucci (fl. Venice 1501–1509, Fossombrone 1511–1520). This sample shows the superius part of the opening Kyrie of Josquin's *Missa l'hommé armé super voces musicales* from the Liber missarum III of 1514. Note the superfluous staff and the overly long ledger lines, features often associated with the multiple-impression process.

sion process: the first for the staves, the second for the notes and musical signs, and the third for the texts, initials, and folios.

Movable type, invented by the Chinese in the eleventh century, was first used in music publishing by Pierre Attaingnant for his *Chansons nouvelles en musique* (Paris, 1527–28). It remained the dominant type of letterpress in seventeenth-century music publishing and was still used widely in Mozart's day. Music printed with movable type could often be completed with just a single impression. Each piece of type included a note positioned on a staff and its rhythmic value. After the pieces of type were assembled in lines, they would be inked and a page would be pressed upon them. The look of movable type on the page is highly distinctive: Since the staff lines are not continuous, slight breaks are visible between each piece of type in the channel (see Figure 2). John Playford (1623–1686) and his

Figure 2. The bass part shown here from Orlando di Lasso's six-voice madrigal "Tanto e quel bene" was set in movable type. In this method, the individual notes and their staffs are printed in a single impression; however, small gaps often appear between adjacent pieces of type. The semiminims toward the end of the third line exhibit this telltale sign. Note also that separate flags are assigned to the individual semiminims.

son Henry (1657–ca. 1707) were among the most important English publishers who used movable type printing. Henry produced fine examples of the technique with his publication of the collections *Harmonia sacra* and *Orpheus Britannicus* of Henry Purcell (1659–1695).

Mosaic type was developed during the 1750s by Johann Gottlob Immanuel Breitkopf. In this process, the staff lines, stems, and flags were divided into separate units to allow beaming and other constellations of notes commonly used in music manuscripts.

The Linotype machine, invented in 1884, dominated typesetting for decades. It produced one-line slugs automatically justified in length. The slugs were first assembled into galleys (oblong trays), and galley proofs were printed for inspection by the proofreader (and sometimes the author) so that corrections could be made. Newspaper galleys were usually one column wide; page layout was determined by a makeup expert, and the galleys were assembled, or broken up and reassembled, to form the definitive pages. Book and magazine galleys were of page width; they were broken up into page lengths that were provided with page numbers and running heads—often the book title on the left-hand *(verso)* page and the title of the chapter or other subdivision on the right-hand *(recto)* page. Page proofs were printed for making any final corrections. At this point, an index could be made.

Except for very small print runs and hand-set jobs, letterpress and Linotype machines are now seldom used. Computers have made the craft of typesetting obsolete.

166   Engraving

In engraving (also known as gravure or intaglio; see Figure 3), the image is etched into a metal plate, often by means of a stylus dipped into sulfuric acid—a slight variant on the fountain-pen-and-inkwell idea. The plate is next covered completely with ink and then wiped clean, leaving the etched depressions filled with ink. Paper brought into contact with the plate pulls the ink out onto the sheet.

Although the engraving process was used in the Netherlands just several years after its appearance in England in 1612, the technique did not appear in France or Germany until the second half of the seventeenth century. Engraving was the dominant method of music publishing in the eigh-

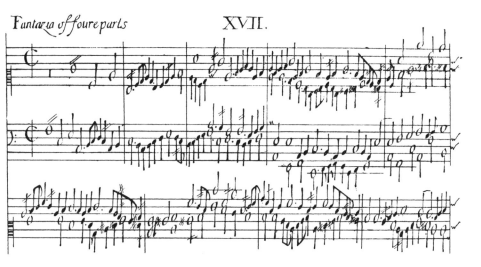

Figure 3. Engraving was first used for music in the first half of the sixteenth century in Francesco da Milano's *Intabolatura de leuto* (1536?); the earliest example that appeared in England was *Parthenia; or, The Maydenhead of the First Musicke That Ever Was Printed for the Virginalis* (1612–13), from which this excerpt from Orlando Gibbons's Fantasia of Foure Parts is taken.

111

teenth century. Estienne Roger (ca. 1665–1722), the first publisher to use plate numbers, issued many important engraved works by Arcangelo Corelli, Antonio Vivaldi, and other Baroque masters from his shop in Amsterdam.

In later examples of engraving, the metal plate was thin enough to be curved around a cylinder in a rotary press, which facilitated inking of the plate. Photogravure and rotogravure are special methods for printing faithful reproductions of photographic subjects.

167 Lithography

The technique of lithography, developed around 1796 by the playwright Aloys Senefelder, depends upon the incompatibility of oil and water. The image to be printed is neither raised (as in letterpress) nor depressed (as in engraving) but is impressed with greasy ink onto a flat dry surface—a stone in its earliest applications. The ink is continuously renewed by a roller, but the vacant portions of the surface are kept wet so that the ink will be repelled.

Lithography is widely used for the reproduction of art works because the process can reproduce the details of almost any artistic medium: the strokes of a brush, the lines of a pencil or pen, or even the mottled appearance of crayon. Fine lithographs are usually numbered individually with the number of the particular lithograph and the total number of copies produced, thus: 17/125. The smaller the number to the left of the virgule, the higher the quality of the lithograph. A relatively small number to the right of the virgule gives an indication that the print is one of relatively few in existence. Currier and Ives, Delacroix, Goya, Manet, and Whistler are just a few of the distinguished artists who used lithography in their work.

Lithography was first applied to the printing of music in the late eighteenth century. Haydn published three sonatas dedicated to the Princess Marie Esterházy (Hob. XVI/40, 41, 42) using the technique. These sonatas, issued in Munich by the firm of Falter in 1797, are outstanding examples of elegant manuscript and clarity of musical detail. Soon, other music publishers began to use lithography, which was cheaper, faster, and far less hazardous than engraving.

The same principle is now used in offset printing. Photolithography merely employs modern photochemical methods for producing the lithographic plates.

168   Offset printing

Surprisingly, the lithographic method produces better results when the image is offset onto the paper by means of an intermediary hard rubber blanket. In the rotary press, the litho plate revolves on a cylinder against a rubber blanket on a second cylinder, which in turn prints the paper as it passes over a third (or impression) cylinder. The litho plate is prepared photochemically from an original, which may consist of text, music, or illustrative material such as photographs, sketches, paintings, or drawings.

169   Illustrations: Basic considerations

Illustrations enliven any text, whether it be an essay of ten pages or a 400-page book. Often, an image conveys the substance of an idea in a way that prose simply cannot. At the same time, the use of illustrations adds considerably to the time, effort, and expense of producing a document.

A high-quality image must be obtained if an illustration is to achieve its full impact. Discard any images that are underexposed, overexposed, double-exposed, blurry, out of focus, or in any way less than perfect. Beware also of ruining good images by writing on them anywhere. Obviously, it will not do to write on the face of an image; but even a word or two written on the reverse of a print or photostat may be visible through the face-up side, or leave an impression on the face-up side. The safest procedure is to write any essential annotations onto Post-it notes (which are pre-glued with a non-drying glue) and then to transfer these notes to the backs of the images.

Like written prose, visual images are subject to copyright restrictions (see Appendix Two for details). Before you decide to use an image, make certain that you can, in fact, procure a usable copy of the image as well as permission to reproduce it. In some cases, you will be charged a fee. Remember, too, that reproduction of illustrations is not as easily accomplished as reproduction of text. Special copying procedures are often required.

Choose illustrations with great care. Photographs, for example, frequently contain hidden messages—messages that we may not intend to communicate in our writing. Ask yourself these questions when considering an image: Does the illustration show only children? Only adults? Only elderly people? Are all the persons in the image of one race or gender? Sometimes the answer will and should be yes. If your topic invites such a circumscription of subjects, as it might if you were writing about music for male chorus, or singing techniques for the young vocalist, then the image is appropriate. Use it! If, on the other hand, the image is arbitrarily exclusive, it should be replaced by a more suitable image.

When you settle on an image, be sure to supply a courtesy line specifying the source. This may be an individual, an organization, or an institution, such as a museum or library. It is commonplace for suppliers of images to stipulate the precise wording of the courtesy line.

One final but very important consideration relates to orientation: Do not assume that a reader will just know, or that you will always remember, exactly how an image is supposed to appear on the page. Devise some method of keeping track of the top, bottom, left-hand, and right-hand positioning of your image. References in the text to an image that appears reversed on the page will discredit you and confuse the reader.

170   Line drawings, halftones

Images are likely to be either black line (for black-on-white drawings or diagrams) or halftone (reproductions of photographs, wash drawings, or anything involving different degrees of shading).

When preparing material for reproduction or publication, use a good-quality ink that will give bold, black lines. Note, however, that inks containing high amounts of carbon have a tendency to clog pens. After using a pen, clean it thoroughly.

Make line drawings larger than needed. Intricate details will be shown with greater accuracy, and minor defects will be eliminated when the image is reduced to its intended size. It is not essential to use the same scale for all oversized drawings, charts, and diagrams, as they will not necessarily be subjected to the same reduction.

Photographs and illustrations in shades of gray are said to be of continuous tone. Halftones have been broken up into dots, or screened. The dots are necessary because, although offset printing cannot reproduce continuous tones, it *is* accurate enough to hold and print series of very small dots, which to our eye look continuous or smooth. The number of dots per inch depends upon the screen used in the photochemical printing process: 85-line screen is used in newspapers; 133- or 150-line screen is common in book printing; and 175- and even up to 400-line screen may be used for very fine detail. The individual dots vary in size according to the tone values (dark, shaded, or light) of the original, creating an illusion of black where they are large, and gray tones where they are smaller. Halftone illustrations must be made from an original photograph; do not rely upon a printed picture as the results will be disappointing.

171   Typographic terms

It may be helpful to have an understanding of the technical vocabulary used in word processing and by professional printers and editors. The following terms are a starting point:

point

A unit of measurement, as for type sizes. There are approximately 72 points to an inch (1 point = 0.0138 inch). The main text of a book is likely to be set in 12-point (formerly called pica), 11-point (small pica), or 10-point (long primer) type, with reduced matter set in type a size or two smaller than the main text. The smallest type sizes (9-, 8-, 7-, 6-, or even 5-point) are hard on the eyes. Larger sizes (14-, 18- [great primer], 24-, 30-, 36-point) are appropriate for display headings. For newspaper banner headlines, printers use types as large as 72-point.

kern

A section of some letter or symbol that extends beyond the edge of its principal area in such a way that it overlaps with adjacent type, whether preceding or following. Kerning refers to the subtle adjustment of spaces between characters in a line of type. Such adjustments are most often required with italic type, especially when it is followed by punctuation. For this reason, the first punctuation mark following a word in italics will usually be set in italics as well.

em and en

An em is a unit of linear measurement equal to the point size of the type being used. Thus for 12-point type, an em is 12 points, for 10-point type, 10 points, and so on. An en is equal to one-half of an em. Different lengths of dashes are available in printing. Examples for 12-point type include the en dash (6 points; slightly longer than a hyphen); em dash (12 points); two-em dash (24 points); and three-em dash (36 points). See rule 34 for a discussion of these various dashes.

leading

When type is set solid, the shoulders of the types themselves provide a certain amount of space between lines. More space can be inserted between lines for legibility or elegance. A lead (pronounced like the metal) is usually 2 points thick, and matter so spaced is said to be 2-point leaded. There are also leads 1 point or 3 points thick. Where extra space is needed, 6- or 12-point leading is used.

CHAPTER 13

The Thesis

Final copies of a completed thesis, dissertation, or book should be submitted as loose sheets, never bound or punched. Each copy should be packaged in its own sturdy envelope, box, or folder with an elastic strap or tie cord to secure the loose flap. An exact copy of the full-title page—the title, subtitle (if any), and author's name—should be firmly pasted on the outside of the container.

For journal articles and books, or for theses or dissertations being prepared by a professional printer, it is the author's responsibility to provide a computer disk containing the entire document (save, of course, for illustrations that will be submitted as hard copy). Before creating such a disk, determine which program, format, and disk type are required. Not all computer software is interchangeable; if there is any question whatsoever about the compatibility of softwares and hardwares, send a sample disk to your publisher or printer. Be certain to include a printout along with the disk so that the accurate reproduction of diacritical marks, typefaces, super- and subscripts, and other details can be verified. Nothing is more unfortunate than missing an opportunity to publish your work because of a silly computer glitch.

172 Etiquette

Remember that format will vary from one country to another, from one institution to another, and from one publisher to another. Make every effort to comply with your advisor's or editor's instructions if you are asked to bring your document into conformity with a house style. In most cases, you will find your "mission accomplished" even though the protocol may be slightly different: Carpenters measuring by inches and feet can build houses just as well as those using centimeters and meters!

173   Arrangement

The following order of arrangement conforms in general to that of printed books. For theses, however, it is recommended that a preface (if any) immediately precede the main text. Note: A slightly different arrangement may be prescribed by your thesis or dissertation advisor, your editor, or the author's guide issued by the organization, institution, or journal for whom you are writing.

> *Front matter*
>> title page
>> table of contents
>> other lists as needed (plates, illustrations, figures, tables,
>>> musical examples)
>> preface (optional)
>> acknowledgments (if not included in a preface)
>
> *Main text*
>> (with suitable divisions into chapters)
>
> *Reference matter*
>> appendix(es)
>> glossary
>> cumulated musical examples
>> endnotes (if footnotes are not used)
>> bibliography
>> index

Front Matter

174   Numbering

Front matter is customarily numbered in small Roman numerals. There is no prescribed formula for front matter. A book, for example, may have a map covering the *verso* of the cover and the opposing *recto*. Following that map may be a blank *verso*, and a note indicating the significance and source of the map on the opposing *recto*. At that point, the bastard-title page may appear, followed by a blank *verso*. Next in order is the full-title page. Perhaps the table of contents follows. To this possible arrangement of front matter, one might add a frontispiece or some other illustrative material. Regardless of what ultimately appears as the front matter, each page independent of the binding should be counted.

175   Title page

Printed books have two title pages: the bastard-title page, which gives only the main title without indication of authorship, and the full-title page, which gives the main title, subtitle (if any), and the name of the author.

For a thesis or dissertation, you will normally begin with a full-title page that also includes the name of the academic institution to which the document is being submitted; the degree program in which the candidate is enrolled; and the statement that the document fulfills partially the requirements of a particular degree. Your advisor or academic institution can provide sample title pages for your information. The format of these title pages must be reproduced in every detail.

176   Contents

List the headings of each major division: preface (if any); each chapter of the main text (by chapter number and chapter title); the subheads and paragraph heads of each chapter; and each distinct subdivision of the reference matter. After each heading, carry leaders across to a page number (in a vertically aligned column at the right margin) indicating where that heading may be found (with precisely the same wording!) in the manuscript.

The table of contents, taken by itself, should provide a good preliminary overview of the subject and indicate clearly how the writer proposes to organize the material. Chapter titles, subheads, and paragraph headings should therefore be crisp and informative. Plan a sufficient number of chapters so that the table of contents will show the main elements in the discussion.

177   Other lists

Where it appears desirable to provide a guide to the location of illustrative material in the manuscript, one or more appropriate lists or tables may be given after the table of contents, set up in the same general form. Plates and figures may be combined under the general heading "Illustrations." Separate lists of plates and figures are appropriate only if the document contains a great many images.

Musical examples are not ordinarily tabulated in the front matter, though this may be appropriate if you are presenting what amounts to an anthology of musical examples and text commentary within a single volume.

Lists of contributors, abbreviations, weights, and measures are all other possibilities. A list of tables should be provided if these are numerous or important in the manuscript.

178   Preface

A preface, as the term implies, is a preliminary statement that you might like to make before launching with full energy into the main subject. A preface may be somewhat less formal in tone than the main text. One's personal involvement with the subject, memorable experiences in the research process, and important sources of information make good topics for discussion in the preface. It is also an excellent opportunity to explain how the main body of the discussion is laid out and to call attention to features of special interest, such as appendixes, useful lists, and so on. Acknowledgments (without any special heading) may be incorporated into the preface, usually toward the end. A well-written preface puts the reader into a receptive frame of mind.

A preface is most appropriate for documents of considerable length and complexity. Books, dissertations, and theses are all likely candidates for some preliminary remarks, but a preface is not obligatory even for these documents. A preface would be out of place in a brief piece, such as a term paper, essay, or journal article.

If you do choose to include a preface, keep it brief and to-the-point. The most effective introductory remarks are just two or three pages long; those that go on for dozens of pages do nothing more than alert the reader to an author's proclivity to blather!

179   Acknowledgments

Acknowledgments are appropriate for published books written by a single author. For theses or dissertations, acknowledgments are best avoided. On the other hand, it is quite proper (and rather expected) to provide a brief paragraph or two giving credit to those who have inspired or assisted you with your work. If such credits are not included in a preface, they may be put on a special page headed "Acknowledgments."

In both dedications and acknowledgments, maintain a restrained and dignified tone, avoiding flowery language; mention professors who have given advice, and any persons from whom you have obtained special information (as through interviews or by correspondence). Where permission has been obtained to reproduce copyrighted materials, this should be acknowledged. Librarians, performing artists, administrators, and other professionals may well be acknowledged. It is also essential to recognize any institutional aid or grants that may have been awarded.

Main Text

180   Chapter headings

When you are entering your text on a disk, it is impossible to determine just how each page will finally appear with footnotes (if you are not using endnotes), with headers and footers, with space provided for musical examples and illustrative material, and with the removal of widows and orphans from the layout. (A widow is a single line from the end of a paragraph appearing at the top of a new page; conversely, an orphan is the first line of a new paragraph appearing at the bottom of a page.) It is best to use an abstract plan consistently, regardless of how page breaks appear on your computer screen. After several draft copies have been reviewed for accuracy, adjustments to the layout can be made with certainty.

For the beginning of each major subdivision (for example, the preface and individual chapters), allow a separation of three double-spaces. Use larger type for the chapter number and chapter title (14-point titles will sufficiently contrast with 12-point text). Perhaps you will add boldface to the chapter titles and subheads. Use conventional title capitalization without terminal punctuation.

A chapter number appearing on a separate line takes no punctuation; but if it is followed on the same line by the beginning of the chapter title, punctuation is required: Use a colon if the chapter title does not contain one; if it does, use a period. Leave two double-spaces between the chapter heading and the first line of text.

In printed books, pages bearing chapter titles usually do not have an Arabic number, even though they are counted in the pagination. Such an unnumbered page is called a blind folio. Since most word-processing programs allow for pagination either in headers or footers, it is safe to place all page numbers in the footers. In this way, the pagination will be consistent, and a conflict between chapter headings and page numbers at the top of the page will be avoided.

Writing convincing chapter titles is an art in itself. See rules 200 and 209.

181 Introductory remarks

The first few pages of an essay, or the first chapter in a thesis, dissertation, or book, may be introductory in nature, providing a general orientation to the subject. Give general observations concerning the background and nature of the subject about to be discussed; review the pertinent literature; isolate and define the specific problem that has motivated the research; explain the purpose of the investigation; identify several of the most important conclusions that have been reached; and mention the kinds of sources used and the methods employed in arriving at conclusions.

Toward the end of the introductory remarks, give a brief preview of the ensuing discussion: Explain briefly what is to be covered and what further information is to be found in appendixes, glossaries, or the like.

Do not be evasive about methodology! Each author approaches a particular subject in a different way. The focus of the study will depend upon the writer's own strengths—and weaknesses. One discussion may be primarily historical; in another, theoretical and analytical details may play a more significant part. Analysis often presumes some type of comparative assessment whereby the structure of the repertoire under consideration is viewed in a larger context. Many studies rely upon some sort of statistical survey that has already been undertaken, whether formally or informally. Ultimately, though, the writer must exercise critical judgment to evaluate the significance of the data.

Do not be surprised to discover that your investigation contains elements of various methodologies. Indeed, a variety of perspectives ensures a thorough and thoughtful coverage of the topic. At the same time, the projected length of the study will impose restrictions. If time, space, and resources are considerations—as they almost invariably will be—plan your investigation with those factors in mind. Do not attempt to crash through a host of complex issues in a fast and furious manner! Instead, identify the most important issues associated with the topic; consider frankly and honestly your own expertise in dealing with those issues; and determine what resources are available to you.

Remember that the heading "Chapter One: Introduction"—although it may be appropriate—tells the reader nothing. Even an introductory chapter should have a descriptive title that gives a precise idea of its content.

182 Chapter arrangement

In a lengthy study, one could expect at least four or five chapters, and conceivably many more. Each chapter represents a major subdivision of the subject treated. The chapter titles, taken successively, should form a logical framework of organization. Chapters toward the beginning of a thesis may depend somewhat more upon secondary sources and previous investigations, but as one proceeds, there should be a crescendo of emphasis upon the writer's own observations and an increase in the amount of detailed evidence presented.

183   Sections within chapters

For articulation of subdivisions within chapters, section headings—generally called subheads—may be used. It is usually unnecessary to assign numbers to such subdivisions. Optionally, subheads may be carried in the table of contents, typed below their respective chapter titles. Depending on the number of chapters and subheads within them, it may be more practical either to place subheads below chapter titles with generous hanging indentation; or, to type continuous lines below chapter titles with the subheads separated by sentence punctuation. In either method, use conventional title capitalization:

Chapter 1: The Nature of Early Chamber Music
Instruments and Instrumentation
Early Consort Music
The Rise of Polyphony
Sonata Repertoire to 1750

Chapter 1: The Nature of Early Chamber Music
Haut and *bas* Instruments. Instrumentation in the Music of the Late Medieval Era and the Renaissance. Early Musical Instruments. The Broken and Full Consorts. Chamber Music Based on Imitative Polyphony: The Canzona and the Ricercar. Ricercar-Type Pieces. The *In nomine.* Early Baroque Sonatas. The Sonata *da chiesa.* The Sonata *da camera.* The Concerto *da camera.* The Keyboard Part in Baroque Sonatas.

184   Conclusions

The word "conclusion" has two meanings: It may designate the end of something—a book, a film, a relationship; or, deductions resulting from the evaluation of data. In scholarly research, we are generally concerned with the second type of conclusion.

Although researchers generally make various deductions during the course of investigation, it is customary to present these in review at the end (the conclusion!) of the essay. In this respect, conclusions are indeed what we encounter last.

In conveying the results of your investigation to others, it is helpful to let the reader know at once (toward the very beginning of the essay) what it is that you have discovered. Such a preview of results does not take the wind out of your sails. On the contrary, if you take a definite and immediate stand, the reader is likely to read your arguments with even greater interest. Equipped with such a preview, the detailed lines of thought and the complex presentation of evidence will cease to be trivia and will become instead vital information.

Nevertheless, most readers would probably like to find at the end of the main text a major subdivision devoted to conclusions, restating in condensed form the ground covered, with possible passing commentary concerning how all this might influence our thinking in relation to the subject, scholarship to date, and additional research needed before closure can be reached. In a thesis, dissertation, or book-length study, a summary of this sort may well occupy the entire last chapter. In less expansive documents, a section bearing the subhead "Conclusions" might be more appropriate.

185 Special cases

In those rare instances where the material does not seem divisible into chapters, some alternative system may be used. Thus, if a subject falls into only two major subdivisions, consider Part 1 and Part 2 (with Roman numerals, if you prefer), with liberal provision for section headings in each part.

Sometimes the principal substance of a thesis is in musical notation, as in the case of a transcription, modern edition, or even an original composition with prefatory remarks. If the manuscript portion is too brief to divide up into chapters, it may be presented as an "Introduction," paginated with small Roman numerals. The musical portion can then begin with a subsidiary title page and (Arabic) page numbers of its own.

Reference Matter

186 Appendixes

Any homogeneous block of material that does not fit gracefully into the main text, but which ought to be available for reference, may be put into a subdivision headed "Appendix." There may be as many appendixes (headed "Appendix 1/A/I," "Appendix 2/B/II," etc.) as there are distinct blocks of material. Each appendix should carry a title that accurately describes its content. Such appendixes should be listed in the table of contents.

Remember: Your reader will not assume the presence of such appendixes. They will be of little value unless you point them out at appropriate moments in the body of the text, instructing your readers, for instance, to "consult Appendix B for details."

187 Glossary

Technical terms—that exclusive and often pretentious chit-chat known as jargon—should be avoided. Still, a technical term will often convey in a word or two complex ideas that might require several paragraphs of detailed prose. Where special or unusual terminology is an important factor in the thesis, consider bringing all such terms together into an alphabetical dictionary headed "Glossary," or "Vocabulary."

A glossary is primarily for reference. Its presence does not release the writer from the responsibility to communicate. Each of the terms that appears in the glossary should be carefully introduced in the body of the text. When the term first appears, it should be thoroughly explained. If the term is to be used consistently, it is a good idea to alert the reader by putting it in quotation marks or italics. Consider providing a note indicating that "words in italics (or 'in quotation marks,' or 'marked by an asterisk') are listed in the Glossary."

Glossaries are generally used in book-length studies. They are not practical for articles, term papers, or essays. Similarly, if such terms are so few in number that a special glossary would seem ridiculous, put them instead at some appropriate place in the main text. A table or a section, perhaps headed "Definitions," might be a viable alternative.

188 Cumulated musical examples

Ideally, each musical example appears on the same page as (or on the page following) the passage in the main text where it is first discussed. Sometimes, because of technical problems of makeup or copyright restrictions, it may be more convenient to cumulate all musical examples in a special subdivision, headed "Musical Examples," as reference matter.

The examples must be carefully numbered and captioned, and cues for each example must appear in the text (see rule 160). Specify the pages where the discussions of the examples are to be found.

189 Index

The function of an index is to direct readers to information. The validity of the research is altogether unrelated to the presence (or absence) of an index. Consequently, an index is an optional, though phenomenally useful, element.

For brief studies, an index would be impractical. Most institutions do not require indexes for theses or dissertations, though they would doubtless be welcome additions should authors have the incentive to provide them. Formerly, books without indexes were common, but in modern times, a scholarly book without an index is unthinkable.

Professional indexing services are available—at a hefty per-page price. Authors preparing indexes must decide whether they will limit the index to names or if they will also include subjects. The index of names is more straightforward, and unless a very detailed index is required, subjects are best avoided, especially if the contents of each chapter is listed in the table of contents.

Indexes, like bibliographies, may be unified (a listing in dictionary fashion of names and subjects) or classified (separate indexes for names, subjects, and perhaps even "Works Discussed").

One final consideration has to do with alphabetization. The two standard methods are to alphabetize word by word or letter by letter. In either method, the initial articles "a," "an," or "the" (or their counterparts in other languages) should be disregarded.

Alphabetizing word by word or letter by letter will be the same when single words are involved; however, when alphabetizing elements consisting of more than one word, variants arise.

In both systems, hyphens, apostrophes, and commas are overlooked. The entry "diminished-seventh chord" would therefore be alphabetized as though spelled "diminishedseventh chord."

Most American and English dictionaries ignore diacritical marks in both word-by-word and letter-by-letter alphabetization. For example, umlauted vowels in German have the effect of adding an "e" after the umlauted vowel: In its original spelling, Arnold Schönberg's name would appear somewhere between the entries for Percy Scholes and *Die schöne Müllerin* as follows:

Scholes, Percy
Schönberg, Arnold
Die schöne Müllerin

When the umlaut is spelled out, the name appears *before* that of Scholes.

Schoenberg, Arnold
Scholes, Percy
Die schöne Müllerin

In word-by-word alphabetization, each word in the element being alphabetized is treated as a separate unit. Alphabetizing begins anew with the second word. Words after the initial word come into consideration only when the initial word or name is identical. The following list of elements is alphabetized word by word.

Old Hall Manuscript
Old Hundredth
Old Roman chant
Old Vic
Oldberg, Arne
Oldham, Arthur
Oldman, Cecil Bernard
Oldroyd, George

In alphabetizing letter by letter, spaces between words are ignored; however, at a point of punctuation or an inversion introduced by a comma, alphabetizing begins anew. In the following list, the words in the previous example are alphabetized letter by letter.

Oldberg, Arne
Old Hall Manuscript
Oldham, Arthur
Old Hundredth
Oldman, Cecil Bernard
Old Roman chant
Oldroyd, George
Old Vic

PART TWO

Writing Skills

Prelude to Part Two

Part One dealt with the more or less mechanical aspects of manuscript style. Part Two deals briefly with the vehicle of communication itself, namely, literary style. Music students are likely to expend the greater part of their energies—and rightly so—in mastering the language of music. Only rarely does the musician have the opportunity to study and practice the skills of written English in a measure comparable, say, to the student of literature, philosophy, or history. It seems appropriate to gather together here for ready reference a few hints and suggestions—some new, some old—that may help students improve their written communication.

The handling of direct quotations is usually treated as something purely mechanical or perfunctory. This subject, along with the vitally important questions of abstracting and paraphrasing, is treated in Chapter 14.

The other sections can be referred to individually, as needed. Chapter 15, "Organization of the Document," is perhaps closest to the immediate challenge of getting a paper written. For a review of the structural components of language—words, phrases, clauses, sentences, paragraphs—see Chapter 16. Students who feel that their writing lacks sparkle, vitality, and conviction may be encouraged by looking at Chapter 17. If the problem is how to get hold of the subject, consider the various kinds of writing reviewed in Chapter 18.

Publication, like being born, is a different experience for each individual. It seems not altogether inappropriate, however, that today's student (who may be tomorrow's author!) should have an early opportunity to consider the possibilities, as in Chapter 19, "Writing for Publication."

CHAPTER 14

Abstract, Paraphrase, Direct Quotation

190 Rationale

Academic writing at its best shows that the author has carefully studied the subject and has shed light on it by examining a wide variety of attendant sources—which in order of priority take their place somewhere behind the primary subject. Enriching though they may be, such sources should function as a supporting actor, who lends emphasis to the principal *dramatis personae* and helps the audience to sympathize with and understand the characters who are central to the drama. Good scholarly writing must never become preoccupied with attendant sources at the expense of the main subject. Nevertheless, when a writer assembles the data collected from attendant sources, and uses that data like an illuminating spotlight, the reader sees the subject with an unprecedented intensity.

Because historians rely so much on the accounts of others, information often assumes the form of an abstract or paraphrase of the original. Direct quotation should be reserved for special situations. The rapport between the writer (you) and the reader is momentarily suspended each time you direct attention to someone else's words by quoting directly. If this is done too often, or without real plan or reason, the reader will think of you as a nonentity, or a parrot, or both, and your paper, a patchwork of catchy phrases, will ultimately fail to communicate effectively.

Writing ought at all times to be a direct expression of the writer's own personality. "Say it in your own words" is a magic formula that time and again cuts through whole jungles of vagueness and misunderstanding. It matters not whether one's own words are simple and homely, or precociously sesquipedalian (see rule 237): Truths have been uttered in all manner of language.

Inexperienced writers are too easily overwhelmed and seduced by the literary skill of whatever author they happen to be reading at the moment. This or that expression or turn of phrase—indeed, whole passages—are borrowed with the mistaken notion that one's own writing will benefit in the process.

Even though the pursuit of information will lead the researcher through the writings of a multitude of authors, it is yet possible for each scholar to have a distinctive and sincere voice. If you choose to imitate the style of a writer whose work you admire, look at broad constructive principles rather than localized details. Feel free to adapt structural and organizational concepts to meet the needs of your work. Remember that every person learns by imitation: If you imitate sound models, you will develop a sound style. Eventually, as you customize your imitations, they will cease to be servile reproductions of another's work, and they will become characteristic of *you!*

The art of abstracting and paraphrasing is crucial to good writing. If the word "art" seems to be too much, then call them disciplines. After all is said and done, the truth is that abstracting and paraphrasing require concentration, evaluation, and self-control. Understanding and brevity are their touchstones. Can you understand a 300-page argument? Can you present the essence of that argument in two or three paragraphs?

The comparatively easy process of extracting direct quotations can produce spectacular results when it is done skillfully and judiciously. Unsophisticated overuse of direct quotation, on the other hand, smothers whatever literary style one may have more quickly than wild morning-glories smother a summer garden.

191 Abstract

An abstract is a condensed summary of the main gist of some longer passage, or section, or even a whole article or book. The purpose of an abstract is to generalize an attitude or a contribution. Since any abstract should be in your own words, it should be fitted smoothly into your (double-spaced) main text.

Abstracting is one of the most important procedures in scholarly writing; for when writers are not bringing into sharp focus the information and commentary provided by others, they are condensing into usable form their own thoughts, observations, and experiences.

When you present someone else's ideas in abstract, provide a reference, just as you would for a direct quotation, mentioning the inclusive pages of the whole passage abstracted. (An abstract of an entire book requires no page reference.)

Special case: Doctoral candidates are usually asked to prepare for publication an abstract of the dissertation, in which case the whole content of a study perhaps running to hundreds of pages may need to be stated in not more than 600 words.

192   Paraphrase

A paraphrase is a free rendering or rephrasing of a passage, retaining the exact meaning but using a different wording. The purpose of a paraphrase is to reproduce the details of an argument or train of thought. The paraphrase may be longer than the original (as when the original is condensed and packed with meaning), or briefer than the original (as when the original is prolix and slow in coming to the point).

Technical words, or words possessing an exact shade of meaning, may be borrowed from the original, but the word order, sentence structure, and emphasis should be purposefully altered, showing that you understand the meaning (not merely the wording) of the passage.

Paraphrasing affords an opportunity to clarify and explain the original, and to adjust the content to your own particular literary style and intentions. In "adjusting" the content, never read into a passage something that is not there.

If you wish to interject comments of your own, you must learn to turn the paraphrase "on" and "off." It is "on" when you mention the author's name and continue as if you were retelling what he or she said. It is "off" when you make a positive statement that obviously conflicts with, or modifies, the original author's intentions. To turn the paraphrase back on, reintroduce either the author's name or a pronoun representing the author. Indirect discourse may be helpful: "The argument later approaches the absurd."

The whole purpose and nature of a paraphrase is such that it must be run into your double-spaced main text. Cite the source, just as you would for a direct quotation or an abstract.

For carrying on an argument with an author, it may be convenient to put the paraphrase in the main text and your running commentary in a series of notes.

Direct Quotations

193 Spacing

Direct quotations, or extracts—any material extracted verbatim from its source—may be treated in one of two ways. The material may either be enclosed in quotation marks and run into the double-spaced text; or be set off from the main text in a manner corresponding to the use of smaller type in a book: single-spaced, without quotation marks, and with recessed left margin. The first method is preferable for brief quotations (approximately five lines), or even for longer quotations when they are frequently interrupted by your own running comments. The second method is preferable when the quotation is long enough to involve possible confusion with your own text, or where it is presented as an exhibit.

194 Selectivity

Avoid verbatim quotation of commonplace thoughts, or long, wordy passages that could be more concisely stated in your own words. (In such cases, an abstract or paraphrase is more effective.) Reserve the use of direct quotation for these special occasions: when the statement is more concise and authoritative, coming from its author, than it could possibly be paraphrased in your own words; when an extended line of close reasoning can be grasped only when the complete original text is seen; or when one is consistently using primary sources containing new or otherwise valuable information that ought to be recorded as fully and exactly as possible.

195 Accuracy

Conform exactly to the original in wording, spelling, and internal punctuation. To call attention to an inaccuracy in the original, put [*sic*] or [!] in brackets after the word or statement involved. (The Latin word *sic* means "thus it is"; in other words, you are telling the reader, "It really says this in the original!")

If the error in the passage cited might cause problems if left uncorrected, by all means, put your correction in brackets. It is customary to preface such corrections with the Latin word *recte* ("rightly"; in other words, "It should *rightly* read"):

Henry Purcell lived from 1658 to 1695 [*recte* 1659–1695].

If you italicize words of the original for emphasis, modernize the spelling, or change the typeface, style, or size, then you must notify the reader of these modifications and explain *why* you have made them. Ideally, the reader should be able to reconstruct the original from what you have provided. On the other hand, you may want to assure the reader of "italics in the original," or "spelling as in the original" in a note or in brackets.

196 Interpolations

Use brackets to elucidate vague or ambiguous words not elsewhere explained, or to enclose comments of your own that you wish to interpolate in quoted matter. Never use parentheses!

In his treatise entitled *Eine Mittheilung and meine Freunde* (A communication to my friends, 1851), Wagner discusses the origins of his libretto for *Die Feen*. At one point, he says, "What took my fancy about the tale of Gozzi was not only its adaptability as a libretto for an opera, but the interesting nature of the matter in and of itself." But what is the tale of Gozzi? A responsible writer will take the time to inform the reader and will cite the passage as follows:

> What took my fancy about the tale of Gozzi [*La donna serpente*] was not only its adaptability as a libretto for an opera, but the interesting nature of the matter in and of itself.

On rare occasions you may have to warn the reader of "brackets in the original" and avoid using them yourself. In such cases, any necessary supplemental commentary may be given in a note.

197 Ellipses

A quotation can often be improved by omitting portions that are not significant, so that the main point is made with a minimum of words. Put an ellipsis . . . (three spaced dots) where something has been left out. If the omission occurs after what might stand as a complete sentence, the ellipsis follows the sentence period. . . .

The three dots are the same no matter how much, or how little, has been omitted. Exceptions: A typed line of spaced periods indicates omission of one or more lines of verse (in poetry), or one or more paragraphs (in lengthy prose quotations).

Leaving out a few words is quite different from leaving out several pages of text. It may be more instructive—and more honest—to interrupt the quotation in some way: "Later in the essay, Fétis reverses himself." Depending on how accurate you want to be, you could modify such a lead-in phrase with precise details: "Three paragraphs later, Fétis reverses himself."

Note: An ellipsis is different from the sign for suspension points (see rule 42). When the writer invites the reader to imagine the conclusion of a statement, suspension points must be used. These are three unspaced dots. Suspension points are never followed by any punctuation.

198 Opening a quotation

A direct quotation should not be dropped into the midst of one's text like some foreign substance. Provide a smooth transition. The first word of a quotation may be adjusted from uppercase to lowercase, or from lowercase to uppercase, to suit the situation.

When quotations appear as portions of your own sentences, run into text, two possible methods of treatment are possible: Start your own sentence and lead "directly (lowercase) into the quotation"; or, "Start (capitalized) with the quotation," close quotes to identify the speaker or otherwise explain the excerpt, and "continue the quotation later in the sentence if you like."

Normally, only quotations of five lines or more are set off from the text. Use single-spacing and set left-hand indentation for a broader margin.

Consider the possibilities for punctuation preceding a direct quotation. If your words of introduction form a complete sentence, put a colon or a period. Open the quotation with a capital if it begins with what can be construed as a complete sentence. If the opening of the quotation is a sentence fragment, you may wish to complete the sentence with a few introductory words of your own, in brackets. The first word in brackets may then be capitalized.

Words of introduction that lead naturally into the quotation, without a break, should have a comma or no punctuation at all. In such cases, you will probably start with a sentence fragment and a lowercase letter for the first word of the extract.

The choice of punctuation really depends upon the tone that you wish to establish and the format of the information that follows. Do you want an official pronouncement? Are you introducing a formal list?

If so, here is what you must do:

Perhaps you desire a more gentle tone, one less formal and intimidating.

In such cases,

199 Foreign-language quotations

Foreign words appearing in an English context should be italicized, but a quotation given entirely in the original language need not be. Treat such a passage just as you would a quotation in English.

As a courtesy to the reader, foreign-language extracts should be presented in English translation. For very brief quotations, either give the original language first, followed immediately by the English translation in parentheses, with or without quotation marks; or, give the translation first with the original language in italics and enclosed in parentheses. If economy is a concern, you can save space by giving the English translation in the body of the text with the original text in a note. If the foreign texts are very extensive, consider placing them in an appendix.

Occasionally, where a comparison of meanings is important, the original quotation and English translation may be set side by side, in parallel columns. Alternatively, use an interlinear arrangement, with the original text in Roman type and the translation beneath it in italics. Musicians will be familiar with this format, an accepted standard in scores of vocal works with English translations. Interlinear format is especially effective when you want to show the precise meaning of each word of the text. Performers with limited familiarity with foreign languages will be grateful for such precise information about the text and its meaning.

If the issue hinges on a single word, you may give a standard English translation:

> In his treatise entitled *Das Kunstwerk der Zukunft* (The artwork of the future), Wagner writes: "The path of science leads from error to knowledge, from imagination (*Vorstellung*) to reality."

Indicate clearly who is responsible for all translations of foreign-language texts. If all or most of the work is your own, simply state at the first opportunity, "Translations in this essay are mine unless otherwise noted."

CHAPTER 15

Organization of the Document

200   Subject matter, title

A report, term paper, or thesis is the *intensive* result of an *extensive* background of study. The subject should therefore be limited in scope, its nature clearly expressed in the title, and the paper should include only material that is closely related to the central theme. A good paper gives the impression that its author has purposely limited the material, giving the reader a maximum of highly pertinent information with a minimum of words. The resulting document, then, represents only a sampling of the author's more detailed and extensive knowledge.

The title must be meaningful (never vague), bring the reader's attention sharply into focus, and provide a sense of direction for the entire paper. Study published titles, and observe how they are constructed. Titles usually omit finite verbs and consist of one or more substantives (nouns or proper names) qualified by modifiers (adjectives, phrases, and possibly a subtitle). On rare occasions, verbals (participles, gerunds, infinitives) are used as substantives and modified by adverbs. Keep titles short. If they must be long, choose the chief substantives carefully. Do not tuck important issues away into obscure corners of long modifying phrases.

Formulate a title before beginning to write the paper, and bear it constantly in mind so that the paper will have a sense of direction. After the paper is written, reconsider the title to see if it expresses the completed achievement, not merely your original intention. Make up ten or so tentative new titles, and select the one that is most convincing.

The routine paper deserves a title and byline just as surely as the formal report, thesis, dissertation, or book; any literary "package" should be clearly labeled as to content and manufacturer. Formal titles, degrees earned, and other accretions to the author's name should not be included in the byline.

201 Direction, relevance, coherence

The governing principles of organization are direction, relevance, and coherence. A sense of direction in any piece of writing means a pull toward some goal. Within the first page or two, the reader should already feel that the discussion is leading somewhere, that it is pointed in some definite direction. As the discussion unfolds, this sense of purposefulness creates a kind of magnetic field which pulls the reader along. Side excursions to explain supplementary matters should be either very brief or else carefully oriented to avoid loss of momentum. Continuous queries—Where am I going? What steps do I take to get there?—can be among the most potent of organizing forces.

Journalists speak of "slant." The skillful writer attempting anything more than dull reporting views the subject from some particular angle or point of view. Scholarly writing, despite its reputation for cold objectivity, is just as likely to be slanted as any other kind of writing. Avoid sensationalism, and try not to twist the facts. When arguing a point of view, be equipped with evidence to support your contention. Anticipate possible objections, and, if possible, defuse them in an expedient manner.

Relevance means sticking to the subject, or at least not wandering too far from it. Many inexperienced writers tend to put down everything that comes to mind. Others fail because of a mental block, becoming critical of every paragraph, every phrase, every word that they write. Remember: It is easier to edit twenty pages of rambling prose than to edit nothing. Perhaps the twenty pages, when edited, will yield eight solid, informative, well-written pages. Writing a research paper is like trimming a tree: Prune away all the extraneous, wild growth, leaving a strong, vigorous shape.

In editing, remember that the things you omit today may perhaps flourish in their own right on some other occasion. Do not discard data that may not fit into the context of the essay at hand. Take Beethoven's lead, and keep these tidbits in storage, just as he kept bits of musical inspiration in various sketch books. When the right time comes, yesterday's scraps may become the foundation of your *magnum opus*.

Coherence is the connective tissue that holds a discourse together. Present each idea clearly, and show its logical relationship to the next step in the argument. At the local level, this process depends upon well-constructed sentences and paragraphs. In the broader scheme, coherence will come from whole sections fitted together to advance a single, dynamic hypothesis. Even assuming direction and relevance are present, coherence is necessary to make writing "jell."

202 Tone, stance

The facts of reality, as best we can determine them, form the foundation of all expository writing. In presenting those facts, authors must establish a characteristic voice. Tone depends upon many different factors: the choice of words and punctuation, the pace of the argument, the details of style. Certainly, these vary from one author to another; nevertheless, writers can be confident that their thoughts will be taken seriously if they maintain a professional tone. The presentation should be concise, not prolix. It should be interesting, but not dramatic. The writing style should certainly be elegant, but poetic or rhetorical language is inappropriate. Avoid alliteration, apostrophe, assonance, euphemism, hyperbole, litotes, onomatopoeia, oxymoron, and personification. Save these techniques for poems and eulogies! In scholarly writing, they are ineffective, potentially confusing, and—ultimately—annoying.

Stance is an equally important consideration. Do not assert your own views aggressively; the reader should be focused on the subject, not on your persona as the author. Similarly, when the presentation reaches a point where you may appropriately draw some conclusions, do not back away. If you find yourself using words or phrases like "perhaps," "it may be suggested," or "one might think," then stop and consider carefully. Do you have anything to say? If your argument is so weak that you are unable to draw a single solid conclusion, then go back and reconsider the viability of your research techniques, sources, and argumentation—even, possibly, the topic itself.

203 Sequence of ideas

Do not plan your discussion primarily as a string of words, but rather as a sequence of ideas. Review each word, each sentence, each paragraph, to see that the text is transparent enough to let the ideas shine through. Too often, when we are too lazy to think, we reach for an easy cliché or habitual stock phrase, which may not convey our precise meaning.

Language that is turbid (muddy), turgid (bloated), or prolix (longwinded) induces boredom as well as misunderstandings. Ideas must be clearly stated: They must move smoothly and logically from one to another. Where a sentence or paragraph, or for that matter a whole paper, does not seem to succeed, strip down the wording to basic ideas to see if the order of presentation is faulty.

204   The brief

A brief is a condensed version of the train of thought to be presented in a paper. In contrast to an outline, which is made up of key words or phrases in a coordinate-subordinate arrangement, a brief consists of short but complete sentences, each stating an important idea to be explored and developed. The sentences succeed one another as in an abstract. In an outline, you leave yourself uncommitted. Mere mention of a word or phrase does not indicate what stand you are going to take in relation to it.

In a brief, with a subject and predicate for each major idea, you force yourself to take a stand. Though writing a brief can be difficult, especially if you find the subject intimidating (like music history, music theory, or analysis), it is still excellent discipline. The best way to assemble and clarify one's ideas is to maneuver them into proper sequence. Also, it is far easier to arrange and rearrange experimentally a dozen sentences, for purposes of organization, than a dozen pages of text.

Consider writing a brief before tackling the first draft of your paper. If this does not seem possible, go ahead and write the first draft, then reduce this draft to the form of a brief—in other words, make an abstract of it. This reduction will lay bare the skeleton of the organization. Review this brief for any flaws in logic and for possible rearrangement of the sequence of ideas. The brief can usually be adjusted to make it more convincing and can then function as a guide to revising the paper.

205   Expanding the brief

The simplest procedure for expanding the brief into a paper is as follows. Each positive statement in the brief serves as a topic sentence for a paragraph in the paper. For example, if the paper ought to contain about ten paragraphs, make up a brief with ten sentences, each suitable for a topic sentence. In writing the brief, one can make terse, positive statements, knowing that each will be explained at length in a fully developed paragraph.

In practice, this simple procedure is often modified in the interests of good literary style. A sentence that is quite at home in a brief may have to be reworded when it is transplanted into the paragraph it is supposed to govern. Paragraph prose differs in rhythm and flow from the prose of abstracts and briefs.

The same general principle can be used at different structural levels. Thus, a sentence in a brief might be called upon to govern a whole section or chapter of a longer document.

206 Opening statement

To illustrate, let us assume a paper of short to moderate length, with the first two paragraphs devoted to opening remarks. The preliminary material is to get the reader's thoughts turned in the right direction before plunging into the subject. The opening statement is difficult to formulate. After the rest of the paper is completed, always go back and review the opening. Typically, drastic revision may be needed to make it serve its purpose.

The opening should be the most tightly constructed part of the paper, because of the necessity for getting quickly into the subject. At the same time, you must write convincing prose to attract the reader. The extent of opening commentary will depend upon a proper balance between these two factors. You cannot afford to rush the reader; neither can you dawdle over long, eloquent pronouncements.

To begin, back away from your topic enough to show your subject in some kind of context. That context may be exclusively musical; it may encompass other performing and creative arts; it may be broadly humanistic; it may consider the topic within a sweeping view of culture, commerce, and technology. Thus, if you are writing about one aspect of a thing, mention first its other aspects, even if you drop them in the ensuing discussion.

Such magisterial opening statements require thoughtful consideration and substantial knowledge. One terrible mistake beginners make is to delve into fields with which they are only vaguely familiar. For a confident start, begin from the perspective of your own knowledge and experience.

Assuming a standard two-paragraph opening, devote the first paragraph to the broader implications of your subject, giving the reader a chance to get accustomed to your literary style. In a second, transitional paragraph, work around to a more precise explanation of the task at hand. Define the subject and tell how you propose to deal with it. Explain important technical terms. If you like, give a brief preview of the layout of the rest of the paper, so that the reader will know what to expect.

Remember: The title stands alone as a kind of label. It is not part of the text. The text itself, therefore, must introduce and elucidate the ideas contained in the title—usually in a paraphrased or restated version. Once the reader has read the opening remarks, the significance of the title should be clear.

Experiment with different types of openings. For a dramatic opening, you may either begin with a startling or paradoxical statement, which you are fully able to justify as the opening remarks proceed; or begin by describing vividly some small, fascinating detail and go on to explain its relevance to the main subject. In either case, you surprise the reader by apparently departing from the subject as announced in the title. Naturally, by the end of the whole opening statement, the surprise opener must be fully reconciled with the title.

The experienced writer who is weary of standard openings might try a more abrupt beginning and come to grips with the heart of the matter in the very first sentence. This approach is more likely to succeed if the title conveys an immediate message requiring little or no explanation; if the subject is sufficiently self-contained to dispense with tie-ins to related matters; and if one knows for certain that the audience is made up of experts who will appreciate your skipping the preliminaries. The method may also be appropriate for some narratives. Most narratives, however, need preparation: Begin with background or a condensed synopsis, and start the narrative only at some point where it is really interesting.

Avoid an opening quotation. The inexperienced writer is tempted to open with an isolated and unexplained direct quotation from his favorite author, for dramatic effect. Don't! It is ridiculous to present your title, put in your byline, and then start off with someone else's words. It is quite a different matter if the author quoted is properly introduced (see rule 198).

207   Paragraph sequence

After the opening remarks, paragraphs should follow one another in orderly sequence. Where there is a choice, shorter paragraphs are preferable to long, rambling ones. Each new paragraph provides a breathing space and gives the eye a momentary rest. Where the flow of ideas has sufficient momentum, no special effort is needed to make paragraphs connect—especially if they are short.

With long paragraphs, or where the complex of ideas necessarily requires a slower pace, transitions are needed. A transition consists of a sentence or two for switching over from one train of thought to another. The transition should come at the end of one paragraph and prepare for the topic sentence that begins the next.

At times a paragraph is purposely put out of sequence. In pressing forward with main ideas, the discussion may have omitted some essential background information. Take time out to provide such information precisely where it is most needed. In other words, the main ideas must be in proper sequence, but secondary and supporting ideas need not follow any order of their own; they may be interjected wherever they are useful. The wording must be subtly constructed so the reader will know when you are going back to fill us in, and when you are returning to the main track. If days, months, and years are involved in the discussion, be sure to reiterate these as often as necessary to eliminate any possibility of confusion.

Occasional digressions can be very effective, but only if they are that: occasional. When the technique is overdone, it will quickly make a shambles of your whole organization.

208   Sections

Lengthy studies may be subdivided into sections by various means: Some scholars use Roman numerals; others use a series of asterisks, bullets, or other symbols. None of these can communicate as effectively as carefully chosen words. Select a subhead thoughtfully, just as you would select an essay title, and use the same procedure for capitalization that you would use for the main title.

Each section introduced by a new heading will normally comprise several pages. Correspondingly, subheadings will be followed by several paragraphs. Subheads—the term used to refer to all levels of headings, subheadings, and sub-subheadings—can be very helpful in revealing the organization of the subject matter: They tend to fix in the reader's mind the larger units of the discussion. Since they identify the progress of the argument, there is no need to indent the first line following a subhead. Of course, all paragraphs after the first should be indented as usual.

Just as the single-sentence paragraph has little purpose or meaning, the subdivided text should contain at least two sections. Subheads should appear on a separate line. For the first level of text division, use the basic font and point size in boldface type. For subdivisions within the first level, use the basic font and size—again on a separate line—in italics.

On some occasions, paragraph headings may be preferred to, or used in addition to, subheads. A paragraph heading is italicized and followed by a period at the beginning of the paragraph. Proceed immediately (in Roman type) with the body of the text. The term "run-in sidehead" is sometimes used to designate a paragraph heading.

All titles and subheads should be typed flush with the left margin; paragraph headings should conform with conventional paragraph indentation.

Frequently enough, a paper (or chapter) can achieve perfect clarity without any subheadings at all. Do not use them unless they serve some real purpose.

209 Chapters

Chapters are appropriate only in lengthy documents, such as theses, dissertations, and books. The chapter title should provide a careful and accurate announcement of the content of the chapter. All chapter titles taken together (as in a table of contents) must convey a meaningful overview of the gist of the study as a whole. Indeed, manipulating chapter titles is an excellent way of controlling the broader elements of organization. Similarly, perusing chapter titles in a table of contents is a good method for evaluating the potential relevance and usefulness of a source.

The various chapters ought to carry approximately equal weight, which is not quite the same as saying they must be of equal length. An average comfortable length is perhaps twelve to fifteen pages—longer, if there is more to be said; shorter, if everything has been said. Where a chapter rambles on, the reader tires and receptivity decreases at an alarming rate. Each new chapter, on the other hand, induces a fresh burst of attentive energy.

CHAPTER 16

Communication of Ideas: Words, Sentences, Paragraphs

For improvement of writing skills, keep constantly in mind the crucial importance of individual words. Where words are strong, vital, and packed with meaning, they are workers. Where they are commonplace, colorless, and hackneyed, they become drones. However skillfully constructed the sentences and paragraphs may be, they will fall flat without the support of effective wording.

210   Synonyms

Synonyms are words that have approximately the same meaning—with subtle differences. To increase your word power, make a habit of searching mentally for all possible synonyms for any word you are about to use and select the word with just the right shade of meaning. Similarly, avoid using the same word over and over by alternating it with one or more suitable synonyms. It may be challenging, at first, to find several words that can be used more or less interchangeably. If you find yourself having difficulty, do not despair: Try writing a paper with a thesaurus at your side. You will never be content to work without one again!

211   Parts of speech

Most of us use language instinctively, and the language that we use most is spoken rather than written. Since spoken language is ephemeral, we usually are not too concerned about being elegant or accurate in our expression. The goal is to get the job done: Communicate the essential message, and be done with it! As a consequence, our vocabulary, grammar, and syntax can quickly become sloppy. The expression of ideas in writing, however, is a more formal matter—especially when we are submitting those ideas for review by an instructor for a grade, or for consideration by an editor for publication. When we know that our words will become both public and permanent, even the most loquacious among us becomes considerably more circumspect.

Our ability to use formal language effectively depends upon our understanding of the principal agents of discourse: words. Words are generally grouped into seven categories—nouns, verbs, pronouns, adjectives, adverbs, prepositions, and conjunctions—called parts of speech.

212 Nouns

Nouns are sometimes called substantives. Proper nouns (capitalized) are names of particular persons, places, or things. Common nouns may be concrete (names of objects), collective (names of groups of things regarded as a unit), or abstract (names of qualities, general ideas). Do not capitalize common nouns for emphasis; it gives the text an antiquated, almost humorous appearance.

References to genres should be capitalized only when linked to a specific work and accompanied by such information as the composer's name, a key, and an opus number. Subsequent references, even to a specific piece previously mentioned, should not be capitalized:

> One of Schubert's best-known chamber works is his Quintet in A major, Op. 114. This quintet is commonly known as the *Trout Quintet*, so called because its fourth movement is a set of variations on Schubert's song "Die Forelle" (The trout).

References to specific periods in music history—Baroque, Classical, Romantic—should always be capitalized. When they appear without capitalization, such terms should be understood as they are used in common parlance. Consider the ambiguity of the following example:

> One of Mozart's most beautiful arias is "Porgi, amor, qualche ristoro" (Grant, love, some relief), which derives its emotional force not only from the excellence of the writing but also from the romantic character of the music.

Is the writer suggesting that the aria has musical characteristics associated with Romanticism? Or is the idea that the aria deals with an ardent emotional attachment of a romantic sort? The use of capitals to designate periods ensures clarity.

213   Verbs

Among parts of speech, verbs are easily the most complex. They show intent and give our prose commitment; our use of them must therefore be precise. To achieve that precision, let us consider the rich variety of verbs and verb forms available in the English language.

Verbs can show activity (*run; jump; move*) or state of being (*am; are; is*). They may be grouped into two classifications: finite verbs and non-finite verbs, or infinitives.

Finite verbs presume a subject in the first or third person singular or plural (*I; s/he; it; we; they*). Infinitives, on the other hand, may not have a subject. Infinitives are always apparent from the marker word "to," and they should never be split. (How strange "To be or to not be" sounds!)

Finite verbs differ dramatically from infinitives because finite verbs are normally presented within a chronological context whereas infinitives are not. Finite verbs have four principal characteristics: tense, aspect, voice, and mood. They may be either transitive or intransitive. Transitive verbs can take an object; intransitive verbs cannot.

The tense of a verb indicates the time of an event in relation to the time of the utterance made about the event. Time may be past, present, or future. There are four absolute tenses and two relative tenses. The absolute tenses denote the temporal aspects of an action only in relation to the moment in which the utterance is made. These are present, past, present perfect (an enduring action in the past that is over and done at present), and future. The two relative tenses are past perfect and future perfect. With these relative tenses, some relative chronological point will be involved:

> By age twenty, Mozart *had composed* approximately 250 works in an incredibly wide variety of genres. [past perfect]

The tense of a verb depends upon the particular inflected form of that verb in its conjugation. Verbs that follow a consistent pattern in the formation of the various tenses are called regular: *I compose* [present], *I am composing* [progressive], *I composed* [past], *I have composed* [past perfect]. The corresponding tenses of irregular verbs assume different forms in their principal parts: *I sing, I am singing, I sang, I have sung.*

Aspect describes the status of the verb (the action or state of being), indicating whether it is consummated or in progress, occurring only once or many times, having a consequence or no consequence, and so on. We can describe verb tenses as being perfect or progressive. When we use the word "perfect," we mean that the action has been completed at the time of utterance (in absolute tenses) or by the specified time (in relative tenses). Completion may occur in the past, present, or future:

> Purcell *had composed* quite a bit of theater music by 1690. [past perfect]

> I *have finished* my arrangement of "Kum ba Yah." [present perfect]

> James Levine *will have returned* from Japan by the time the Metropolitan Opera season opens in the fall. [future perfect]

Progressive (or imperfect) tenses indicate that the event under consideration is in progress. An unfolding event may occur within the context of the past, present, or future:

> For the most part, Purcell *was composing* theater music during the 1690s. [past progressive]

> I *am finishing* my arrangement of "Kum ba Yah." [present progressive]

> James Levine *will be returning* from Japan in the next few weeks. [future progressive]

Aspect is perhaps the most subtle characteristic of a verb. It is possible to focus on the beginning of an event (ingressive aspect); the continuity of an event (durative aspect); the repetitious or habitual character of an event (iterative aspect); the final consequence of an event (effective aspect); or the nature of an event as it unfolds from beginning to end (terminate aspect).

> Mozart *began composing* when he was but a child. [ingressive aspect]

> He *continued composing* works at an astounding rate of about twenty-five pieces per year. [durative aspect]

Note: Here, the gerund object ("composing") might well be replaced by the infinitive complement ("to compose") depending on whether the verb ("continued") is perceived as transitive or intransitive.

> Bach *revised* the music of the B-minor Mass *again and again*. [iterative aspect]

> Brahms *finally completed* his Symphony No. 1 in C minor in 1876. [effective aspect]

In 1825, Beethoven *put* the finishing touches on his String
Quartet in E-flat, Op. 127. [terminate aspect]

Besides infinitives, the other so-called infinite (unchanging) parts of verbs
are participles ("writing," "written"), gerunds ("writing," as verbal
noun), and gerundives ("writing," as a verbal adjective).

The two voices of verbs are active and passive. Verbs that view actions
from the point of origin are described as active voice; verbs that consider
the recipient of the action or its consequences are described as passive
voice:

After the disastrous first performance by Ignaz Schuppanzigh
and his quartet, Beethoven *insisted* that Joseph Böhm give the
"official" premiere of his String Quartet Op. 127. [active voice]

Haydn *was not granted* the position as the music director at the
Esterházy court until the death of Gregor Joseph Werner.
[passive voice]

To maintain a vigorous, lively, and interesting tone, writers should use
active voice. Still, the passive voice may be useful in some situations. If, for
example, the point is to show that Haydn, despite his humble background,
his diligent efforts, his loyal service to the Esterházy court, and his total
commitment to his work, was basely abused and scorned by this older
composer, who was doubtless jealous of this very capable young man,
then the passive voice effectively channels the reader's sympathies toward
the innocent victim of exploitation.

Passive voice can also be effective in situations where the embarrassing abstract third person singular pronoun would normally be required.
For instance:

The reader will derive the most benefit from the text that *he is
reading* if its vocabulary is clear, direct, and unbiased. [active
voice with abstract third person singular pronoun]

The reader will derive the most benefit from the text that *is
being read* if its vocabulary is clear, direct, and unbiased.
[passive voice with third person singular pronoun deleted]

The three moods of verbs are indicative, subjunctive, and imperative.
The indicative mood is used to indicate a fact or statement, or to ask a
question that will probably be answered with a simple yes or no, or with
some definitive statement.

The subjunctive is used to express a possibility, wish, or doubt, or to inquire about some situation or circumstance that will require an answer involving speculation, hypothesis, or conjecture.

The imperative mood expresses a command and is often closely related to the subjunctive. The old saying "Your wish is my command" perfectly demonstrates the fine line that separates an earnest desire from a command. Similarly, the difference between "requesting" (subjunctive) a person's resignation and "firing" (imperative) that same individual is, in many cases, a matter of protocol. In other cases, the decision will depend upon the rank of the person making the alleged request and the comparative rank of the person of whom the request is made.

The term "indicative mood" is, perhaps, a bit misleading: When we say "indicate," we mean "to show the way," "to point out," or "to state as fact":

> Mozart's career as a composer began when he was
> approximately ten years old.

The indicative mood may also be used to make an inquiry:

> Approximately when did Mozart's career as a composer begin?

Verbs in the indicative mood are far more common in present-day English than either subjunctive or imperative mood verbs. The indicative mood appears in all tenses with equal frequency.

Control over various verb forms contributes to both subtlety and accuracy of expression. Sometimes ideas that we express are not facts: They may be fantasies, things wished for, or possibilities. Such ideas may be worded with verbs in the subjunctive mood, thus highlighting the speaker's departure from the world of facts and data.

When making statements in the subjunctive—in the realm of imagination and possibility—the likelihood or unlikelihood of the realization of these possibilities must be considered. If the coin toss falls in favor of likelihood, the realm of possibilities is usually discussed using verbs in the indicative mood:

> Because of the presence of Purcell's characteristic manner of
> writing the small letter "r" backward, it is very likely that this is
> a genuine Purcell holograph manuscript.

Note: Even though the word "likely" suggests an element of uncertainty here, the verb form "is" shows that the probability is approaching certainty.

If, on the other hand, the speaker is inclined to be skeptical of the authenticity of the document under consideration, the sentence might be something like this:

> If this *were* a genuine Purcell holograph manuscript, I should have expected to see his characteristic manner of writing the small letter "r" backward.

The use of the subjunctive form of the verb "to be" ("were") is a red flag: It conveys powerfully the skepticism of a hypothesis that is probably erroneous.

Some uses of the subjunctive are intended to establish a hypothetical situation for the sake of argument. This type of subjunctive (often called the subjunctive of logical reasoning) is routine in classrooms and lecture halls:

> *Let us suppose* a tonality of C minor, and *let us* further *suppose* that an augmented-sixth chord containing the tones A-flat, C, E-flat, and F-sharp occurs within the passage. If that chord *were allowed* to progress to its customary resolution, A-flat *would move* downward to G while F-sharp *would move* upward to G. The remaining tones, C and E-flat, *would move* down to B-natural and D respectively, forming the dominant-seventh chord of the tonic.

Another form of the subjunctive that still appears in day-to-day parlance is the hortatory subjunctive. Any situation in which we make an exhortation or urgent appeal would be an appropriate context for the hortatory subjunctive:

> And God said, *"Let there be* light." (Genesis I: 3)

> Lord *have* mercy upon us. (Ordinary of the Mass)

In both these examples, and particularly in the second, the fine line that separates the subjunctive from the imperative is apparent. Note: In the second example, no comma follows the word "Lord"; hence, the construction is a genuine hortatory subjunctive, meaning "*May* the Lord have mercy upon us!" On the other hand, the passage appears commonly enough with a comma following the word "Lord," in which case, the meaning is the imperative "Lord, *you must have* mercy upon us!"

When the statement that is to follow the verb is clearly a contradiction of actual circumstances or conditions, the subjunctive form of the verb should be used:

> If I *were* the conductor of the Berlin Philharmonic, I would open the season with a Bruckner symphony.

The subjunctive mood is appropriate in many circumstances; but sadly, the trend in English usage has been to use some indicative verb form where formerly the subjunctive was found. In common parlance this laxity causes no problems, but in scholarly writing and legal documents, precision is more than merely desirable: It is a fundamental prerequisite.

214 Pronouns

Personal pronouns frequently change form depending on their case, whether nominative, genitive, dative, or accusative. The pronouns and their associated adjectival forms seldom give trouble in the first person (*I, my, mine, me; we, our, ours, us*) and second person (*you, your, yours*); it is the third person (*he, his, him; she, her, hers; it, its; they, their, theirs, them*) that is potentially confusing—unless the reference (the substantive for which the pronoun stands) is unmistakably clear. An impersonal third person is also available. Impersonal pronouns and their adjectival forms may be in the singular form (*one; one's*), or they may appear in the plural (*they; their; theirs; them*).

Relative pronouns (*who; which; that*) are used to introduce either adjectival or relative clauses or phrases. "Who" is used for persons, "that" is used for things:

The man *who* wrote the libretto is himself a composer.

The libretto *that* Stephen Sondheim wrote for the musical brought him instant acclaim.

See also rule 225.

Demonstrative pronouns (*this; these; that; those*) must be distinguished from so-called limiting adjectives ("*this* book"; "*that* flower"). Where a demonstrative pronoun refers to a whole concept, the reference must be clear:

Composers, after writing several overtures, often turn to the symphony. *This* is to be expected.

Sometimes a demonstrative pronoun does not refer back to an antecedent; rather, it is immediately explained in an adjectival clause:

That *which comes easiest* may not always be the best.

Those *who think carefully* will agree.

Indefinite pronouns may stand either as subject (*) or object (§):

Given the amount of poetry written by the Goliards, a correspondingly rich number of musical settings must have existed; however, to date, *no one** has found *any*§ to speak of.

*Everyone** knows that one hymn tune can easily be exchanged for *another*§ if their musical structures match the structures of the poetic texts being set.

Numeral pronouns are cardinal (*) or ordinal (§) numbers. Cardinal numbers indicate "how many." Ordinal numbers, as the name implies, show a particular place in an ordered sequence:

Four* of Beethoven's symphonies contain variations. The Third§, Fifth§, Seventh§, and Ninth§ offer a virtual compendium of early nineteenth-century variation technique.

Personal pronouns can be transformed into reflexive or intensive pronouns by the addition of the suffix *-self* or *-selves:*

When the prince married a young woman who was not much interested in music, Bach recognized that he had to find *himself* a new position. [reflexive]

In many cases, Bach wrote out the performing parts *himself*. [intensive].

The reciprocal pronouns are "each other" where only two things are involved, and "one another" for more than two.

Interrogative pronouns are usually avoided in expository writing. The exception might be a rhetorical question for which the answer will be supplied:

Which of Beethoven's symphonies departs from the Classical four-movement design?

What are the pitches of a Neapolitan sixth chord if the key is F major?

215 Adjectives

Adjectives are used to describe, modify, or qualify nouns or pronouns, either as attributes (next to the subject or object) or as predicates (connected with the subject by means of a verb). Proper adjectives are derived from proper nouns that name a particular person, place, or thing: *Shakespeare, Shakespearean; France, French; Trinity, Trinitarian.* Proper adjectives should always be capitalized.

Practically speaking, Dmitri Shostakovich (1906–1975) was a *Soviet*—not *Russian*—composer. [attributive proper adjectives]

Regardless of political circumstances, it is clear—both from his memoirs and from his music—that he was *sincere*. [predicate adjective]

When used appropriately and accurately, adjectives are perhaps our most powerful resource for developing a vigorous style, but their force is quickly depleted by overuse. One must constantly look for new ones and resist the temptation to use modifiers that are trite or colloquial.

Through judicious use of adjectives, several ordinary sentences may be transformed into a single enriched sentence:

The common transverse flute, with its three-octave range, is distinguished by the lyric quality of its middle register; the haunting, silvery brilliance of the uppermost octave; and the velvety, sensuous charm—despite its weak, breathy quality—of the lowest octave.

Compare:

The flutes that are most common are played sideways. They have a range of three octaves. The middle register has a lyric quality. The higher notes sound brilliant and silvery. They have a haunting quality. The lowest notes cannot be played forcefully, and sound breathy. They nevertheless have a certain charm that is velvety and sensuous.

See rule 227 for other ways to enrich sentences.

216 Adverbs

Inexperienced writers tend to forget all about adverbs and their potential. When we have found the right verb, we tend to rush on to the rest of the predicate; but could the verb be given more precise meaning if we were to modify it adverbially? Adjectives may be similarly touched up by adverbial modifiers. One adverb may also modify another adverb ("*quite happily* ascended").

Adverbs, adverbial clauses, and prepositional phrases functioning as adverbs may be found or tested by asking questions:

How?	*Quickly, suddenly, slowly.* He plays *without any expression.* She sang *as if she were choking.*
How much?	*Scarcely, equally, more, less, completely, extremely.* Recently he has been performing *more than ever.*

Where?	The conductor looked *heavenward*. The choir performed *in Carnegie Hall*.
When?	*Often, seldom, always, never, soon, later, finally*. The second violins entered *early*. A reception for the composer will be held *after the concert*.
Why?	Bruckner was forced to conduct the premiere of his Third Symphony *because the conductor who was to have done so died suddenly*.
Conditions attached?	*Yes, no, surely, perhaps, possibly, certainly, doubtless, absolutely*. Schönberg *probably* would have remained in Germany for his entire career *if Hitler had not come to power*.

An adverb may also govern a whole sentence:

First, Handel studied with Friedrich Zachow (1663–1712) to become a good eighteenth-century church musician. *Unfortunately*, circumstances at the Cathedral of Halle were not to Handel's liking. *Later*, he decided to relocate in Hamburg and try his hand at opera. *There* he found his true calling.

217 Prepositions

A preposition (*pre*, "before"; *ponere*, "to place in some location or position") comes at the head of a phrase, to hold the phrase together and indicate its function in the sentence. The English language is rich in prepositions.

Some prepositions appear as single words: *across, after, against, at, before, behind, below, beside, between, by, during, from, for, in, into, on, onto, opposite, to, up, upon, toward, with*. Prepositional word groups are also common: *according to, because of, by means of, due to, in place of, out of, owing to, up to*.

Prepositions themselves do not give much trouble (as long as one understands the functions of prepositional phrases); nevertheless, one can renew one's vocabulary from time to time, even for these modest parts of speech.

Ending a sentence with a preposition may be awkward:

What did you bring that book I didn't want to be read to out of up for?

In such cases, reword the sentence. On the other hand, if the sentence seems less stilted or forced with the preposition last, there is nothing to be afraid of.

218   Conjunctions

Coordinating conjunctions hold together individual words or phrases ("ham *and* eggs"; "sudden, *yet* not entirely unexpected"), or main clauses in compound sentences. When coordinating conjunctions connect two independent clauses, place a comma before the conjunction:

> The plainchants for the Mass are contained in books called graduals, *and* the chants for the Divine Office are in antiphoners.

Subordinating conjunctions tie dependent clauses to their main clauses. Conjunctive adverbs tie together the independent clauses of a compound sentence, or a new sentence to its predecessor. Use any of these connectives accurately, so that they express precisely the relationship between the elements connected.

> *Because* he was an enthusiastic Hungarian nationalist, Bartók chose to attend the Budapest Conservatory rather than the Vienna Conservatory.

Copulative conjunctions and correlative conjunctions normally appear in pairs. They differ insofar as copulative conjunctions present two substantives of equal importance in tandem. Note: The juxtaposition of the two substantives may be within either a positive or a negative context.

> *Both* Bach *and* Rameau capitalized on the potential of unlimited tonal mobility.

> *Neither* just intonation *nor* mean-tone temperament afforded the tonal potential that Bach exploited in these twenty-four preludes and fugues.

Correlative conjunctions differ subtly in that the second element of the pair they combine usually represents an intensification of sentiment:

> Nadia Boulanger's submission of an instrumental fugue for the Prix de Rome offended Camille Saint-Saëns enormously, *not only* because Boulanger, a woman, had ventured to enter the competition along with male students, *but also* because she

had dared to violate the rule requiring a fugue scored for a
vocal ensemble.

Because they establish a hierarchy of events leading to a climax, correlative conjunctions can build dynamic tension into what might otherwise be a routine iteration of facts.

219 Articles

Articles are a specific type of adjective. The indefinite articles are "a" and "an." The definite article is "the." "A" is used before indefinite substantives beginning with a consonant sound, including the "yoo" sound of some vowels: *a* book; *a* yacht; *a* euphemism; *a* ukulele. "An" is used before all words beginning with a vowel sound: *an* actor; *an* element; *an* uncle.

Initial aspirated (pronounced) "h" takes "a": *a* hero; *a* handbell; *a* harpsichord. Aspirated "h" in an initial unaccented syllable may take either "a" or "an": *a* or *an* historical account; *a* or *an* historian. In American usage, "a" is preferred; the British usage of "an" may be a remnant of earlier times when such an "h" was not pronounced. Where initial "h" is not pronounced use "an": *an* honor; *an* hour.

"The" may be used before singular or plural nouns. Omit "the" before a plural noun used in a general sense:

Fugues are often prefaced by toccatas, preludes, fantasias, or other free-form pieces.

Include "the" wherever you could substitute "these" or "those": "*the* fugues in volume one"; "*the* choral movements in *the* oratorios."

One may occasionally use the comparative form "the . . . the":

The more I hear Berg's music, *the* better I like it.

Nouns in a series may or may not repeat the article, depending on the shade of emphasis desired:

She performs the toccatas and fugues of Bach.

She performs the toccatas and the fugues of Bach.

220 Interjections

In its simplest form, an interjection is any word or short phrase thrown in merely to express emotion:

Alas, it was too late.

Ah, the sweet music that was made!

Good for you!

What nonsense!

In a looser sense, one may break off a connected discussion momentarily to interject a passing comment, usually emotional or argumentative:

The last three pieces are trivial indeed. *Why do they write such stuff?* They depend upon special sound effects that are by now quite hackneyed.

As you have probably guessed, interpolated exclamations are not in the best taste in formal writing; here, passing comments are more likely to take the less emotional form of "momentary digressions." In informal writing, and if you are sure of your audience—go for it!

221 Simple sentences

A simple sentence consists of a single main clause, with a subject and predicate. The subject will be a noun, pronoun, or occasionally a noun phrase or noun clause. The predicate must always contain a finite verb, which may be transitive or intransitive, and in the active or passive voice. Strong, meaningful verbs tighten the pace of good prose. Overuse of the verb "to be" produces a vapid style, just as overuse of the passive voice makes ideas seem too weak to take any action. In short sentences, the verb may be enough to complete the meaning:

Hanson offered Bartók a position on the Eastman composition faculty. Bartók *refused.*

Sentences constructed in this fashion are sometimes called elliptical sentences, since they leave out words that the reader or listener will assume. Stated fully, the second sentence of the example would read, "Bartók refused the position."

Usually the predicate includes material that describes the subject, or one or more direct or indirect objects of the verb, or adverbial modifiers of the verb itself. Additional words may be used to modify any element in the sentence, but as long as there is only one main clause (without any modifying dependent clauses), it remains a simple sentence.

When using a pronoun as subject or object, make sure that the antecedent of the pronoun is unambiguous. The "unidentifiable pronoun" is a dangerous booby trap. Consider all nouns within striking distance and make adjustments if necessary, forestalling any possibility that the reader's mind might jump from the pronoun back to the wrong noun.

Passive voice of verbs may be used to turn the sentence around for better emphasis, or to eliminate awkward pronouns, especially the first person and the abstract third person.

The last movement *adds* a contrabassoon. [active]

A contrabassoon *is added* in the last movement. [passive]

They performed Beethoven's Sixth Symphony on 22 December at the Theater an der Wien. [active]

Beethoven's Sixth Symphony *was performed* on 22 December at the Theater an der Wien. [passive]

I found an example in measure 10. [active]

An example *may be found* in measure 10. [passive]

222   Incomplete sentences

Check every sentence to see that it contains a finite verb. No verb, no sentence—or rather an incomplete sentence, like this one. At times the verb may be purposely suppressed to produce a special kind of emphasis. Or a livelier pace. Caution: This device should be used only on rare occasions, and even then, some readers may object.

223   Compound sentences

A compound sentence contains two or more main clauses with no subordinate clauses. Two main clauses placed together without a connective are called contact clauses; they should be separated by a semicolon. More often, connectives are used to join the main clauses.

Coordinating conjunctions are strong connectives, such as *and, but, for, or, nor, yet*. These pull the main clauses closely together and are usually preceded only by a comma. In very short compound sentences, even the comma is sometimes omitted; but, when the two clauses are lengthy, or if they contain commas already, it may be more prudent to use a semicolon before the conjunction.

Conjunctive adverbs are weaker connectives, such as *accordingly, also, anyhow, besides, consequently, furthermore, hence, however, indeed, instead, likewise, moreover, namely, nevertheless, so, still, then, therefore, thus.* These adverbs call for a slight pause in the flow of ideas. They should be separated from the preceding main clause by a semicolon, and from the following main clause by a comma.

224 Complex sentences

The addition of one or more subordinate (dependent) clauses changes a simple sentence into a complex sentence, and a compound sentence into a compound-complex sentence.

> Because the musical organization at the Court of Dresden was frequently disrupted by the Thirty Years' War (1618–1648), Schütz occasionally fled to the more tranquil environment of the Court of Copenhagen.

> Because the musical organization at the Court of Dresden was frequently disrupted by the Thirty Years' War (1618–1648), Schütz occasionally fled to the Court of Copenhagen; there he found a more tranquil environment.

225 Subordinate clauses

A subordinate clause must always have a subject and a finite verb. If the verb is omitted, you have only a phrase. Subordinate clauses are used as modifiers and may function in three ways.

Adverbial clauses typically modify a verb (sometimes an adjective or adverb). Adverbial clauses usually begin with a subordinating conjunction, such as *after, although, as, as if, as long as, because, before, how, if, in order that, since, so that, though, unless, until, when, where, whereas, while, why.* In the following example, the dependent clause is italicized and the word modified is bracketed:

> *When the singer missed his cue,* the conductor [stopped] the orchestra. He asked the first clarinet to play louder and began again. "That was [better]," he said, *"because you came in on time."*

Adverbial clauses are sometimes introduced by prepositions:

> Carl Philipp Emanuel Bach (1714–1788) was born *during* Johann Sebastian Bach's tenure at the Court of Weimar (1708–1717).

Adjectival clauses modify a noun or pronoun and are introduced by a relative pronoun, such as *who, which, that* (nominative); *whose, of which* (genitive); *to whom, for which* (dative); *whom, which, that* (accusative). They tend to specify essential details relating to the person, place, or thing under consideration; therefore, they should not be set off by commas:

> Composers *who write avant-garde music* have a tough time of it.

Relative clauses and phrases generally provide supplemental information and are therefore set off by commas:

> Augmented-sixth chords, *which became common in the early nineteenth century,* are rare in the music of J. S. Bach.

A noun clause substitutes for a noun as subject, object, indirect object, or object of the preposition. Noun clauses are most often introduced by *that, what, who,* or *whoever.*

> *That Schütz had an instinctive understanding of music* was indisputable. Gabrieli gave his young German pupil *what he needed:* a thorough training in the fundamentals of harmony and counterpoint. Schütz's glorious Madrigals, Op. 1 (1611) are really dedicated to *whoever understands the beauty of Renaissance polyphony* written in the strict style.

The elliptical clause implies but does not state the verb, which will be readily understood by the reader. Elliptical clauses depend upon their context for comprehensibility and must, therefore, be preserved in that context when they are excerpted for quotation:

> Ockeghem wrote about nine motets, Obrecht about thirty, and Josquin more than a hundred.

226 Phrases

The word "phrase" has several meanings: a style of diction ("long-winded phrases"; "a well-turned phrase"); a group of words that makes sense without a finite verb ("good morning"; "out of sight, out of mind"); and a group of words less than a clause that functions collectively as a sentence element. In the following examples, the phrase's function is given in brackets.

> The *quick brown fox* jumped over the lazy dog. [subject]

> We found *several extant versions.* [object]

> Pierre Monteux, *the famous conductor,* died in 1964. [appositive]

Her eyes swollen with grief, Helen picked up her manuscript and left the professor's office. [adjective]

The examples *could have been made* more intelligible. [verbal]

We run across these things *time and time again.* [adverbial]

But in spite of these sad conditions, one must carry on. [conjunctive]

The concert being over, we went out into the street, *walking slowly along toward Piccadilly.* [absolute: the phrases modify the entire main clause]

More specifically, a phrase is a group of words introduced by a preposition, or by a verbal—a participle, gerund, or infinitive. Such a phrase contains neither a finite verb, which would make it a clause, nor a subject: It takes an object.

Prepositional phrases begin with a preposition and may function as adjectives, adverbs, or more rarely as nouns:

"I Dream of Jeanie *with the Light Brown Hair"* [adjective]

Stravinsky wrote *in elegant manuscript.* [adverb]

Without the pedal is preferable. [noun]

Participle phrases contain a participle derived from a verb and are used as adjectives:

A composer *writing a string quartet* needs concentration.

The symphony *heard last week* was better.

Gerunds are part noun and part verb, and they are formed by adding the suffix *-ing* to the infinitive form of the verb (without the infinitive marker "to"): *sing, singing; compose, composing; perform, performing.* Gerund phrases always function as nouns:

Composing a string quartet requires concentration.

Hearing her new symphony was a great pleasure.

Infinitive phrases begin with an infinitive and function as nouns:

To understand Messiaen's music is not easy.

We all like *to perform Schubert's Trout Quintet.*

Your aim should be *to achieve perfection.*

165

227 Enriched sentences

A writer with natural talent or acquired experience ought to feel at ease writing sentences of any length—short and crisp, medium, or long and involved. This versatility is needed for the sake of variety and for control over pace and rhythm. In the first draft, keep sentences short so that the main ideas are clear and uninvolved. In subsequent revisions, the sentence structure can be built up, elaborated, and enlarged as much as you like. Do not, of course, exceed the practical limits of intelligibility.

Having control over sentences means being consciously aware of how they are constructed. Several means of enrichment are available. One easy device, often overlooked, is to bring two simple sentences together as main clauses in a compound sentence. Another is to incorporate dual and multiple sentence elements. A sentence need not be restricted to one subject and one verb. Two, or even more, of each sentence element may be present, provided the meaning remains clear.

> For Wagner, etiquette and music were entirely separate:
> He would not hesitate for a moment to call on friends, acquaintances, and even enemies if he thought that they could assist him artistically or support him financially in achieving his artistic goals.

Adding modifiers is another way to enrich your sentences. Important ideas should be described or qualified through the subject-predicate relationship of a main clause. Lesser ideas or individual sentence elements may be freely modified by means of words, phrases, or subordinate clauses. Test each sentence to see if it can be made more vivid by adding modifiers:

> Purcell composed songs and anthems.

> Purcell composed *secular* songs and *sacred* anthems. [words]

> Purcell, *composing with the theater in mind,* wrote songs *for the London stage while simultaneously writing sacred* anthems *for use at the court chapel.* [phrases]

> Purcell, *who finally found a capable librettist in the person of John Dryden,* composed songs *that appeal to attentive listeners instantly, while continuing to write profoundly expressive sacred* anthems. [clauses]

Modifiers may be strung together in word chains—like a litany—when a special circumstance merits such a dramatic tone:

166

The long, tortuous, lugubrious theme rambles on interminably, but finally and mercifully ends in a passage that is brighter, firmer, more intelligible, and on the whole more convincing.

Phrases too may appear in chains, either to modify main-clause elements [a], or to modify another phrase [b].

Musicians *of lesser reputation* and *without any secure income* usually subsisted *in those times* upon employment *at local taverns.* [a]

Those proficient on instruments *of the wind family* could participate in festive occasions *involving open-air entertainment of various kinds.* [b]

Finally, subordinate clauses may be cumulated to modify a main-clause element [a], or to permit one subordinate clause to modify another [b].

The performer *who has any sense of artistry,* and *whose technique is proficient,* studies a passage *until its musical meaning becomes clear.* [a]

A mechanical performer, who is satisfied *merely with playing all the notes,* may nevertheless impress listeners simply *because they do not know any better.* [b]

228   Paragraph building

Construct the paragraph around a central idea, one that is clear in your own mind before you begin to write. State the central idea in a topic sentence, and develop that idea in the rest of the paragraph. Plan a smooth and purposeful flow of thought from sentence to sentence.

The topic sentence will usually appear at the beginning of the paragraph: The exceptional case will save the topic sentence as the grand finale of the paragraph—usually when you are reasonably sure that your reader will have reached the topic statement as a logical result of the data presented during the course of the paragraph.

The development of the central idea may consist in restating the topic sentence in a more detailed, paraphrased version; analyzing the idea in terms of its component parts; illustrating the idea by describing specific examples; giving the detailed sequence of events that led up to a situation; or presenting the steps in an argument that led to a conclusion.

Avoid inserting irrelevant remarks that disrupt the development of the main idea. Beware of facile words and phrases that seem to write themselves; they will usually lead you off the track. Keep firm control over the wording and phrasing so that these are at all times subservient to the thought to be expressed. Study the effects of rhythm and pace—in words and ideas—to give your writing vitality.

The relationship of one paragraph to another must be logical and coherent. The central ideas of successive paragraphs should be connected smoothly. Where ideas do not flow naturally, supply transitional sentences to guide the reader through the argument. A simple test: Can an orderly abstract of the paper be made by lifting out only the topic sentences?

Paragraphs should be of an appropriate length—neither too long (stodgy) nor too short (journalistic). A good practical rule: Every double-spaced page ought to contain at least one new paragraph.

CHAPTER 17

Control of Literary Style

229 Literary style in general

Ideas flow through our minds in a chaotic jumble. Novelists sometimes use the stream-of-consciousness technique to exploit this desultory activity, so characteristic of the human mind. When we mumble to ourselves or jot down little memoranda, the thoughts expressed are likely to be fragmentary and, to the observer, incoherent.

We bring our ideas into focus when we perform a task requiring concentration: reading instructions for installing new computer software, following a recipe from a cookbook, and so on. When we engage in conversation, a further effort must be made: We get our ideas in order, *and* we must communicate them. In any piece of writing, the writer is engaged in a one-sided conversation with potential readers. Writing is more formal than ordinary conversation—and more permanent. Written language must be more carefully considered than ephemeral conversation.

The "literary" part of writing is the use of words and language to express ideas. Compare "literate," as meaning "able to read and write," or as a modest way of saying "well read, and able to express oneself effectively." The "style" part of writing is really a blend of two things: those qualities which, beyond the bare communication of ideas, induce in the reader a kind of aesthetic satisfaction; and those manners of expression which give writing the stamp of its author's personality. The corresponding strategy must therefore be first to arouse in the reader a glow of appreciation (even if subconscious) at the aptness of the literary vehicle; and second, to maintain the integrity of the author's own literary personality, whether this is accomplished unobtrusively, in the background, or occasionally by stepping boldly forward into the discussion.

Any creation that is well made and bears evidence of inventive authorship has style. We speak of clothes as having style; literary style, though, is different. With clothing, one can lounge around every day in jeans and dress up only for special occasions, but people who use words as part of their daily work must continuously refine their skills, from the first waking moment in the morning until they fall asleep at night. There was once a preacher who, to amuse his friends in conversation, often used the phrase "All ye feak and weeble sinners." One day, from force of habit and without thinking, he used the expression in the midst of a solemn sermon. (Note: The unintentional or humorous exchange of the initial sounds of two words is known as a spoonerism, after the Reverend William A. Spooner, 1844–1930.)

The tape recorder is a handy device that enables us to hear ourselves as others hear us. For self-training, an inexpensive model will do. Practice oral communication with your tape recorder. The playback will give you insights, and encourage better habits of diction and style, which can be transferred to the writing process. Many professional "writers" use dictating machines, so that all their literary composition is in fact oral. It is up to the typist, then, to transcribe the material to manuscript.

230   Diction

Singers will think of good diction as synonymous with clear and correct enunciation of words in a song or aria, whatever the language. Diction, in both speaking and writing, can also refer to the choice of words.

In written language, words ought to communicate effectively with the reader. In spoken language, sonority also comes into play. If written words fail to convey the intended meaning fully or accurately, or if they communicate effectively but sound poorly when spoken, the diction is flawed. Expository prose is intended to communicate information and explain its significance; nevertheless, anyone preparing an oral presentation must be sensitive to potential misunderstandings (especially when homonyms are involved) and instances where a particular phonetic configuration is just downright ugly:

> Berlioz's and Brahms's Requiems' sacramental associations are
> certainly minimal.

231   Economy

If brevity is the soul of wit, it follows that witty writers will set down their principal message in the fewest possible words. This does not relieve them of the obligation to explain things thoroughly, but explanations can be terse and to the point.

Your text is a kind of *cantus firmus* against which the reader's mind is constantly weaving, voluntarily or involuntarily, in counterpoints of its own. If your *cantus firmus* is long-winded, your readers will start improvising, and their minds will wander. Economical wording, on the other hand, forces the reader to pay strict attention to your message.

The short paper is a good starting point for beginning writers. A typical assignment may take two weeks to research, but the student must report the results in two or three pages—no more! Such exercises quickly teach us how to sort out the essential from the unessential, and to search for economic means of expression. When one tackles a long term paper or thesis, the good habits already formed lend crispness and vitality to the style.

If upon self-analysis you find that your writing is wordy, learn to wield an editorial red pen. Cut out words that contribute nothing to the meaning: Superfluous words frequently appear in the opening paragraphs or pages of papers, as authors look for ways to embark upon the actual topic. It is perfectly normal for writers to lack focus at first, so feel free to roam as you please with your prose until you strike upon the topic sentence of the opening paragraph. Then go back and delete the pages of wandering.

Wordiness can also be reduced by consolidating ideas into enriched sentences. For colorless or ambiguous words, find substitutes that convey meanings more accurately. Be sure to consult a thesaurus before deciding upon the right word.

232 Rhythm

As in music, rhythm is an important element in literary style. Poetry, of course, has rhythm—usually metered. Prose too has its own sense of rhythm, less regular than that of poetry, but effective in its own way.

Words fall naturally into patterns. The following sentence is in a regular 3/8 meter:

Where can we / find something / suitable?

If we inserted bar lines into prose passages, we should probably find a fluctuating meter: 3/8, 4/8, 2/8, 3/8, 5/8. Careful examination might disclose other subtleties, such as upbeats and downbeats, syncopation for emphasis, triplets (in duple time) for speeding up, duplets (in triple time) for slowing down the rhythm. All forms of accentuation (tonic, agogic, expressive, and so on) also pertain to rhythm. Any prose is bound to have its lesser and greater accents, its smaller and larger climaxes.

In rapid reading of prose, we pay little conscious attention to such matters, but the rhythmic undercurrent is there nevertheless. An effective style will hold speech rhythm under some measure of control, just as the recitative passages of Baroque and Classical operas do.

Each sentence ends with a full stop (period). Therefore, the only place we can control rhythm is within the sentence itself. Test your writing from time to time by reading it aloud for musical quality in terms of rhythm. Sometimes, where a sentence does not come off, the fault lies in its rhythm, which is out of step with the prevailing flow or pace. Deletion or addition of even a single word may do the trick. Some sentences may need reconstructing so that accents will fall at the right places.

233   Flow

We are here reserving the word "flow" to describe a succession of ideas. To simplify, let us say that ideas come in different sizes: phrase-length, clause-length, sentence-length, and paragraph-length. These ideas should flow smoothly one into another, forming associations and groupings among themselves as they move along. It takes at least a split second, if not longer, for the reader to grasp each idea as the procession passes by. Some kind of suitable spacing is needed.

Fortunately, ideas come "packed" in words, and this packing material automatically spaces the ideas to some extent. In general, the size of the "package" should be proportional to the importance of the idea. For big ideas, let the words accumulate until they carry real weight. For lesser ideas, trim the wording according to the degree of impact sought. Occasionally, this principle is reversed: A big idea is exploded like a bombshell in one brief statement. The reverse, letting some picayune idea monopolize a whole paragraph, is not recommended—unless, of course, your literary style gives the readers such aesthetic pleasure that they do not mind.

Test samples of your own writing by putting a mark at each place where an idea seems to crystallize. Are the ideas suitably spaced? Is the flow smooth and even or jerky and distraught? Does the flow of ideas cooperate with sentence rhythm and pace? If the flow is faulty because of logic, reorganize. If the trouble is spacing, trim the wording around lesser ideas and build up the larger ones. By "build up" we do not mean mere padding: You have probably left something out, because big ideas require precise definitions or more detailed investigation.

234   Pace

Pace in writing is like tempo in music. It should normally be *allegro* or *moderato*. Upon occasion, *lento* is called for; detailed narratives or broad concepts that require time to soak in benefit from a slower pace. *Presto* suits rapid, staccato passages that can be quickly absorbed. Evaluate the nature of the ideas under consideration. Do not inundate the reader with a flood of intricate, complex, or unfamiliar material. Instead, allow a comfortable ebb and flow of concepts that calls the reader at one moment to exert full concentration, but then allows a certain respite for more relaxed contemplation. Too much too fast will simply overwhelm your audience, and the natural instinct for self-preservation will quickly numb their minds to such an unwelcome assault upon the intellect.

The pace, or speed, that you settle upon influences both the sentence rhythm and the flow of ideas. These matters are powerful factors in the control of literary style, and anyone who aspires to be a real writer must consider them carefully.

One may alter the pace, just as one may have an *accelerando* or a *ritardando* in music. An abrupt change of pace (as when a new section or chapter is begun) may act like a *volti subito* upon the reader's attention. A tight (brisk) pace is most often associated with shorter sentences. A sustained (leisurely) pace calls for longer, compound or complex sentences. If it helps, keep in mind the musical analogy: Fast tempo? Shorter phrases, with frequent breaths. Long, sustained melody? Let the theme unfold gently, gliding smoothly from phrase to phrase.

235   Imagery

Writing that comes from the intellect naturally embodies much abstract thinking but may tend to lack imagery. An image is precisely that: a visual, aural, tactual, kinesthetic, or emotional pattern or experience that the reader can call vividly to mind. Use of imagery supplements and supports the train of thought. "Sensational" writing draws heavily upon imagery, often titillating or morbid. "Dull, scholarly" writing, on the other hand, sometimes squeezes out every bit of imagery as "unworthy." Some middle course between these two extremes is preferred.

Indeed, one picture is often worth a thousand words. Even the most serious of authors, at times, might want to write so that the less-well-informed can understand. The broader public (and here I am tempted to define "public" as any one or more persons *other than the person writing!*) is better able to think when given something concrete to hold onto, to feel, or to visualize.

Cultivate the art of evoking the right images in the reader's mind, ones that are appropriate and in good taste. Avoid expressions that are trite or cute. Remember, too, that an evocative image is like a splash of bright color on a dark canvas. A few images—carefully chosen—will add interest and vitality to your prose, but overuse of imagery will become irksome to the reader.

The trick in manipulating imagery is to employ a stimulus in *one* arena of experience that evokes an image in *some other* arena. Thus, music (aural) can induce recall of emotive states, or even visual scenes. The sight of a flower brings to mind a line of verse. And so on. Writing, which is a verbal means of expression, ought therefore to seek its imagery in the aural, visual, kinesthetic, tactual, or emotive realms.

The verbal-to-aural channel needs special attention. In writing about music, we must frequently recall music through the use of words. "The first theme appears in the oboe" is not enough. It tells us neither what the theme is like nor what particular oboe tone is meant. "Theme" alone is an abstract concept. Suppose readers have never heard this particular theme. How can they follow you unless you provide clues about how the theme sounds? Each clue supplied, each aptly chosen descriptive word, brings them closer to the approximate effect. The image you concoct may persuade your readers to seek out and listen to the *real* theme. On the other hand, if in your paper you reduce the Funeral March of Beethoven's *Eroica Symphony* to a dreary succession of "Theme A, theme B, second countersubject in the violas, with a half-cadence in C minor," your reader may only yawn distractedly.

As for the "oboe," the tone quality varies, depending on register, attack, dynamics, and so on. Here are some evocative words for a range of oboe timbres and effects, culled from an orchestration treatise: *spicy, nasal, cutting, poignant, pastoral, legato, staccato, incisive, tiresome, thick, coarse, honky, ultra-reedy, primitive, thinner, less pungent, sensitive.*

The other channels—verbal-to-visual, verbal-to-kinesthetic, verbal-to-tactual, verbal-to-emotive—are chiefly cultivated to maintain an active undercurrent of live interest. The human mind so functions that the reader must inevitably and continuously supply autonomous commentary to your discussion. If you provide your readers with appropriate images out of their own experiences, they will remain actively involved in your presentation. (Be wary of ambiguous imagery—the double-entendre!)

Since music is closely associated with eurhythmics and dance, verbal-to-kinesthetic imagery can be extremely helpful in describing music. We bipeds naturally move in duple meter; it is hardly surprising, therefore, that marches are most often in 2/4 time. When tempo, meter, and accentuation coalesce to mimic the human gait—as in the last variation of the third movement of Beethoven's String Quartet Op. 18, No. 5 in A major—

do not hesitate to note how the vigorous downbeats capture the strength of the left foot placed firmly forward in an exuberant military march.

Imagery may be controlled through word association, illustration, or analogy. Some words are richer and more intense in imagery than others. The evocative word triggers associations, which flash vividly upon the screen of consciousness or surge up just below the threshold of consciousness. In the mature mind, vast quantities of verbal, sensory, and emotive data are stored in the memory. Take for example the musician who, when given the simple verbal cue "Chopin, Op. 10, No. 12," or the aural stimulus of the first few notes, can recall and "play back" mentally the entire "Revolutionary Étude." For some, the recalled images are eidetic—almost as vivid as the original experience.

The term "illustration" refers to the construction of an image through the use of words. Illustration anticipates the reader's reaction: "All right, I think I understand what you mean. Now give me an example!" When we summarize knowledge, define terms, or explain principles, our language tends to be abstract, but when we select a typical example and describe it clearly, the subject becomes more concrete. Any cogent discussion will alternate judiciously between abstractions (principles) and concretions (examples), recognizing the reader's two channels of understanding—intellect and imagery. Switch back and forth between these channels, deliberately and with due attention to flow and pace. This fluctuation provides moments of rest, with renewed alertness, in the respective segments of the reader's mind.

An example is a verbal illustration drawn from the subject being discussed. An analogy, on the other hand, borrows material from an unrelated field. When you discuss an unfamiliar topic, consider whether, in some totally different field, you might find a comparable circumstance more certain to tap vivid recollections in your reader. If you build upon experiences with which the reader feels comfortable, you have a much better chance of being understood.

General principles may also be clarified by interdisciplinary borrowing: If Principle X is obscure, perhaps Principle Y in some other field operates in the same way and is easier to grasp. Suppose that I advise you, in writing a paper, to stay on the main trail and not go wandering up side trails; to avoid getting entangled in the underbrush of wordy rhetoric; and not to dawdle along the way lest you be overtaken by nightfall. I have merely borrowed the analogy of the hiker to suggest, in more vivid terms, the abstract principles of maintaining a sense of direction and a suitable pace in your composition.

Analogies come to us by inspiration; with practice, they flow freely.

But one must develop a sharp critical sense for testing their appropriateness: Analogies must be highly accurate and used sparingly, reserved only for very special occasions.

236 Figures of speech

Figures of speech are a part of our ordinary conversation. Such devices of rhetoric—the art of expressive speech or literary composition—were already well known to the ancient Greeks. The following classification and order of rhetorical devices—word association, comparison, overstatement, understatement, arrangement, and dramatization—does not necessarily agree with the standard presentation of rhetoric textbooks.

Three devices concerned with word association are onomatopoeia, metonymy, and synecdoche. Onomatopoeia (*onomatos*, "a name"; *poiein*, "to make") refers to the use of words whose sounds contribute to the meaning. Philologists preempted the term to denote words that imitate natural sounds. One may use normal vocabulary or artificially constructed expressions or exhalations: *buzz, hiss, whine, screech, gurgle, guzzle, plunk, thump, achoo, whew.*

Metonymy (*meta*, "beyond," "over," denoting a change of position or condition; *onyma*, "name") names the cause for the effect, or vice versa; the sign for the thing signified; the container for the thing contained—in the manner of a caricature: "some Beethoven" (meaning his music); "all the missing notes" (a slovenly performance); "Signor Crescendo" (Rossini, in whose music the crescendo is a cliché); "Wizard of Wahnfried" (Wagner, whose villa at Bayreuth was called Wahnfried).

Synecdoche (*syn*, "together"; *ekdechesthai*, "to receive") is closely related to metonymy. A part named signifies the whole: "they had words" (an altercation); "the strings" (the instruments, not merely the strings on the instruments). More rarely, the whole signifies a part: "the city slept" (or rather, the people in it); "war came to our village" (not the whole war, but some local skirmish).

A simile (neuter form of *similis*, "resembling") is an imaginative comparison, formally introduced with "like" or "as." The given object, action, or relation is compared in one or more aspects with some other thing of different kind or quality:

She sang like an angel.

He wandered as in a dream.

Themes scurry in and out like mice in a pantry.

Another form of comparison, metaphor (*meta*, "beyond," "over"; *pherein*, "to bring"), substitutes a description of something, which the reader is expected to apply directly to the thing being discussed. A simple metaphor is a compressed simile that omits "like" or "as":

Drunken rhythms stumble along for another six measures.

Sometimes the metaphor may be sustained for cumulative effect:

The composer saved his heavy artillery until the end, when he proceeded to bombard the audience with a barrage of brass and percussion that splattered sonic shrapnel into the topmost gallery.

Prolonged metaphor may turn into allegory, a whole series of actions (symbolizing other actions) with an imagined cast of characters. A fable is an imaginary narration to enforce some useful truth or concept, often with animals or inanimate objects speaking and acting like humans. A parable, on the other hand, is a brief narrative, involving simple, everyday things and people, intended to convey some important moral or spiritual truth.

Do not mix metaphors:

From the scrapheap of outworn forms, a new star arose that blossomed overnight and spread like wildfire, capturing the hearts of all who were tuned in.

Horrible!

Overstatement often takes the form of hyperbole (*hyper*, "above"; *ballein*, "to throw"), which device employs extravagant exaggeration for expressive emphasis:

Karajan holds the final fermata of *Tristan und Isolde* forever and a day.

Hyperbole may be combined with simile or metaphor:

Beethoven was like a colossus, overshadowing all his contemporaries.

Beethoven was a colossus, overshadowing all his contemporaries.

Understatement is accomplished with the rhetorical device of litotes (from *litos*, "plain," "simple"). Description is purposely kept modest, or overmodest, in hopes that the reader will rebound sharply and magnify the statement to its true dimensions:

We are grateful to Bach for having written a few good pieces.

On occasion, statements may be kept modest to avoid censure. Scholarly writing is expected to underplay, rather than overplay—unless, of course, one can be absolutely certain, and hence explicit. If your data leave room for doubt or alternative interpretations, be truthful and communicate your uncertainty to the reader by using words ("perhaps") or phrases ("it may be that"; "at least some of these") as qualifiers. On the other hand, do not be overly cautious. Readers will quickly lose confidence in you if your every phrase contains an emergency exit!

The purpose of a euphemism (*eu*, "well"; *phanai*, "to speak") is to substitute a milder, more agreeable word or expression for something ugly, harsh, unpleasant, or indelicate:

His playing suggested some modest potential.

Clichés such as "he passed away" are so overworked that it is a relief to hear "he died." In expository writing, euphemisms should generally be avoided; however, they are suitable for reviews and other evaluations of creative activities—by persons who may ultimately learn of your critical remarks.

Irony (*eironeia*, "dissimulation") achieves its effect by stating the opposite of what is intended:

Wagner, who is well known for his brevity, wrote what are undoubtedly the most succinct operas of the Romantic era in his famous trilogy, *Der Ring des Nibelungen.*

The effect of irony can range from humor to light sarcasm to ridicule. Unless you are certain that your audience will understand the genuine intention, it is best to avoid irony.

Oxymoron (*oxys*, "sharply," "pointedly"; *moros*, "foolish," "ridiculous") is a type of irony that combines contradictory ideas or terms:

Make haste slowly.

The concerto was met with thunderous silence.

When ideas or propositions are so arranged that each succeeding one rises in impressiveness or force, the resulting figure of speech is called climax (*klimax*, "ladder," "staircase"):

Interest engenders curiosity, curiosity leads to diligent searching, and searching sooner or later points the way to knowledge.

When ideas are ordered so that each is less dignified or striking than its predecessor, the resulting figure of speech is anticlimax *(anti,* "against," "opposite"):

> At the age of eight, he was a wunderkind; at eighteen, he gave an occasional concert; at thirty, he was playing in backstreet bars.

The term "anticlimax" is often used to denote faulty writing, where ideas have not been put into proper sequence. When legitimately employed as a figure of speech, anticlimax serves a clear purpose.

Another sort of arrangement is antithesis *(anti,* "against," "opposite"; *tithenai,* "to set"), in which the opposition of ideas is emphasized by coupling contrasting words within the same sentence, or by placing them in corresponding positions in successive sentences:

> Webern was frugal with his talent; Wagner was prodigal.

Rhetorical devices for achieving dramatization of the text must be used sparingly and judiciously. One of the more common is exclamation, a sudden utterance expressive of strong feeling. Another is interrogation, which, though ostensibly a question, has in fact the force of an emphatic affirmation or denial. Personification imbues an inanimate object or abstract idea with a personality possessing human attributes. Prosopopoeia *(prosopon,* "a face"; *poiein,* "to make") refers to the representation of a deceased or absent person as being alive or present. In an apostrophe, the writer or speaker turns from the audience to address directly a person (dead or absent), an imaginary object, or abstract idea. The device of vision presents some past or imagined scene or event as though it were present and visible.

237   Some faults of style

Critics often use the descriptive terms that follow to describe bad prose. Telltale signs of these stylistic lapses are offered here to heighten your sensitivity to their potentially dangerous consequences.

When writing is branded "academic," the implication is that the style is more impersonal than it need be, unpleasantly abstract, aloof, dull, or lacking in vitality. Otherwise, good academic writing is the preferred means of communication among scholars, teachers, and research workers, and is characterized by a certain formal dignity, scrupulous documentation, and serious attention to worthy matters. Academic writing is contrasted with an easygoing, popular style intended to instruct a broader public, or with the products of creative literature, such as novels, plays, or poetry.

Bathos (from the Greek for "depth") denotes a disappointing letdown in style—perhaps a sudden false pathos (straining for pathetic effect), or a switch to dull, low, and commonplace subject matter or style, especially following, in ludicrous contrast, something sublime. This striking juxtaposition of the elegant and the mundane can, at times, be effective. Moreover, its use is not limited to the written word: Mahler, in particular, was fond of following deeply moving and serious passages with dance tunes, military music, bird calls, folk songs, and the like. Use such juxtapositions purposefully!

Colloquial language is the informal, everyday speech that people use on the streets. It is not appropriate for formal, written communication. Dictionaries usually indicate which words and expressions are colloquialisms, slang, or dialect.

Dated writing uses words, expressions, or syntactical configurations of words that are characteristic of some earlier time. Good prose is ageless, to be sure, but an obsolete usage may now strike us as pretentious or comical. Avoid modes of expression that have gone out of fashion.

Inflated style, marked by ostentation and self-importance, is pompous, verbose, bombastic, grandiloquent, and turgid. Vocabulary appears to have been chosen primarily to impress readers rather than for the sake of communicating with them.

Insipid writing lacks taste or savor. It is vapid, flat, dull, weak, and lifeless.

The word "juvenile," when used in a pejorative sense, indicates writing that is underdeveloped, unsophisticated, and unworthy of an adult in vocabulary, subject matter, or intellect. On the other hand, effective writing for a juvenile audience requires special aptitude, skill, and experience. Educators and authors of books for children take their writing tasks very seriously.

Laconic writing is sparing of words. It may also be sparing in the expression of emotion or emphasis, in the manner of the Laconians (Spartans). Pithy writing turns this mild fault into a virtue.

Prose that is Malapropian (after Mrs. Malaprop, a character in Richard B. Sheridan's play *The Rivals,* 1775) is characterized by grotesque misuse of words, as for example when a table of contents tells us that a "Forward" rather than a "Foreword" opens a book. Frequently heard phrases are often botched in this fashion: "for all intensive purposes" (meaning "for all *intents and* purposes").

The Latin term *non sequitur* ("it does not follow") indicates faulty logic: The evidence given does not support the conclusions offered.

Obscure writing hides the intended meaning (or lack thereof) behind a smoke screen of words. A style is enigmatic when we have to puzzle out its meaning as though it were some kind of riddle.

A purple patch refers, in a pejorative sense, to a passage that is obtrusively ornate. The term is also used as an antithesis to bathos, denoting a passage distinguished by brilliance or effectiveness in the midst of a work that is otherwise commonplace and straightforward.

Sesquipedalian writing is characterized by the use of long words. The word "sesquipedalian" is itself humorous hyperbole, meaning words a foot and a half long.

A staccato style employs short, rapid-fire sentences (often exclamations or interrogations) and vigorous verbs, and tends to omit connectives between statements. It is very effective for short passages of special stress, but it becomes a fault when overdone.

Telegraphic style appears frequently in newspaper headlines. The essentials are present, but without the usual comforts of more leisurely prose. Telegraphic prose can be ambiguous, as when we have to read a headline several times to grasp its meaning.

CHAPTER 18

Kinds of Writing

238 Audience

Composers must consider the constitution of the ensembles for whom they are writing: Chamber music is different from symphonic music; solo vocal music is not quite the same as choral music; and pieces that combine vocal and instrumental resources involve still different restrictions and possibilities.

The communication of information through words is similarly diverse. The intended audience may consist of highly trained professionals, persons with keen interest but modest training, or novices. No one style of presentation is best; each will exhibit distinctive features to suit the intended audience.

Sometimes we share our knowledge through spoken presentations, whether informal (with the text largely improvised at the time) or formal (with a text that is to be read aloud). Spoken presentations may involve a live audience, or they might be videotaped for airing at some later time.

The potential audience of a paper meant purely for written communication may be very small, as when a term paper is read by a professor and handed back with comments. Even under such circumstances, you might like to visualize a larger audience, as if rehearsing your manner of communicating as a teacher, as a lecturer, or eventually as a published writer.

Toward what kind of audience is each particular piece of writing specifically directed? Before you begin to write, take the time to form in your mind a clear image of the group you are addressing. Are you more at ease with a select handful of your own contemporaries? Does a larger assemblage of, say, a hundred provide a more resonant sounding board for your ideas, force you to enunciate more clearly and with better diction, and help you to adjust rhythm, flow, and pace to the reverberation time of a larger hall?

How well prepared is the imaginary audience to assimilate what is presented? Assume that your auditors are intelligent and knowledgeable, but remember—they are not mind readers. If they are to know what you are thinking, you must tell them. You have the advantage: You have just come from your workshop, where you have been devoting your undivided attention to the subject. They too may know something about the subject, but in all probability, they have been busy with other investigations.

The successful presentation begins by giving the audience a frame of reference. Remind them of what they ought to remember, and redefine the terms that you will use in the discussion.

If your presentation is being taped for later viewing, avoid references to the date, the time of day, the weather, your location, and so on. These sorts of details may be inappropriate—or downright ridiculous—when your lecture is presented to an audience.

239   Technical writing

When a report is likely to appeal chiefly to a select group of experts, the writing may be uninhibitedly technical in tone. One draws freely upon the specialized vocabulary of the particular field. The pace will be brisk, since you know that the audience will readily follow the flow of ideas.

In such technical writing, you must "speak the language" fluently, with complete mastery of the terminology and with convincing presentation of evidence, illustrations, and conclusions. If you are not yourself a member of the select circle addressed, you must at least know all the passwords so as not to be laughed off the rostrum.

Gear imagery to needs. For abstract subjects, very little imagery is required; any audience of experts is quite accustomed to manipulating abstract ideas. For more concrete subjects, the imagery of illustration is approached not from the point of view of a spectator, but as an expert would handle the materials.

240   Nontechnical writing

A wider audience will sometimes criticize a music lecture or essay as being "too technical," signaling that the listener or reader has not been able to follow what you have said. On these occasions, one must be prepared to carry on a discussion in more general, nontechnical language. This is not to say that the general public should be treated like children. Bear in mind that your potential readers may be far more competent in their own particular fields of endeavor than you are in yours. They may even be quite experienced as direct consumers of music, having attended operas and concerts, collected recordings, and so on. They have merely not had the specialized training necessary to follow a technical conversation about music.

To adjust to a general audience, observe a few simple precautions. Always include a *few* technical terms, but explain them thoroughly. Lay persons are always grateful for this; it admits them to the inner circle of the initiated, makes them feel wanted, and enables them to understand by intellect what they had formerly perceived primarily by intuition.

Keep the flow of ideas slow enough to make sure that your audience is always with you, but lively enough that readers will not get bogged down with unnecessary details.

State and restate complex ideas in paraphrased versions. If we miss one wording, the next wording may convey the message.

Cultivate verbal description. In a lecture, you can always play a musical illustration; but in written or published matter, the general reader will probably not be fluent enough to form an aural image merely by looking at a musical example.

Use analogies much more freely than you would in addressing a trained audience. Some operating principle, or interrelationship of parts, which "everybody" understands may be the key to unlocking the mystery of some complex musical process.

Addressing an audience of experts is like speaking to professionals at a business meeting in a conference room. The general reader, on the other hand, you are inviting into your home, as it were. As any good host or hostess knows, it is essential to put guests at their ease, to show them around and make them feel comfortable. Their visit with your subject matter will be more relaxed if, for instance, you occasionally interject some relevant personal anecdote, or rhetorical question, or describe how they might react in a given situation.

Remember that *music* is the reason you are writing. Provide at least one musical example for your audience, sooner rather than later in the presentation. If the repertoire is unfamiliar or esoteric, more examples will be needed. Select these examples purposefully, and either tell your listeners in advance what they should notice about them; or, if time permits, invite their active participation by inquiring of them afterward what they perceived as noteworthy or distinctive about the examples.

Finally, as a test of whether you are getting your message across, read your paper aloud to one or more intelligent lay persons of your acquaintance. If they understand you and are impressed, all is well. If not, they may have some very good suggestions for improving communications.

241 Factual writing

In factual writing, we attempt to record reality accurately, either as exist-
ing in the present, or as reconstructed from the past. Reality comprises
things, persons, places, events, circumstances, conditions, qualities, relationships, and so on, which can be directly observed, or for which reliable
evidence is obtainable. The scholar is expected to assemble all facts relevant to a particular inquiry, to present them clearly, and to indicate precisely where they were obtained. Writers may arrange the facts into some
logical order, and they may make inferences and draw conclusions from
the facts presented. They ought not to suppress any facts embarrassing to
the principal inferences or conclusions of the essay.

One can scarcely avoid mingling some opinions with the facts presented—as long as the distinction between what is stated as fact and what
is stated as opinion is clearly maintained.

242 Expression of opinion

Statements of opinion sometimes assume primary importance, notably in
the case of critical writing, where the opinion of the critic (whether valid
or invalid) may be of equal or even greater interest than the thing criticized. Accounts of past events too may be tinged by an author's own views
of the matter, requiring us to sort out facts from personal opinion. To
have opinions is perfectly natural; there is nothing wrong or indecent
about them, and hence no need to hide them or cover them up in shame.
It is simply a matter of asking oneself firmly: Am I here primarily concerned with facts, or with opinions? If they *are* opinions, whose are they?
Do they stem from some other source or are they my own? Remember
that fine distinctions of this sort may hinder the progress of your argument. Provide as much detail as necessary, even if it means adding more
notes.

243 Forms of discourse

By the time they reach the stage of wanting to write about music seriously,
students of music too often have forgotten the forms of discourse they
were supposed to have learned during their earlier schooling in English
composition. Traditionally, these are exposition, narration, description,
argumentation, and criticism. An entire paper may be in one form of discourse. It is also possible for the approach to change as one deals with
the various subdivisions of the subject, in chapters, sections, or even pas-

sages. To find a sense of direction, ask yourself: Which form of discourse shall I pursue in this particular paper? or section? or passage?

Exposition is intended to present data and to explain the significance of that data. Simple exposition is the most basic form of writing to convey information. When the subject is difficult to understand, it is "exposed" by the orderly analysis of its parts and the use of typical illustrations or familiar analogies. In a narrower sense, exposition may mean the first setting forth of the meaning and purpose of a piece of writing, an expounding of one's intentions.

Narration recounts a series of events in chronological order. The result may be a narrative (with incidental descriptive writing as needed), an account (less formal in tone), or a recital of events (with considerable attention to details). The main gist of the story (continuous, or in successive episodes) must be in correct chronological order; however, a skillful narrator can incorporate descriptive detail or other digressions, such as flashback and foreshadowing, without doing violence to the forward progression of the narrative.

Description is useful for representing to the reader something that the writer has observed—an object, a scene, a person, a sensation. The writer's task is to build up a careful and vivid image of the thing described in the mind of the reader. Such a portrayal need not depend upon adjectives alone. Often a verb, or a verb with an adverb, may serve an admirably descriptive function. In most writing, description appears in certain sections or passages as a support and supplement to some other, main form of discourse; however, a paper devoted to old instruments, for example, might be very largely descriptive.

The term "description" is sometimes loosely used for narrative or expository writing. Many words, if indeed not most, have different shades of meaning—at one moment precise, then more general, and at times even ambiguous. When circumstances require, meanings should be brought into sharp focus. On other occasions, the meaning is usually sufficiently clear from the context.

As a nine-to-five word, "argumentation" implies a dispute, disagreement, altercation, or even wrangling and bickering. The true meaning, for use in formal discourse, is more sedate. To argue is to present reasons or evidence in proof of something, to convince someone, or to persuade people to act in some particular way. Argumentation is writing in which the process of reasoning is the controlling factor. The line of reasoning may be inductive or deductive.

Induction starts with individual facts that are observed or known and then organizes them in such a way that inferences can be drawn from them. If the inductive process is carried a step farther, it arrives (at least tentatively) at general principles or truths. A general law or principle thus established is a hypothesis (a provisional conjecture) until it has been sufficiently verified by repeated testing to be considered a theory. Induction leads upward, like addition; one assembles various parts to form a whole.

Deduction—the opposite process—begins with some general idea, proposition, or principle, and then examines how it applies in specific cases. Deduction leads downward, like subtraction or selection; one begins with a whole and drops down to a consideration of one or more of its parts. The term is often used in a loose sense: We say that Sherlock Holmes "made deductions," when in fact he made inferences from the evidence given.

One ought not entirely to forget the other meaning of argumentation: debate or controversy. The intelligent reader may think of various objections to your line of reasoning. It is up to you to anticipate all possible counter arguments, to bring them into the discussion, and to dispose of them convincingly.

Criticism presents the writer's evaluations and judgments regarding the beauties and faults of works of art; the validity and appropriateness of actions or procedures; or the style, content, method, and theories of other writers. The critic examines, judges, and forms an opinion. The resulting piece of writing is a critique, or a review, or perhaps a critical essay.

Just critics keep in mind two frames of reference: their own knowledge, experience, and understanding; and the circumstances under which the thing criticized was produced. In the former context, critics must ask themselves whether their personal experience and knowledge is adequate for the task of criticism. In the latter, we ought to consider what the intent of the work's creator or author was. Has the objective been accomplished? Was the intent valid?

The self-willed critic often pronounces judgment without full explanation of the reasons involved. The wise critic, aiming to convince, mingles argumentation with criticism, explaining how the particular judgment has been deduced from a set of standards, and anticipating possible objections from readers whose tastes may differ from the critic's. Recall, moreover, that the purpose of criticism is both to evaluate and to disseminate information. If, for example, a piece of scholarship has failed to take into account some important study that recently appeared in print, rather than berating the author for the gross omission, simply call that study to the reader's attention and get on with your review. If, in your review, you repeatedly note oversights of this sort, your readers will quickly determine that the source under consideration is a poor piece of scholarship.

CHAPTER 19

Writing for Publication

244 News release

Arts organizations, universities, and other special interest groups often have an elected or appointed officer who handles publicity. The preparation and dissemination of news releases are an important part of the publicist's work.

When you are involved with the sponsorship of a concert, lecture, or any kind of meeting to which the public is invited, see that all local newspapers are notified well in advance of the event. If possible, include photographs, discographies, thumbnail biographies of the performers, and other, supplemental material from which editors may choose in accordance with their interests, space allocations, and publication schedules.

A news release must be brief. It should quickly present the information that makes it news: Who? What? When? Where? Why? How? If there is to be a paid admission, how much, and where can tickets be obtained? If the presentation is free, say so. The reader wants to know what will take place, who is sponsoring the event, and who is performing in it. If you expect people to come, you must make it easy for them to find the right place at the right time. Give the day of the week, the date, and the time of day. Include the address of—and even directions to—the venue, indicate whether parking is available, and mention other conveniences. Is there anything particularly noteworthy about the event? Does it make available something to which the public seldom has access? Is it an annual (or otherwise recurring) tradition or series; a commemoration of a special occasion; a benefit for a worthy cause; or in honor of some person or persons? The manner of conducting the event may be of interest: a performance in costume; a lecture with film taken on a recent trip; a recital upon a genuine Stradivarius.

Word count depends partly upon the type size used for the newspaper. In Newspaper A, a page has eight columns in 10-point type; one full column of solid matter (that is to say, not counting headings and subheads) would therefore run to about 650 words. Newspaper B has six columns in 9-point type, and a column takes about 1100 words. Translated to manuscript pages, a full column in Newspaper A can take two or two and a half pages of double-spaced type. For Newspaper B, three or four pages of double-spaced matter could be fit into a comparable space. The average news release, however, will be allotted perhaps four or five column-inches of space: One must say all that is to be said on a single double-spaced page.

Several things may happen to your news release: It may go into the editor's wastebasket; it may be published exactly as submitted; or it may run with several paragraphs rewritten by the editor, or cut for lack of space. In view of this last possibility, it is helpful to indicate optional cuts that may be made without spoiling the text.

As a heading, put FOR IMMEDIATE RELEASE. If the news is to be kept confidential until a certain date, indicate, for instance, FOR RELEASE 15 JANUARY. At the end of the statement, type your name, address, telephone number, fax number, and e-mail address. Mention your official capacity, such as principal conductor, president, business manager, or secretary.

245 Feature story

A feature story or article includes a byline. Most feature stories in newspapers are written by staff writers or by freelance writers whose names are familiar to the subscribers. Occasionally, though, a guest writer is invited to provide a feature story.

The average feature story will run to about 500 words, the equivalent of about two pages of double-spaced manuscript. For the Sunday supplement, the feature story could be a little longer. The editor who invites you to write a piece will specify how many words are allowed, and the question of photographs or other illustrations should be discussed in detail.

Editors of major newspapers are usually too busy to look at unsolicited submissions. Smaller papers are more likely to need extra material occasionally. Enclose a stamped, self-addressed envelope for the return of the manuscript. It is also prudent to give a phone number, fax number, and e-mail address in case the editor wants to discuss your contribution.

Feature stories about music and musicians ought certainly to help inform and educate the general public. Remember that you are writing for the general public. The story must be lively and interesting, should tell the readers something they will be glad to know, and may be more informal in style than the typical textbook or article in a scholarly journal.

246   Program notes

The development of writing skill brings with it an urge to communicate with a public. Program notes are a readily accessible and satisfying outlet. Many concerts and performances are sufficiently elaborate to include a signed commentary in the printed program. Sometimes no one thinks of this possibility until the last moment; then whoever appears most willing is given the assignment, with only a few hours to prepare the material for the printer. The writer who has practiced this sort of thing for some time is more likely to meet the challenge successfully. Program notes may seem like a modest form of writing, but when well done, they are appreciated by a very real audience.

Economy is vital. The space allotted to program notes is usually limited by the cost of printing, and the audience will have only a few minutes, at most, to read and digest the commentary between the time of arrival and the beginning of the performance. The notes must therefore be concise, clearly worded, and readily understandable. The writer must know the music that is being described, and must be able to visualize how it will appear to the audience in performance. Details that will not be heard are not worth mentioning. On the other hand, one may assume the role of critic, if necessary, to point out important features of the music and prepare the audience to grasp its main intent and meaning.

Do not fall into the trap of providing too much background, such as a long biography of the composer. One sentence is usually enough to identify the composer. The second sentence might tell where and when the work was composed, or first performed, but the third sentence should probably come face to face with the problem of listening to and understanding the work itself. Where you can indulge in the luxury of lengthy program notes, put the essentials in the first paragraph, and let the concertgoer take the program home and study it at leisure for the erudite content of your later paragraphs.

247   Reviews

Many periodicals carry reviews of recently published books and music, or of newly issued recordings. Publishers furnish periodicals with copies of the material in the hope of eliciting reviews that will stimulate sales. The reviewer's function is that of a critic: The primary obligation is to inform readers and turn their attention to valuable and useful publications. The reviewer wields tremendous power in this regard, and reviews are of crucial importance to many authors and performers.

Periodicals usually have a review editor who may either write the reviews or assign topics to specialists in those areas. An invitation to write a review typically comes quite unexpectedly, with an early deadline attached. One must be prepared to drop other things and give concentrated attention to the task of reading the book, or studying the music or the recording. Although one is not likely to be asked to review something until one has already developed some skill in making judgments and in writing effectively, nothing should deter the ambitious student from writing practice reviews for amusement and edification. This kind of self-assignment is strongly recommended as an auxiliary discipline to supplement other kinds of writing.

Reviews of live performances depend upon whether an editor is willing to assign space in a publication. Here too, the "dry run" is good practice.

248 Articles

When you have written a paper that you consider publishable, get one or more responsible persons to read and criticize it. If your paper has merit, they may be able to suggest a suitable publication.

Study carefully three or four recent issues of several periodicals. Get a clear sense of their intended audience, subject matter, and typical article length—short, medium, or long. Unless your paper fits all three categories, there is no point in submitting it.

Begin by sending a brief letter (not more than a page) to the editor, asking whether your article might be of interest. Indicate the title, topic, and basic methodology of the paper, and give an estimated word count. Another sentence or two may be added to describe some distinctive features of your study, such as special sources to which you had access. If there is blank space left over, and if you enclose a stamped self-addressed envelope, some editors may immediately write an answer on the same sheet and send it back. This saves them the trouble of drafting a reply. If the editor is not interested, make inquiries elsewhere.

If the editor invites you to submit your article, obtain a copy of the periodical's style sheet. In general, notes are typed double-spaced at the end of the paper; illustrative material is on separate sheets. Type your name and address on the title page (upper left corner), and your name on each page. Mail the article in a manuscript-sized envelope, enclosing a stamped self-addressed manuscript-size envelope. It may take months before the editor makes a final decision. Do not become anxious: A long wait usually means that your contribution is being given serious consideration.

Put the number of words on the title page (upper right corner). Average length depends upon the particular periodical. Let us assume that an average article runs from 3000 words (approximately ten to twelve double-spaced pages) to 5000 words (fifteen to twenty double-spaced pages). A short article would comprise fewer than 3000 words, a long article, more than 5000 words.

Once an article is accepted, there may be another long wait before it appears in print. (A year or even several years is not unusual, especially in scholarly journals.) Most publishers will furnish you at least one copy of the issue in which your article appears. Some periodicals provide offprints—extra copies of the pages containing the article, printed and stapled together. Find out at the time of acceptance how many offprints are furnished gratis, or whether you have to pay for them. If, say, ten copies are supplied free, it may be possible to order extra copies in advance, for a small charge. Budding young authors always like to distribute their offprints to all their friends. Experienced writers trade them (like stamp collectors) for offprints from other writers.

249 Books

Publishers must be confident that the book you propose has a healthy market potential. Even university presses, which traditionally enjoyed institutional support, generally insist that a publication repay the substantial costs of editing, printing, and distribution, and perhaps even go beyond the break-even point to return a small profit. If your book is to be published, there must be a need for it. The publisher may even expect you to prove that a market for your book exists, to indicate precisely what segments of the buying public will be interested, and what their total number will be. (The publishers, of course, will also make their own estimates; that is their business.) A well-written basic textbook, for example, finds a market more readily than a highly literate critical essay. Popular writing has a wider appeal than academic writing; and yet the publisher may expect very high quality in popular titles (trade books) so as not to compromise the firm's reputation. In brief, it is not the author who seeks a publisher: It is the publisher who is constantly looking for suitable material to fill a need, to reflect credit upon the firm, and to generate at least enough revenue to cover production costs.

An author usually seeks publication by making an inquiry and submitting a proposal. First address an inquiry to the editor of the firm you have in mind. The inquiry should be brief. Ask if there would be interest in a manuscript (give the word count) on such-and-such a subject. If no interest is expressed, you must believe that the editor is an experienced person who probably knows a great deal about books and their potential market. If the editor is interested, you will be asked to submit a proposal—not the entire manuscript.

Editors will describe exactly what they want in a proposal. Generally, this will be a title page, with your title and byline, and any other information that is legitimate for a formal title page (plus your name and address in an upper corner); a preface, which, since it will have to explain your book to the reader, might also serve to explain it to the editor; a table of contents in which, under each chapter heading, you include half a dozen subheads or statements that show clearly what will be covered; and a sample chapter or two, to show your literary style and manner of handling the subject. Do not submit the first chapter, since it is usually preliminary in nature and does not indicate what happens when you come to grips with more involved aspects of the subject.

Thus far, you will not have been sending back and forth a bulky document, but only letters and a reduced sampling. Before one goes to the trouble of writing an entire book, it is wise to find out if it is likely to be published. If an editor expresses an interest in seeing the complete manuscript, while this is of course no guarantee of publication, it is at least encouragement to go ahead and write the book.

Established professional writers may be able to obtain a contract with the publisher on the basis of the proposal. Assuming that you are not an established writer with a contract in your pocket, the editor will first want to see your complete document. Editors typically have submissions read by one or more experts who not only know the subject but can be relied upon to judge the potential market. This takes time. Allow several months before getting impatient to know whether your manuscript has been accepted or rejected.

If your manuscript is accepted, you had best do whatever the editor suggests from then on. Writing styles and formats may vary considerably, so do not be surprised when you are asked to make certain modifications. Remember, too, that budgetary constraints are a reality of editing and publishing. If a publisher cannot cooperate with some request or suggestion of yours, do not assume that your idea was a poor one: It may simply have been an expensive one! Whenever possible, cooperate with your editors and publishers. You are all working for a common purpose and goal.

PART THREE

Combining Words and Music

Prelude to Part Three

The first two parts of this book covered the techniques of documentation and literary style. In addition to these, writing about music requires mastery of another important set of skills, pertaining to the combination of words and music.

The writer must decide when to use words, when to use musical examples, and when to combine the two in an apparently seamless unity. That decision will depend, in part, on the makeup of the intended audience. Most people who enjoy music as a pastime do not have significant skills in transforming written notes into an imagined sound. When writing for the amateur, therefore, you will probably want to use words as much as possible. On the other hand, if your primary audience will consist of trained musicians and professionals, a musical example may be the best way to communicate your ideas.

For the most part, words will take the place of music. We mention an arpeggio in E-flat minor, the tempo of minuet, or a modulation from tonic to dominant. Musicians will understand these words as though they were musical notation—but only if our words are unambiguous and consistent. Chapter 20, "Words as Music," offers some procedures for writing commentary of this sort.

When the decision falls in favor of citing a musical excerpt, authors must be certain that it makes the intended point. Music notation software of varying levels of refinement and complexity is currently available; but the computer can print out only what the author indicates, and most people who write about music—although they have had considerable musical training—learned to put musical signs on the page by osmosis, not as an independent discipline. Chapter 21, "Fundamentals of Music Notation," provides some basic information about the preparation of clear, concise, and accurate musical examples.

The notation of music has changed dramatically over the centuries, just as it continues to change in progressive twentieth-century music. In many cases, it is impossible for the scholar to avoid discussion of notational details since the *way* a composer chooses to write music often reveals its essence. In Chapter 22, these various types of scores, both ancient and modern, are explained.

The final chapter of Part Three identifies some distinctive features of musical sources. These features enable us to trace the evolution of a piece of music as though it were a living organism and to establish the authority of specific sources.

Musical examples—whether communicated in prose, in musical notation, or by means of live or recorded performances—are essential to any piece of writing about music. The ability to move back and forth from expository writing to authentic musical experiences is one that develops with practice; nevertheless, the guidelines contained in this final portion of *Writing about Music* should expedite that process.

CHAPTER 20

Words as Music

250 Pitch names

Solfège, the practice of assigning syllables to pitches, dates back to the eleventh century, when Guido of Arezzo assigned the syllables *ut, re, mi, fa, sol,* and *la* to the six tones of the hexachord. At present, seven syllables are used to represent the diatonic pitches of the major and minor scales. These syllables are *do, re, mi, fa, sol, la,* and *ti* in the major scale, and *la, ti, do, re, mi, fa,* and *sol* in the minor scale. Note: European solfège frequently replaces *ti* with *si*.

Chromatically altered notes that are raised a semitone change the usual vowel of the syllable to "i"; hence, an ascending chromatic scale would be *do, di, re, ri, mi, fa, fi, sol, si, la, li, ti*. Note that *mi* and *ti*, since they already move by semitone to the next scale degree, require no modification. For lowered scale degrees, the vowels change to "e," except in the case of *re*, which, since it already ends in "e," changes to "a"; hence, a descending scale would be *do, ti, te, la, le, sol, se, fa, mi, me, re, ra*. When basing the minor scale on *do*, the lowered forms of the third, sixth, and seventh scale degrees should be used.

Solfège can be helpful in teaching melodies without written music—especially since Rodgers and Hammerstein provided us with the popular song "Do-Re-Mi." The two systems of solfège are fixed *do* and movable *do*. In the fixed-*do* system, syllables correspond directly to specific notes in the key of C: *do* is C, *re* is D, *mi* is E, and so on. In the movable-*do* system, the configuration of half steps and whole steps (or semitones and whole tones) represented by the particular syllables is maintained regardless of any transposition; hence, the syllables *do, mi, sol* would represent a major tonic triad in any key. In some cases, it will be important to indicate which system of solfège you are using. In other instances, it will be of no consequence:

One of the stock figurations in keyboard music of the later eighteenth century is the Alberti bass (named after Domenico

Alberti, 1710–1740). In this left-hand pattern, the tones of a triad are stated in linear succession rather than as a harmonic block. Typically, the chord tones are arranged in the configuration *do, sol, mi, sol,* and so on.

The custom of naming pitches with letters of the alphabet dates back at least to the time of the *Scolia enchiriadis* and *Musica enchiriadis* (ca. 900). Whether these documents were written by Hucbald, a monk active at the abbey of St. Amand at Tournai, or by Otgerus (at the same abbey), we cannot determine. In any case, the author's intention was to group chant melodies according to their finals—D, E, F, and G. The association of pitches and letters subsequently appeared in other early sources, such as the tonary of St. Bénigne of Dijon, H. 159 Montpellier, which even offers a subtle distinction between B-flat (written as a Roman lowercase letter "i") and B-natural (written as an italic lowercase letter "i").

Letters of the alphabet have become the standard indicators of pitch names. The diatonic C-major scale consists of the tones C, D, E, F, G, A, and B. The succession of letters makes more sense in the natural minor scale on A, which consists of the tones A, B, C, D, E, F, and G.

When citing alphabetical names, the words "sharp" and "flat" are used to indicate chromatic alterations. If a sharped or flatted note is the subject of discussion, the capital letter representing the pitch name should be hyphenated to form a closed compound with "sharp," "flat," or "natural" as necessary: ·

The C-sharp in the first measure of the full score appears incorrectly as a C-natural in the first flute part.

The signs for "number" (#) to mean "sharp" or superscript lowercase "b" to mean flat (as in B^b) should be used only where a lengthy succession of pitches is indicated:

An ascending chromatic scale beginning on C would be C, C#, D, D#, E, F, F#, G, G#, A, A#, B.

Note: German usage designates B-natural with the letter "H," B-flat with the letter "B."

When naming pitches within prose, capital letters are always used—eliminating the possibility of confusing the pitch A with the indefinite article "a." Capital letters appearing in this fashion are understood as abstractions rather than pitches appearing in a particular octave.

When letters are used with other words to form compound adjectives, be sure to include a hyphen that will make the compound clear to the reader:

Petroushka's motif, an F-sharp-major chord in first inversion juxtaposed against a C-major chord in root position, is an early example of Stravinsky's use of harmonic and melodic materials derived from the octatonic scale.

The foregoing guidelines apply to situations occurring within prose, but not to those within musical analysis or to analytical examples used as illustrative material within text. In analytical contexts, it is customary to use uppercase letters for major chords and lowercase letters for minor chords.

Since the diatonic scale contains seven tones, the numbers 1 through 7 are frequently used in the same capacity as solfège syllables or alphabetical names. When numbers are used to represent scale degrees, they should be surmounted by a circumflex (^) to distinguish them from Arabic numbers representing harmonic intervals.

In set theory, the chromatic tones are numbered differently. If we assume a chromatic scale ascending from C, then C is 0, C-sharp is 1, D is 2, D-sharp is 3, E is 4, F is 5, F-sharp is 6, and so on. The numbers of an ordered set are usually enclosed within parentheses without the sign ^ over the individual numbers; however, the numbers should be separated from one another by commas. For example, the set (0, 4, 7, 10) would yield the configuration of intervals that, in functional harmonic music, would be a dominant-seventh chord. Although the numbers tell us about the structure of the sonority, they do not represent specific pitches, nor do they indicate how those four tones are distributed in a particular octave or voicing.

In tonal harmony, the tones of the scale may also be indicated by function: tonic, supertonic, mediant, subdominant, dominant, submediant, subtonic, and leading tone respectively. There is no need to capitalize these names. Note further that the seventh scale degree is designated as the subtonic when it is a whole tone below the tonic, but that it must be called the leading tone when it is a semitone below the tonic. Chromatic alterations of the scale degrees may be indicated either with the words "raised" and "lowered," or "sharped" and "flatted." Whichever terminology is elected should be used consistently.

251   Octave designations

Many different systems are used for indicating the disposition of a pitch within a specific octave. The easiest system—and the one that will be used in this book—is as follows.

Designate the octave beginning on middle C by capital letters without super- or subscript Arabic numbers. For octaves above the middle-C octave, add a superscript Arabic numeral 1 for the first octave above, 2 for the second, 3 for the third, and so forth. Those octaves below the middle-C octave should be accompanied by the appropriate subscript to designate the particular octave:

$$C_1 \ D_1 \ E_1 \ F_1 \ G_1 \ A_1 \ B_1$$
octave below middle C

$$C \ D \ E \ F \ G \ A \ B$$
octave of middle C

$$C^1 \ D^1 \ E^1 \ F^1 \ G^1 \ A^1 \ B^1$$
octave above middle C

More complicated than the first system, but widely used nonetheless, is that in which middle C and the tones in its octave are indicated with lowercase letters: c, d, e, f, g, a, b. For each octave above the middle-C octave, a single stroke is added beside the letter, so that the octave above the middle-C octave would be shown as c', d', e', f', g', a', b'; two octave above as c", d", e", f", g", a", b"; and so on. The tones in the octave below middle C are shown in single capital letters (C, D, E, F, G, A, B); those two octaves below in double capitals (CC); those three octaves below in triple capitals (CCC); and so on.

A third system uses signs that are identical to the second system's on the printed page, yet their meanings are very different. In this third system, middle C and the notes in its octave are indicated with lowercase letters accompanied by a single stroke: c', d', e', f', g', a', b'. As the octaves ascend, one stroke is added. The octave below middle C is represented with lowercase letters (c, d, e, f, g, a, b); and the octave below that with capital letters (C, D, E, F, G, A, B). At this point, successively lower octaves are indicated with capital letters and subscript Arabic numbers: $C_1, D_1, E_1, F_1, G_1, A_1, B_1$.

Certain other systems are used for particular instruments. Piano technicians, for example, commonly refer to the bottom three keys of the piano as A0, A-sharp0, and B0. Notes in subsequent octaves are named with the capital letter and an Arabic number placed on the base line beside it: C1, D1, E1, F1, G1, A1, B1, C2, D2, E2, and so on. In this system, middle C is shown as C4. This method of pitch citation is used by the American Acoustic Society and in many classrooms throughout the world. Despite its widespread use, however, this system of pitch identification relies upon the piano keyboard for its point of reference; consequently, the specification of sonorities below A0 is difficult or impossible. The lowest C in the pedal division of an organ with a 64-foot *Gravissima* stop (such as that on the Rufatti organ of Davies Symphony Hall in San Francisco) sounds C_5, the pitch two octaves and a sixth below A0.

Before you begin writing, ascertain from your academic institution or publisher which system is to be used. As a courtesy to the reader, indicate how that system works. This may be done either in the preface or in a note accompanying the first mention of pitches within a specific octave.

Beware: If you are quoting from a source that uses a different system from the one that you use in your own text, explain that system to the reader. It may be most convenient to do this by inserting brackets with some message, such as [our C^3]. If many of your quotations involve conflicting sources, you may prefer to provide appropriate explanatory remarks in a note.

Additional cautions are necessary: We have seen that some systems of octave designation use strokes beside the name of the tone in question. These strokes resemble single or double quotation marks. Avoid ending a quotation within the body of your text with a pitch name accompanied by these strokes. This configuration, for example, is an open invitation for miscommunication:

> Noel Straus praised the newcomer: "The soprano, in a brilliant roulade, brings the entire act to its conclusion on c‴."

252 Scales, modes

In naming any scale, use the capital letter identifying the tonic followed by the indication "major" or "minor." Do not capitalize the words "major" or "minor." When letter names are used with a mode to form a compound adjective, be sure to link the letter and qualifier with a hyphen: A-minor Sonata (*but* Sonata in A minor).

In classic modal theory, four of the eight modes are called authentic modes and four are called plagal modes. The four authentic modes take their names from regions in ancient Greece; hence, the names are proper nouns and they must be capitalized: Dorian, Phrygian, Lydian, and Mixolydian.

The plagal modes are derived from the authentic modes, but the range of each of these modes is a fourth lower than that of the related authentic mode. The prefix *hypo-* ("beneath") appearing in conjunction with the modal designation of the authentic source clarifies the relationship between each authentic mode and its plagal derivative. Note that the plagal modes too are capitalized: Hypodorian, Hypophrygian, Hypolydian, Hypomixolydian.

In many cases, Arabic numbers are used instead of the names. In such cases, the authentic modes are numbered modes 1, 3, 5, and 7 respectively, and the plagal modes are numbered 2, 4, 6, and 8.

Most other scales, such as the whole-tone scale, the pentatonic scale, the octatonic scale, and so on, are not capitalized. Certain specialized scales named after countries or regions should be capitalized. The Scottish scale, for instance, named after the compass of the Highland bagpipe, has a range from G to A^1, with C^1 and F^1 approximately a quarter-tone sharp. Another is the Gypsy, or Hungarian, scale; a Gypsy scale beginning on C consists of the pitches C, D, E^b, F#, G, A^b, and B.

253   Note values

Americans speak of whole notes, half notes, quarter notes, eighth notes, thirty-second notes, and so forth. Any one of these values may be extended by half with the addition of a dot, in which case we would refer to a dotted whole note, a dotted half note, and so on. There is generally no need to hyphenate the two elements of a note value to form a compound noun. Caution is necessary, however, when references to the "eighth" or "sixteenth" are intended as ordinal numbers rather than as arithmetic proportions:

> The violinist was utterly confused when the conductor asked her to resume at the eighth note in the phrase, because every note in the phrase was an eighth note!

Of course, when note values are used as compound adjectives, they require a hyphen:

> The eighth-note pattern in the left hand is an example of an Alberti bass.

Under *no* circumstances should the British designations of semibreve, minim, crotchet, quaver, semiquaver, demisemiquaver, hemidemisemiquaver, and semihemidemisemiquaver be used. Even many British publishers are abandoning this unwieldy manner of indicating note values.

254   Instruments

The names of many instruments are actually foreign words that have long since lost their original meanings. The piano, for example, was originally called the *gravicembalo col piano e forte* ("harpsichord with soft and loud"). Later, the name was shortened to *pianoforte* ("softloud"). Even though, technically speaking, this is the proper name for the instrument, most of us simply use the word "piano." In such cases, the rule of putting foreign words in italics is customarily suspended, even though the word is an Italian one.

This general rule, nevertheless, has exceptions, involving names that have been assimilated into common English usage in combination with an uncommon foreign-language qualifier. In these cases, italics may be used for the foreign-language portion of the name only. Some commonly encountered examples follow:

oboe *da caccia*   viola *d'amore*
oboe *d'amore*   viola *da spalla*
viola *bastarda*   viola *pomposa*
viola *da braccio*   violoncello *piccolo*
viola *da gamba*

Some instruments are named after the countries with which they are associated. The two most common examples are the French horn and the English horn. The English horn is not a horn at all, nor is it particularly English; nevertheless, the convention of capitalizing proper nouns and adjectives should be observed, even in open compounds.

255   Movement designations

When individual movements within a multi-movement composition have distinctive titles, those titles should be in Roman type and enclosed within double quotation marks, even if the movement title happens to be in a foreign language. Never use italics *and* quotation marks!

For movements without distinctive titles, tempo indications normally serve in lieu of a title:

Haydn asked that the Adagio from his Symphony in E minor, Hob. I/44, be played at his funeral, hence its nickname, *Trauersymphonie* (Mourning symphony).

Note: Since the tempo indication functions as a title, it is capitalized. Note, too, that the term is not placed in italics, its Italian etymology notwithstanding.

Sometimes movements have generic names rather than distinctive titles or tempo indications. In these cases, the generic designation should be capitalized:

The Minuet of Haydn's String Quartet, Op. 20 No. 4, shows the influence of Hungarian Gypsy music.

When genres are mentioned in a nonspecific context, do not capitalize:

The minuet was a common dance of the eighteenth century.

256 Dynamics, tempo indications, performance instructions

The conventional Italian words for dynamics, such as *pianissimo, piano, mezzo piano, mezzo forte, forte,* and *fortissimo* should always be spelled out completely. Although these terms are routinely abbreviated in musical scores, those abbreviations are inappropriate in good writing.

Dynamic indications and performance instructions in foreign languages should be put in italics. Tempo words, when they are not being used as movement titles, should also be in italic type:

Liszt's *Salve Regina* for organ solo, a paraphrase of a Gregorian plainchant, begins at a *pianissimo* and never exceeds *piano.* The tempo, *lento assai,* complements the serene character of the chant.

CHAPTER 21

Fundamentals of Music Notation

To be most effective, musical examples should be inserted at the optimal place in the discussion. For copyright restrictions that may affect the inclusion and/or location of examples, see Appendix Two; for the purposes of the present discussion, we will assume that no such restrictions apply.

First determine the format of the musical examples. It is not always necessary to show a full score, and in many cases, a reduced score may be more effective. Music for four-part mixed chorus, for example, can easily be shown on two staffs with the soprano and alto parts written in the top staff and the tenors and basses in the lower staff. If adjacent voices move in the same rhythm, they may share the same stem; if they move independently or cross one another, put stems up for the higher of the two voices and stems down for the lower voice. In cases where the voices are written in the same register and cross frequently, however, this score layout would be unsatisfactory.

In general, use the format that takes the least amount of space on the page. Remember that you can always explain in a note the characteristics of the original layout of the music. When you have done so, ask yourself if the reader could reconstruct the original score exactly from the information that you have given. A musical example that has been condensed effectively loses nothing: It functions in much the same way as an architect's scale model of a building. In both cases, the intention is to demonstrate structural and formal details to persons who are eager to understand your point, but who cannot do so without the aid of some tangible model.

Staffs, clefs, key signatures, meter signatures, and most other notation signs are variable and assume meaning only when placed in a context. Additional signs are used to indicate pitch, duration, intensity, and other musical details. The following guidelines for the placement of these signs should be sufficient for most cases; however, specialized notational signs are frequently encountered in music written in alternative systems of notation—such as tablature, shape-note notation, spatial notation, and so on. Those who require more detailed information concerning the technique, theory, and history of notation may want to consult the following sources:

Apel, Willi. *The Notation of Polyphonic Music, 900–1500;* 5th ed. Cambridge, Massachusetts: Mediaeval Academy, 1953. 464 p.; 64 musical examples.

Boustead, Alan. *Writing down Music: A Practical Guide to Preparing Music Manuscript;* reprint. New York: Oxford University Press, 1990. 137 p.

Caldwell, John. *Editing Early Music;* 2d ed. Oxford: Clarendon Press, 1995. 135 p.

Grier, James. *The Critical Editing of Music: History, Method, and Practice.* New York: Cambridge University Press, 1996. 267 p.

Heussenstam, George. *The Norton Manual of Music Notation.* New York: Norton, 1987. 168 p.

Roemer, Clinton. *The Art of Music Copying;* 2d ed. Sherman Oaks, California: Roerick Music, 1985. 207 p.

257 Staffs, clefs

For most music written from the Renaissance to the present, the five-line staff should be used. Clefs indicate the location of some particular note on the staff. The three clefs normally used are those showing the positions of G, F, and C.

If, for facility of reading, clefs must change in the course of a musical example, we generally put the new clef immediately before the first note that is to be read in that clef (Example 1). An exception is made in the case of a note that is shorter than the note value to which the beat is assigned, and preceded by a rest that completes one beat. In this context, the new clef should appear before the rest.

Example 1. Excerpt from the Ash Wednesday Responsory "Emendemus in melius," with clef change to avoid ledger lines

258   Key signatures

Key signatures are used both for modal and tonal music. Sharps and flats should be placed on the staff in the order of their appearance in the cycle of sharps and flats; namely, as we move upward through the cycle of fifths, we add sharps to the key signatures. The proper sequence of sharps is F#, C#, G#, D#, A#, E#, and B#. As we move from the neutral key of C into keys with flats in their signatures, it is understood that we are moving downward. Flats accrue in the following order: B♭, E♭, A♭, D♭, G♭, C♭, F♭. (See Example 2.)

Example 2. Succession of sharps and flats in key signatures

Key signatures should be repeated on each system of the score. If the key changes, draw a double bar, and put the new key signature *after* the double bar. Cancellation of the original key signature is unnecessary except when the new signature has no sharps or flats, as in C major or A minor. A key change at the start of a new system should be anticipated at the end of the previous system.

259   Meter signatures

Meter signatures should be placed immediately following the key signature. Do not draw a line between the upper and lower number as is customary in writing fractions. Be sure to write the meter signature on each staff of the system. Avoid the trendy practice of writing a single meter signature elongated to extend over two or more staffs.

Unlike key signatures, meter signatures should not be repeated on each system. The original meter will be presumed until a change is indicated.

When the meter changes, put the new meter signature *after* the bar line (Example 3). There is no need to use a double bar for meter changes. When such changes appear, be sure to indicate the relationship of the old beat to the new beat if they are different. In shifting from simple to compound meter, for example, if the quarter note of the former equals the dotted quarter note of the latter, show that proportional relationship directly above the bar line where the meter change is introduced. If these details are your own editorial additions, enclose them in brackets so readers will know they were not shown in the original score.

Example 3. Succession of clef, key signature, and meter signature, with change of meter signatures following the bar line

260   Chromatic alterations

Chromatic alterations—sharps, flats, or naturals not appearing in the principal key signature—traditionally apply only to the measure in which they appear. If an altered note is carried over into the following measure with a tie, the indicated alteration naturally applies to the full duration of the tied notes; however, if the note is to be altered in its subsequent appearances in the measure, the alteration sign must be repeated. If, on the other hand, the note is to return to its status as indicated in the key signature, a courtesy chromatic sign is required (Example 4).

Example 4. Chromatic alterations applied within measure and to specific octave, with courtesy natural signs

    When multiple alterations are performed on a note in a single measure—for instance, if a doubly sharped note is later stated with a single sharp—there is no need to cancel the double sharp by using a natural sign with the single sharp. The same principle applies to doubly flatted notes that are later stated with a single flat.
    Chromatic alterations applied to tones in a chord should begin at the top of the staff and move downward. The top alteration sign should be as close to the note as possible without intruding into the notehead or its stem. Moving down the chord tones, the second alteration sign should be farther to the left than the first. For the third and any remaining odd-numbered alterations, move back as much as possible to the right. For the

210

fourth and any remaining even-numbered alterations, move farther out to the left. If vertical space permits, odd- and even-numbered alteration signs may be arranged in parallel columns.

Chromatic alterations apply only to the specified note in the octave where the alteration is written; therefore, chromatic alterations of that note appearing in different octaves must be specified with the appropriate sign. Remember that chromatic alterations intended to apply to notes written under an *ottava* sign (8va) must be repeated since they are, in fact, octave displacements of the written note. To avoid confusion, be sure to give courtesy chromatic signs when chromatic alterations appearing in one octave are not intended to be used with the appearance of that note in other octaves.

261   Stems, flags, beams

Stems attached to notes above the middle line of the staff should be drawn to the left of the notehead pointing downward through the space of approximately three staff lines. Notes below the middle line should have their stems drawn to the right of the notehead, pointing upward through the space of three staff lines. Notes on the middle line may have either downward or upward stems, depending on the context in which they appear.

Stems for chords require special attention (Example 5). Naturally, the stems will be longer than those for single notes. In general, it is still advisable to maintain the space of three lines above or below the top or bottom note of the chord. Stem direction upward or downward is determined by the correct stemming for the majority of notes in a chord.

Example 5. Elongated stemming to accommodate the majority of notes

When writing two parts on a single staff, use upward stems for the upper voice and downward stems for the lower voice, regardless of the position of the notes on the staff. If the voices cross frequently, consider using a separate staff for each voice. It is generally impractical to attempt showing three voices on a single staff.

Cues are often provided in individual parts (especially in orchestral music) when it would help a player to be aware of a musical event taking place in a different part. To avoid confusion, the notes of a cue should be distinctly smaller. The stems of cue notes are *always* written pointing upward, regardless of their position on—or even above—the staff.

When using flags to show eighth notes, sixteenth notes, and smaller divisions, the flags should always be drawn to the right-hand side of the stem, regardless of whether the stem points upward or downward.

Beams join notes together into groups. Sometimes those groups are based on the meter, sometimes on the intended articulation and phrasing of the notes, and sometimes—in keyboard music for example—on the execution of those notes by the left hand or the right hand. Until recently, beams in vocal music were used to complement text declamation: When a note carried one syllable, it got one stem without a beam to any adjacent note; if, on the other hand, the note appeared in a melisma sung on one syllable, the notes of that melisma would be beamed together according to the meter, indicating that there was no change of text during the singing of the beamed notes. Contemporary practice has been more liberal in using beams, and now, vocal music tends to use the same system of beaming as instrumental music. In this style of notation, slurs can be used to show the continuation of a particular syllable.

When notes are beamed together, the general practice is to show beats. In common meter with a quarter-note pulse, eighth notes would be beamed in pairs, sixteenth notes would be in groups of four, and so on.

It is sometimes necessary to elongate the stems of beamed notes, whether upward or downward, to make a visually pleasing grouping. When more than one beam is used, as will happen with subdivisions smaller than the eighth note, the stems of each note in a beamed group should reach to the farthest beam to form a T-shaped intersection.

In asymmetrical meters, such as measures of five beats, the beams should be drawn to show clearly how the beat subdivisions are grouped. If the measure consists of three eighth-note beats plus two, for instance, the first three eighth notes or their equivalent should be beamed together, and the second two eighth notes or their equivalent should be beamed together.

262   Rests

A whole rest may fill out a measure of any meter; nevertheless, once the measure is divided into beats, the rests, like beams, should reflect the basic beat (Example 6). This axiom has two consequences: Rests are never syncopated; and rests that complete a portion of a beat should be shown even when their value might be assumed into a single rest sign of longer duration. In a measure of simple triple meter with a quarter-note beat, for example, a quarter note would require two quarter-note rests to complete the measure rather than a half-note rest.

Example 6. Rests chosen to show beats

not

When using hooks to show rests having the value of an eighth note or less, draw the hooks in the spaces of the staff, not on the lines. In contemporary practice, rests may be used in place of noteheads within a beamed grouping.

263   Systems, brackets, braces

A system of music shows all music in all voices taking place simultaneously. Systems are indicated by a single line drawn to the left of the staffs being grouped.

Brackets ([ ) within a system show groupings of instruments that function as a homogeneous unit. In a trio sonata for two violins and continuo, for example, the two violin parts should be bracketed together. Brackets would appear for similar groupings, such as a string quintet, a saxophone quartet, or the string choir of an orchestra.

A second bracket sometimes appears when instruments are grouped into pairs. The first and second oboe parts of most Classical orchestral literature, for instance, are usually written on a single staff. Where separate staffs are necessary, they are customarily grouped by a second bracket.

Many students confuse brackets and braces. The brace sign ({) is used to enclose different staffs representing a single musical instrument that plays over a wide range requiring multiple clefs and staffs. In a score for harpsichord, piano, or harp, for example, the treble and bass clefs would be grouped together by a brace.

Bar lines complement brackets. They can be extended through one or more staffs to show groups of performing forces within larger ensembles; hence, the brass choir or string choir of an orchestra would have continuous bar lines, and the bar lines for the system of S-A-T-B chorus with piano accompaniment would run through the four staffs of the chorus, cease in the blank space above the piano part, and intersect both staffs of the piano reduction. Note: Popular editions frequently leave the spaces between choral staffs blank, facilitating text underlay.

264 Ledger lines, octave transpositions

Ledger (sometimes spelled "leger") lines are a projection of lines and spaces that extend beyond the five-line staff. Ledger lines should be spaced at exactly the same distance as the lines of the principal staff.

Ledger lines appear in keyboard music primarily. They also occur in flute and violin parts when an extended passage is written high in the register; in these instances, it may be more convenient to write the music an octave lower and enclose the passage with an *ottava* sign (8va). A string of hyphens usually stretches above the notes in question. To avoid confusion, write the word *loco* ("in place") at the point where the player should begin reading in the indicated octave. This same procedure may be applied to bass lines (Example 7). In those cases, the transposition sign will be the *ottava bassa* (8vb).

Example 7. Octave transposition using *ottava bassa* and *loco*

265 Ties

Whenever possible, draw ties from one note to another, not from stem to stem. For the sake of clarity, ties should not touch the notes they connect. Tie each notehead successively when connecting notes in a series.

For single notes that are tied, the arch of the tie should be in opposition to the note stems: stems up, inverted arch; stems down, upward arch. For multiple notes that are tied, draw the curve of the note at the end of the stem in opposition to the direction of the stem, then draw the remaining outer tie in the opposite direction. For any remaining notes in the chord, place the arch of the tie in opposition to the stem. Exception: Seconds occurring within clusters should be tied in pairs, with the first pair of ties curved outward in opposition to the stem. (See Example 8.)

Chords with notes on both sides of the stem cannot be tied from notehead to notehead in the customary fashion. Do not cross stems with ties; instead, begin or end the tie as necessary at the line or space occupied by the tied note.

Example 8. Ties showing (a) seconds tied in pairs, (b) successive ties in a series of tied notes, and (c) multiple notes tied with an outward curve in opposition to their appropriate stem directions

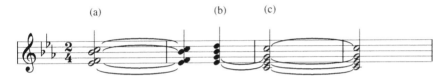

266 Slurs

Whenever possible, draw slurs from one notehead to another, without touching either. Unlike ties, slurs may be drawn from a notehead to a stem, or from a stem to a notehead when necessary. When the slur sign embraces both upward and downward stems, draw the slur line above the notes to be included.

267 Articulation marks

Most articulation marks, such as *staccato* dots, *tenuto* macrons, and *sforzando* wedges, should be placed adjacent to the notehead. Never position these signs by the stems.

Recent scores—roughly since Stravinsky—often have commas indicating a momentary break between individual notes or phrases. The comma should be placed at the end of the space proportionally assigned to the particular value. Commas should normally be placed above the staff but not touching it (Example 9). Exception: When a single staff contains more than one voice and the comma applies to one voice only, position the comma so that its meaning will be clear.

Fermatas should appear at the precise moment where the lengthening of the written value will take place; they should be written above the notes to which they apply. A fermata may be used above a notehead or above a stem. Avoid inverted fermatas.

268 Dynamics, expression indications

Dynamic markings are placed below the line to which they apply—except in keyboard notation (where the indicated dynamic level commonly applies to all staffs enclosed within the brace) and vocal music (where they are placed above the line to which they apply, so they will not be confused with text). Expression indications are placed above the line to which they apply.

Example 9. Placement of articulation marks, dynamics, and expression indications

269 Music with text

Texts should appear beneath the notes of the voice part. If more than a single voice is notated on a single staff, the text may be placed above, below, or between the voices, as clarity demands. If, for example, the soprano and alto parts are written on a single staff and the voices generally have the same text at any given time, the text should appear beneath the staff. On the other hand, if the two voices declaim the text in significantly different ways, it will be better to place the soprano text above the staff and the alto text below the staff. When four parts sing simultaneously, use two staffs. Place the soprano and alto parts in the upper staff and the tenor and bass parts in the lower staff. The text may be centrally located between the two staffs. If the declamation differs from one voice to the next, soprano and tenor texts should appear above the line, alto and bass texts below the line. If parts are divided, or if the texture is very complex, it may be more prudent to use a separate staff for each voice. In such cases, texts must appear beneath each staff—except when the voices are *divisi* and their respective rhythms differ significantly from one another.

Never divide words of a single syllable (regardless of length) or words containing bogus syllables with silent vowels (*asked; dreamed; longed;*

blessed). Exception: When the silent vowel of the conventional spoken language is intended to be sung as a vowel, the word may be divided into syllables. Music written when such pronunciations were current, or music with a deliberately archaic treatment of text will frequently involve such declamation. Church music, in particular, often requires the pronunciation of unvoiced syllables.

When positioning the text for a voice part, the division of words into syllables should conform with the syllabification given in standard dictionaries. Use hyphens to separate words into syllables:

If mu-sic be the food of love, play on.

Hyphens appearing in vocal texts may be followed by as much space as is required before the placement of the next syllable with its concomitant note in the musical line.

Melismas usually require a bit more than a hyphen to show the continuation of a given syllable. In melismatic passages, we use an extender line, directly beside the syllable that is to be prolonged. The extender continues until the point where the syllable changes.

Conventional usage of capitals and lowercase letters should be observed in vocal texts. If text appears in both the original language and in a translation, use Roman type for the original language and italic for the translation.

270   Transposing instruments

Many conventional instruments, such as the clarinet, horn, trumpet, piccolo, and double bass, are in fact transposing instruments. In the cases of the piccolo and the double bass, the transpositions are one octave higher and one octave lower respectively. For these and other instruments that transpose the line by an octave, there is generally no need to state that fact. For instruments whose transpositions are not octave duplications of the written pitches, great caution is necessary. Indicate at the left-hand side of the system the name of the instrument and the key in which it plays: Clarinet in E-flat, Horns in F, and so forth.

For the convenience of the reader, musical examples should generally be given as C scores—that is, with the pitches written accurately reflecting what will be heard as concert pitch. State clearly in a note that the score you are citing is a C score. In specialized studies—a paper concerned exclusively with the horn parts in Beethoven's Ninth Symphony, for instance—transpositions of the original parts should not be made.

271 Instrumentation

To specify the instrumentation of small ensembles, use generic designations, such as trio sonata, string quartet, or piano trio. If the instrumentation is variable, specify the precise instruments used. Remember, for example, that a string quintet may consist of two violins, two violas, and one cello (Mozart's standard string quintet scoring) or two violins, one viola, and two cellos (as in Schubert's String Quintet in C major, Op. 163, D. 956).

For large ensembles, we can use a shorthand method of specifying instrumentation according to orchestral choirs. A conventional symphony orchestra consists of the following sections:

Winds   flutes, oboes, clarinets, bassoons

Brass   horns, trumpets, trombones, tuba

Strings   first violins, second violins, violas, cellos, double basses

Percussion   timpani

Additions to this core ensemble—piccolo, English horn, bass clarinet, contrabassoon, piano, celesta, and organ, for example—are common.

When the discussion requires information about instrumentation, the aforementioned scoring is assumed. You may show the exact constitution of the choirs of winds and brass by giving the number of each type of instrument separated by a period, and the choirs separated by an en dash. When a particular instrument is not included, be certain to show a zero. For example, a wind choir of two flutes, two oboes, no clarinets, and two bassoons—standard for most of Haydn's and Mozart's symphonies—may be shown thus: 2.2.0.2. If to these winds were added two horns, two trumpets, and three trombones, but no tuba, the instrumentation would be given as follows: 2.2.0.2.–2.2.3.0.

Percussion instruments for most eighteenth-century Western European repertoire will simply be a pair of timpani, which detail is best indicated with words.

In nineteenth-century repertoire—and even more so in recent compositions—the percussion family is indeed an orchestral choir; nevertheless, its constitution is variable. Percussion instruments must, therefore, be listed individually after the timpani and before the strings.

Percussion instruments frequently require multiple players. If two, three, or four players are needed in performance, it is helpful to specify the precise number of players involved and to assemble the instruments for each player into groups, thus:

Percussion I   timpani, triangle, tambourine, tam-tam

Percussion II   glockenspiel, chimes, xylophone, marimba

Percussion III   crotales, celesta, piano

Percussion IV   side drum (without snare), side drum (with snare), tenor drum, bass drum

In musical examples, such constellations of percussion instruments should be grouped on staffs using from one to five lines. Certain percussion instruments, such as the marimba, celesta, and piano, require a grand staff.

Precise numbers of strings, for the most part, are given only in some twentieth-century repertoire, where this sort of exactitude is essential. In most cases, an indication such as "strings in four parts" or "strings in five parts" will suffice.

For additional instruments, place the appropriate information in parentheses beside the principal entry. For instance, a wind choir consisting of three flutes plus one piccolo; four oboes; four clarinets plus one bass clarinet; and four bassoons plus one contrabassoon would be shown thus: 3 (1). 4. 4 (1). 4 (1). Additional commentary may be necessary to indicate particular players who perform on more than one instrument, the constitution of the on- or offstage band, and other details.

The extraordinarily elaborate instrumentation of Stravinsky's *L'oiseau de feu* may be shown as follows:

4.4.4.4.–4.3.3.1.–triangle, snare drum, cymbals, bass drum, tam-tam, timpani, glockenspiel, xylophone, celesta, piano– 3 harps and strings of 16.16.14.8.8. Stage band of 3 trumpets, 2 tenor tubas, 2 bass tubas.

When a solo instrument is featured in a concerto-like texture, the solo part should be listed between the percussion and string choirs. If an organ part is included, it may either be listed after the strings or between the celesta and the piano.

272   Jazz, blues, gospel, rock, and Latin idioms

These diverse contemporary styles are a synthesis of Western European music and African music. Since African music evolved out of an aural tradition, and thus is not notated, discussion and representation of it by conventional means is both challenging and a bit misleading.

Pitch—particularly for what are generally called blue notes—varies depending on context. References to pitch are therefore understood to be approximate. The C blues scale, though notated as C, E♭, F, G♭, G, B♭, C, is ordinarily altered in its intonation for expressive purposes. An adjustment to pitch, whether upward or downward, is known as bending.

Improvisation is an important part of this repertoire; musical examples should therefore give chord symbols above any part where improvisation occurs. The recommended chord symbols (using a C chord as the model) are as follows:

C	major triad
C-	minor triad
C°	diminished triad
C+	augmented triad
C MA7	major-major seventh
C7	major-minor seventh (= dominant seventh)
C-7	minor-minor seventh
C-7b5	diminished-minor seventh
C°7	diminished seventh

Upper harmonic extensions can be added as needed: C7(b9,#11).

In improvised passages, chord symbols are often placed over open measures, with slashes (virgules) to designate quarter-note values where the chord is to be repeated. The virgule will always indicate quarter notes and may be used in conjunction with rests (Example 10).

Example 10. Virgules showing quarter-note rhythms of harmonies

The instruments for most ensembles in these styles should be listed in the following order: saxophones, trumpets, trombones, guitar, piano, bass, drum set. List voices, if any, above the instruments.

CHAPTER 22

Types of Scores

When we write about music, we generally imagine a performance that takes place in real time; however, most performances rely upon some sort of score. Scores are the instruction sheets that we follow to realize the composer's conception. In many cases, particularly when we are dealing with early music, we must pay particular attention to the physical details of the scores since they provide crucial information about how an original performance might have taken place.

When discussing musical sources, authors should use the appropriate terminology. The entries that follow explain some of the most common types of scores and score layouts.

273 Choirbook

Choirbooks were used mainly from the late thirteenth to the sixteenth century. Since they were intended to be used by vocal ensembles of, perhaps, a dozen or more singers, they are sometimes very large volumes, often as much as 28 inches high and 20 or more inches wide.

Choirbook layout suited both polyphonic music and the monophonic repertoire. For the polyphonic repertoire of the Notre Dame school, the tenor was usually placed at the bottom of the opened book, running across both pages on one or several staffs. The duplum, which had more syllables as well as more music to accommodate, was placed on the left-hand side; the triplum was on the right-hand side.

274 Cut-away score

Cut-away scores are widely used for twentieth-century ensemble music in full score. The staffs are arranged in their conventional order (see rule 271), but the score shows only the staffs of the instruments or voices that are actually sounding at any moment. Those parts that would be filled by rests in a traditional full score are simply cut away, leaving a blank space on the page. Good examples of cut-away scores may be seen in such late works of Stravinsky as *Movements for Piano and Orchestra* and *Requiem Canticles*.

275   Facsimile

A facsimile (from the Latin *facere*, "to make," and *similis*, "like," "in the manner of") is a reproduction that duplicates the original in every detail. A true facsimile score will reproduce all aspects of the original, including dimensions; paper type; pagination; bindings; and color or colors of ink, pencil, crayon, and other writing media. Errors in the text, physical damage to the document (missing pages, foxing, water stains, bleed-through), and other items that would normally be "corrected" in a practical edition are also reproduced with absolute fidelity.

Viewed in the most naive fashion, a facsimile is essentially a forgery: Counterfeit documents are deliberately made to be indistinguishable from the authentic original, and the better the facsimile, the less easily the counterfeit is spotted. It is, perhaps, ironic that the Roman Catholic Church pioneered the development of the facsimile score. Dom André Macquereau, working with the monks at the abbey of St. Pierre de Solesmes, undertook the publication of the series entitled *Paléographie musicale* beginning in the year 1889. By using photographic reproductions of early plainchant manuscripts, the monks sought both to justify their modern editions of the chant repertoire and to preserve and disseminate those documents among the scholarly community.

Facsimile scores preserve the appearance of a given primary source. They are important not only because they retain the visual details of the original source, but because they also—in a sense—arrest the ravages of time that diminish the usefulness of the original.

276   Full score

A full score contains all the music for all the parts, each displayed separately. This is the type of score that would be used, say, by a conductor leading a performance of a Beethoven symphony.

Except for indicating multiple measures of rest, full scores traditionally show the parts as they would be seen by the individual performers: Parts for trumpets and clarinets in B-flat are written a step higher than those of the C instruments; the English horn line appears a fifth higher than it will actually sound; and so on.

In recent times, composers and publishers have tended to write full scores at concert pitch. Be sure to state whether a score is transposed or uses concert pitch (a C score). If no particulars are given, the presumption is that the score is transposed.

The term "orchestral score" is sometimes used to mean a full score. If the term is to be used accurately, it should be reserved for references to full scores of orchestral works.

277   Open score

In the early seventeenth century, Italian composers of complex polyphonic keyboard music began writing each voice on a separate staff. The custom spread (the German composer Samuel Scheidt chose the open-score format for his three-volume *Tabulatura nova,* published in 1624) and remained popular throughout the Baroque era.

278   Parts, partbooks

When instrumentalists speak of parts, they generally mean the music that is played by a single instrument within an ensemble. A string quartet, for instance, includes parts for first and second violins, viola, and cello. The parts for these instruments will show only the music played by each individual in the ensemble. Cues showing what other instruments in the group are doing may appear from time to time, in small notes with all stems up (see rule 261). These cues clarify the musical context in which each of the parts will be performed. Musical examples written in part format generally need not include cues.

From a functional point of view, partbooks are quite similar to instrumental parts; however, the word "partbook" is usually reserved for vocal repertoire. During the Renaissance, partbooks were the standard format for polyphonic vocal music. The number of partbooks required for a performance will accord with the number of voices in the particular composition; hence, a five-part madrigal will require five partbooks. The individual books are ordinarily called by the name of the specific part (a five-part madrigal might consist of discantus, cantus primus, altus, tenor, and bassus, for example), which nomenclature can be very helpful in determining the chronological and geographical origin of a particular piece of music.

279   Piano reduction

The term "piano reduction" usually means that all music of a larger score has been written on two staffs, with the upper staff using a treble clef and the lower a bass clef. Remember, however, that this term can be misleading since merely condensing the music so that it may be *written* on two staffs in no way guarantees that it may, in fact, be *played* on the piano. A classic example of a piano reduction that is unplayable on that instrument is the tenor aria "Forward into Light" from Charles Ives's cantata *The Celestial Country*. When he issued it as No. 99 of his *114 Songs,* Ives merely crammed the instrumental parts for full orchestra and string quartet onto two staffs!

280   Piano score

A piano score is usually characterized by a layout using two staffs joined by a brace. Many composers (Liszt, Brahms, and Debussy, for example) occasionally used three staffs for their piano works. In a two-staff layout, the normal clefs are treble clef for the upper part and bass clef for the lower.

281   Table book

A good deal of music written during the sixteenth and seventeenth centuries may be performed using different combinations of instruments or voices. Some repertoire of the English lute song school, for instance, may be sung either by solo voice accompanied by the lute, or by a vocal ensemble with or without the accompaniment of the lute. To facilitate diverse types of performances, the melody was printed above the lute accompaniment on the left-hand page. On the right-hand page, a vocal bass part was printed in the central third of the space, but it was positioned to be read by a singer to the left of the lutenist/singer. The tenor and alto parts were printed in the spaces above and below the bass. The tenor part would appear upside-down to the lute player, but to the singer sitting on the opposite side of the table, the music would have been in conventional disposition. This format was used for John Dowland's *Third Book of Songs and Ayres* (London 1603).

282   Vocal score

Most vocal scores show all the vocal parts but give the orchestral music in a piano reduction. For instance, most opera scores are published as vocal scores, for use by singers. In more recent repertoire, the instrumental music may be left out almost entirely. This type of vocal score is usually cued heavily, so that singers may be certain about pitches, tempo, tonality, and other details at the various entry points.

CHAPTER 23

The Nature of Musical Sources

Before performing musicians can intelligently interpret written symbols, they must understand the score before them. As with words written on a page, the presence in a musical score of erasures, marginal notes, and scribbles may indicate that the document represents a work in progress rather than a finished product. Such internal evidence not only allows us to follow the progress of ideas from their earliest manifestation to their final form but also enables us to evaluate the relative authority of source materials. The following terms are widely used by musicians and scholars, but if these words are to communicate effectively, they must be used in a manner that is both precise and consistent.

283   Autograph

The term "autograph" is a combination of the Greek words *autos* ("self") and *graphein* ("to write"), suggesting a document written in one's own hand. Although some scholars restrict the use of the term to mean only an item that is signed by the creator, others recognize the creator's hand, with or without a signature. It is possible to have signed manuscripts, signed typescripts, or even signed printed editions; consequently, the word "autograph" is commonly used in conjunction with other technical terms.

284   Draft

A draft is a work in progress, not a finished document. It is like the finished document insofar as it presents the entire work, essentially, with the general sequence of events as they will appear in the final form. Since a draft is a composition score, it is normal to find shorthand methods of notation, abbreviations, and other time-saving devices. Draft scores very often show a great variety of parts on just two, three, or four staffs. Indications of instrumentation, tempo, and other details may appear from time to time.

285   Fair copy

When a composition is complete, the composer or an assistant will normally make a fair copy showing all details of the piece in exactly the way they are to be rendered in the printed edition of the piece. The fair copy is the document that publishers use as the basis of their publication of that work.

286   Holograph

The Greek words *holos* ("whole," "entire") and *graphein* ("to write") combine to form the word "holograph." A holograph is any document written entirely in the hand of its creator—whether a composer, poet, novelist, essayist, or what have you. The term "holograph" gives no clue about the status of the work, and we have holograph drafts (such as Schubert's draft of the song cycle *Winterreise*) as well as holograph fair copies.

287   Manuscript

When used in the strict sense, the word "manuscript," from the Latin *manus* ("hand") and *scribere* ("to write"), refers to any handwritten document. The simple fact of a document's being handwritten does not necessarily impart to it authority, historical significance, or financial or artistic worth. On the other hand, we have a good deal of information relating to the copyists who assisted many of the great composers. In such cases, the distinctive features of a particular copyist's musical penmanship may provide adequate evidence to establish the authority, historical significance, and cash value of a particular score.

288   Sketch

The typical musical sketch—consisting of a brief melody, a two- or three-note motif, a short succession of chords—may be compared with a single sentence, a clause or phrase, or even a single word. Ideas are not expressed in any particular context, nor is it possible to determine how such fragments will be used in the larger context of a musical composition.

APPENDIX ONE

Sample Paper and Abstract

Formal Paradigms for Monteverdi's "Possente spirto"

Mark A. Radice

"Possente spirto," Monteverdi's virtuoso aria from Act III of L'Orfeo, is a stellar example of the strophic-variation technique beloved of early seventeenth-century Italian composers. In this form the bass line repeats unchanged, or with only slight rhythmic modifications, while above it are distinctive rhythms, predictable phrases, and catchy melodic motifs echoed in witty imitations.

Orfeo's impassioned prayer to Charon is the crux of the drama,[1] and indeed the form of "Possente spirto" is distinctive both for its extraordinary complexity and its dramatic force. Never does Monteverdi repeat the bass line exactly, nor are the strophic modifications slight (see Example 1).[2] Instrumental interludes, over yet another repeating bass line, separate its first four verses, yielding two sets of strophic variations, one vocal and the other instrumental. The fifth stanza is set freely, interrupting the pattern, with a new bass line and a basso continuo accompaniment only. The strophic variation resumes in the sixth and final stanza, with a different versification.

Example 1. Monteverdi, "Possente spirto," bass lines of vocal strophes 1--3

The aria's effect depends equally on its departures from standard strophic-variation design and on its allusions to other contemporaneous vocal music forms. The resulting hybrid, though novel, is sufficiently allied with conventions of the day to have been immediately comprehensible to seventeenth-century listeners. To understand Monteverdi's conception of "Possente spirto," we must know the formal paradigms that were familiar to him.

Text-Tone Relationships in the Later Sixteenth Century: The Falsobordone as a Genre

The reforms of the Council of Trent (1545--1563) made clarity in text setting a central issue for composers working within the Roman Catholic Church. With this emphasis came a burgeoning of falsobordoni: harmonizations of monophonic recitation formulas adorned with sixteenth-century cadential patterns. The recitation patterns of early falsobordoni were Gregorian psalm tones (or near paraphrases); in later repertoire, melodies were newly composed.

Formal Aspects of Plainchant Recitation Formulae and Falsobordoni

At their simplest, falsobordoni are in two sections, each consisting of a recitation on one chord followed by a cadence.[3] Most drop the opening melodic gesture and proceed directly to the first recitation tone, which lasts for a single syllable or longer, depending on the text. Since both segments commence with a recitation, at least two points have variable durations.

Tempo and rhythm too are adaptable. According to Giovanni Luca Conforti, a chorister at the Sistine Chapel and author of several collections of ornamented falsobordoni,

> From the beginning of the verse up to the line with two dots, even if written in measured time, you can sing without [a strict meter], but from these two dots up to the first dot of the words of the verse and of the end you must always sing with a beat. 4

Murray Bradshaw notes that Conforti often "springs" the music from its "metrical straightjacket" by adding notes or even beats to a bar.[5]

Texts

The plainchant model varied depending on the context and genre of the text being sung:

> The tones for the introit are . . . more elaborate than those for the Psalms. . . . Still more elaborate are the tones for the Invitatory. . . . The eight tones for the great responsories . . . are . . . distinctly more elaborate. Intonations, unlike those for the Psalms, are adjusted for text accent. Except in the fifth mode, the reciting pitch is different in the two halves, though the elaborate character of the intonations and cadences greatly reduces the prominence of the reciting tones, especially for shorter texts. 6

Psalms were the texts most often sung as falsobordoni; the tones for

the canticles are similar. The variability of the chant recitations and the
freedom shown by composers in writing falsobordone melodies led to a
"blurring . . . between the halves of the verse, [and a] softening of the
distinction between recitation and cadence."[7]

Performance Practice during the Late Renaissance and Early Baroque
The classic falsobordone with syllabic declamation was an invitation
for improvisation, particularly when lengthy texts necessitated the
repetition of straightforward musical ideas. Even within the plainchant
tradition, elaborate tones were associated with high feast days of
the liturgical year, whereas simple tones were heard on lesser feasts.
The ornamentation of liturgical recitative was, therefore, part of a
continuing tradition rather than a sixteenth-century innovation.

Musicians elaborated polyphonic recitation formulae by
distributing texts among dissimilar forces, such as solo voices and
choral ensembles---the practice of alternatim. Another variant was
for one chorus to sing a simple falsobordone for the odd- or even-
numbered verses and another to sing the alternate verses either in
plainchant (a second falsobordone, resulting in a so-called double tune)
or in a polyphonic setting.

Although it was often included in falsobordoni performances, for
certain austere liturgies the organ remained silent. When organ was
used in alternatim, the organist might imply the unsung texts by using
the appropriate plainchant for interludes between sung verses. It was
also possible to insert an instrumental verset after every other sung
verse.[8] In other words, the singing of the complete text was punctuated
by instrumental ritornellos.

Many title pages invite the addition ad libitum of various instruments to enhance the performance of falsobordoni. Hortensio Naldi says that his falsobordoni are "well suited to be sung by voices or with all sorts of instruments" (tum viva voce tum omni instrumentorum genere cantatu cum commodissimi).[9]Another way of elaborating falsobordoni is to ornament either the recitation formulae themselves or their harmonizations. Both vocalists and instrumentalists may improvise passaggi to highlight a particular word or melodic motif.

Ornamentation of Solo Vocal Falsobordoni: Severi's Salmi passaggiati

The Perugian singer and composer Francesco Severi (b. ca. 1595) is responsible for an especially important collection of ten embellished falsobordoni, published in Rome by Nicolo Borboni in 1615. As Bradshaw observes,

> Conforti's publications were clearly a model for Severi's psalms. . . . [Both] collections . . . are devoted entirely to embellished falsobordoni; . . . both [were] written by members of the Sistine Chapel; both have, to a certain extent, a teaching purpose; both use the ornament sign t for trillo . . . and both are intended for direct use in the liturgy. 10

Severi frequently uses thirty-second notes in his passaggi.[11] In rare instances, the beat is divided as far as the sixty-fourth note.

Apart from their embellishments, Severi's falsobordoni are quite simple. As Example 2 shows, bass lines repeat unchanged or with only slight rhythmic modifications.[12] When the ornamented vocal lines and their bass are combined in performance, however, a more complex design emerges, one that is virtually indistinguishable from that of the strophic variation. Here, then, in the embellished falsobordoni of the late sixteenth and early seventeenth centuries, Monteverdi found his primary model for "Possente spirto."[13]

Example 2. Severi, "Dixit Dominus" from Salmi passaggiati per tutte le voci, bass lines, primo tuono

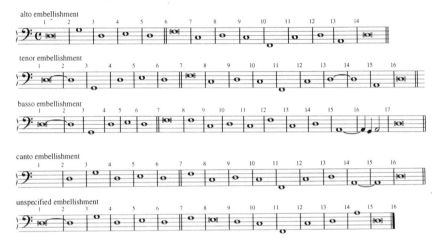

The Relationship between the Falsobordone and "Possente spirto"

The similarities between strophic variations like "Possente spirto" and falsobordone clarify certain structural details. In the case of this aria, the origin of the interludes, which are not ordinarily a part of strophic variation, becomes clear: When psalms were sung in alternatim, the verses of text could either be replaced by, or sung in alternation with, instrumental versets. What is remarkable about Monteverdi's interludes is that they too are built over a recurring bass line of G_2, D_1, C_1, G_2, D_1, G_2.[14] Though the pitch content of this bass line accords with the bass line of the vocal strophes, it is clearly an independent line, not a continuation of the same line.

The text for this aria suggests further associations with psalmody and the falsobordone tradition. The biblical lament is invariably both a song of praise and an appeal for divine intervention; nearly a third of the psalms in the Psalter may be so classified.[15] "Possente spirto" is a lamentation over the death of Euridice, addressed to a deity both as a laud and as a desperate plea for assistance. In fact, Proserpina refers to Orfeo's "lament" in her address to Plutone at the opening of Act IV. Another parallel to psalmody is the reference to the mythological singer Orpheus, who tamed wild beasts with his lyre: He may be compared with the biblical singer David, who soothed Saul with his music.

Distinctive Features of Striggio's Poem

The text of "Possente spirto," by Alessandro Striggio the Younger, is neither taken from the Bible nor adorned with biblical phrases; nevertheless, it is striking---indeed stylized---in its versification and form:

Possente spirto, e formidabil nume,
(Mighty spirit and wondrous deity,
Senza cui far passaggio a l'altra riva
without whom passage to the other shore
Alma da corpo sciolta invan presume,
a spirit separated from the body vainly awaits,)

Non vivo io, no che poi di vita è priva
(I do not live, not I; for since of life deprived is
Mia cara sposa, il cor non è più meco,
my dear wife, my heart no longer is with me,
E senza cor com'esser può ch'io viva?
and without a heart, how can it be possible that I live?)

A lei volt'ho il cammin per l'aer cieco,
(To her I have made my path through the dark air,

A l'inferno non già, ch'ovunque stassi
<u>yet not to hell, for wherever it may be,</u>
Tanta bellezza il paradiso ha seco.
<u>so much beauty is accompanied by paradise.)</u>

Orfeo son io, che d'Euridice i passi
<u>(Orfeo am I, who Euridice's footsteps</u>
Segue per queste tenebrose arene,
<u>follow through this dark wasteland,</u>
Ove già mai per uom mortal non vassi.
<u>where never mortal being has trod.)</u>

O de le luci mie luci serene,
<u>(O of my vision the vision most serene,</u>
S'un vostro sguardo può tornarmi in vita,
<u>if your gaze can return me to life,</u>
Ahi, chi niega il conforto a le mie pene?
<u>ah, who would deny this comfort for my pains?)</u>

Sol tu, nobile Dio, puoi darmi aita,
<u>(Only you, noble god, can give me help.</u>
Né temer dei, ché sopra un'aurea cetra
<u>Nor needest thou fear, o god, since upon the golden lyre</u>
Sol di corde soavi armo le dita
<u>only some sweet strings are the armaments of my fingers</u>
Contra cui rigida alma invan s'impetra.
<u>against which the most impervious soul vainly fortifies itself.)</u>

For the first five verses Striggio chose <u>terza rima,</u> a series of tercets with eleven-syllable lines arranged in pentameter. The stanzas display an interlocking rhyme scheme in the pattern <u>aba</u> I <u>bcb</u> I <u>cdc</u> I <u>ded</u> I <u>efe,</u> which versification is unique to this point in the libretto.

Monteverdi's and Striggio's audience would have been familiar with this versification from Dante's <u>Divine Comedy,</u> which consists of one hundred cantos in <u>terza rima.</u> By the time Striggio wrote the libretto for <u>L'Orfeo,</u> Dante's poem, written between 1314 and 1321, had acquired a literary status something akin to Scripture; it was, in fact, during the sixteenth century that the adjective <u>Divina</u> was added to Dante's original title, <u>Commedia.</u>

Striggio clearly intended to recall Dante. He ensures that the link will be made by quoting, moments before the aria, what is probably the most famous line from Dante's masterpiece: "Abandon all hope, ye who enter" (<u>Lasciate ogni speranza, voi ch'entrate</u>). Striggio knew that <u>terza rima</u> would effectively highlight Orfeo's lament, but Monteverdi, as the composer, required a similarly powerful association for his music. Falsobordone provided exactly that: a musical style that was not only flexible but also rich in associations and allegorical significance.

The stanzaic design of <u>terza rima</u> and the natural division of lines in psalms sung as falsobordone, however, are greatly at odds: Psalm texts often consist of paired sentences built with antecedent and consequent phrases. The tercets of Striggio's poem are not so formally balanced, nor could they be effectively sung to genuine falsobordone patterns. Monteverdi achieved musical balance by inserting the interludes among the first four verses. Each, in effect, compensates for a "missing" line of text. Moreover, he uses the moment at the conclusion of the fourth verse, where an interlude might have occurred, to great effect by plunging headlong into the fifth verse: with a single, unadorned melodic line; the sole accompaniment of basso continuo; and a new bass line that concludes with a chromatic descent beneath the last line of the stanza.

These three changes to musical texture highlight the text. That clarity is appropriate at this point both because the fifth stanza contains Striggio's most powerful lines of poetry and because it states Orfeo's dilemma more succinctly than any other verse of the poem.

In the sixth verse, the original bass line returns, but the poetic form of the stanza is different: Striggio now writes a quatrain with the rhyme scheme fgfg, in which the f rhymes continue the pattern of the interlocking tercets. The quatrain might be viewed as a tercet in terza rima with an added line; however, grammatically, it is clearly a four-line stanza. For the last line of the quatrain, Monteverdi adds seven bass notes---corresponding roughly with the duration of one statement of the interlude---to accommodate the extra line of text.

The dramatic impact of "Possente spirto" is due primarily to Orfeo's circumstances in the unfolding scenario; however, both Striggio and Monteverdi have intensified our perception of his predicament with subtle poetic and musical structures, each with specific associations for the members of the Accademia degl'Invaghiti who attended that first performance in February of 1607. At times, the poetry provides continuity where the music is surprising (in the fifth stanza, where the terza rima continues while the bass line is new); elsewhere the music creates cohesion even as the poetry evades the expected (in the sixth stanza, where the tercets are replaced by a quatrain, but the strophic bass line resumes). (See Example 3.)

Example 3. Monteverdi, "Possente spirto," bass lines from strophes 5 and 6

Implications

The coexistence of two vocal lines in the first four verses of "Possente spirto" has posed problems in performance. Some scholars offer that Monteverdi provided an alternative against the unavailability of a virtuoso singer, others that the ornamented melody is merely a suggested embellishment---not necessarily one that should be followed at each performance.[16] If a performer <u>does</u> use Monteverdi's <u>passaggi</u>---as most modern performers do---is the performer expected to continue with an ornamented vocal line in the last two strophes? Or did Monteverdi intend for the ornaments to stop at this point?

I have already suggested that late sixteenth- and early seventeenth-century church music provided Monteverdi with the falsobordone as the formal model for strophic variation, and <u>salmi passaggiati</u> as the model for virtuosic solo song. The idioms of church music offered a musical language whose affective significance would have been understood by Monteverdi's audience, and the allusion to <u>musica da chiesa</u> would have been strengthened by the sound of the <u>organo di legno</u> required in the score.

If these associations were in Monteverdi's mind as he wrote "Possente spirto," then contemporaneous performance practices of church music might provide answers to our questions. An important clue appears in Adriano Banchieri's <u>Conclusioni nel suono dell'organo</u> (Conclusions for playing the organ), published in Bologna in 1608. Perhaps the unadorned melody that concludes "Possente spirto" was inspired by this custom, described by Banchieri in the expanded 1609 edition:

> In the Requiem Mass one is not to play the organ. . . . It is, however, customary at some funerals of Prelates or principal dignitaries to play the organ, but not as an organ, but rather with a serious, full sound for the devoted people, using the Principal alone, <u>without including diminutions,</u> and with the case-doors closed. 17

This examination of the score and text of "Possente spirto" has pointed out many poetic and musical allusions---references too numerous to be dismissed as coincidental---that were included in L'Orfeo as a means of engaging the listeners in an affective and personal way. Whether conscious of these allusions or not, Monteverdi's early seventeenth-century listeners would have been familiar with the liturgical customs of the church. They could hardly have avoided assuming the emotional posture that these allusions to ecclesiastical music would have suggested. While this <u>favola per musica</u> has long been regarded as a groundbreaking achievement in the annals of opera, it must, at the same time, be recognized that both the poet and the composer spoke to their audience within their own cultural milieu, employing diverse elements of the customs, the rituals, and the traditions of the age; however, their singular achievement is this: They used the familiar for unfamiliar ends, and in so doing, imbued the familiar with an ineffaceable dramatic vitality and an enduring stamp of veracity.

Abstract

Monteverdi intended "Possente spirto" as the dramatic and musical centerpiece of his opera L'Orfeo. An examination of the aria reveals that in it, both he and librettist Alessandro Striggio the Younger used, from their respective arts, established formal features that would have been easily recognized by early seventeenth-century Italian audiences. Monteverdi turned to the florid solo song of the Roman Catholic Church as practiced in the various salmi passaggiati of late Renaissance falsobordoni settings. Here he found not only the model for his vocal ornamentation but also the fundamental architectonics for his set of strophic variations. When viewed as an offshoot of the falsobordone, the structure of "Possente spirto" assumes new significance. Further, documents bearing on early seventeenth-century performance practices for church music provide vital clues both for the performance of this aria and for the interpretation of affective signals embedded within its musical materials.

Notes

1 See Monteverdi's letter of 9 December 1616, probably written to Alessandro Striggio, in Paolo Fabbri, Monteverdi; trans. Tim Carter (Cambridge University Press, 1994), p. 149.
2 The barring in Example 1 is based on Gian Francesco Malipiero, ed., L'Orfeo, vol. 11 in Tutte le opere di Claudio Monteverdi (Vienna: Universal Edition, n.d.), pp. 84--94. I have aligned pitches rather than bars to demonstrate the significantly different durations of particular pitches.
3 Murray C. Bradshaw, "Falsobordone," New Grove Dictionary of Music and Musicians; ed. Stanley Sadie (London: Macmillan, 1980), vol. 6, p. 375.
4 Cited and translated by Murray C. Bradshaw in Giovanni Luca Conforti: Salmi passaggiati 1601--1603 (Stuttgart: Hänssler Verlag, 1985), p. li.
5 Ibid., p. lii.
6 Richard F. French, "Psalm Tone," The New Harvard Dictionary of Music (Cambridge, Massachusetts: Belknap Press of Harvard University Press, 1986), p. 667.
7 Murray C. Bradshaw, The Falsobordone (Stuttgart: Hänssler Verlag, 1978), p. 78. Though here he speaks of keyboard intonation, Bradshaw's comments are equally valid when applied to other mutations of the falsobordone.

8 Murray C. Bradshaw, ed. Francesco Severi: Salmi passaggiati, Vol. 38 (Madison, Wisconsin: A-R Editions, 1981), in Recent Researches in the Music of the Baroque Era, p. xiii.

9 Hortensio Naldi, Psalmi omnes (Venice: Ricciardo Amadino, 1606).

10 Bradshaw, Francesco Severi: Salmi passaggiati, p. x.

11 Ibid. Bradshaw reproduces as Plate V a page from the 1615 edition of Severi's psalms, in which thirty-second notes and the t for trillo are clearly visible.

12 Ibid. The bass lines in Example 2 are as given in Bradshaw's edition of Severi; see note 8 for a full citation of this source.

13 Monteverdi would have been well acquainted with falsobordone by the time he composed L'Orfeo. See John Bettley, "North Italian Falsobordone and Its Relevance to the Early stile recitativo," Proceedings of the Royal Music Association 103 (1996--97), 10.

14 Capital letters denote tones in the octave of middle C; subscript numbers designate octaves below.

15 Arthur Weiser, The Psalms; trans. Herbert Hartwell (Philadelphia: Westminster Press, 1962), p. 66.

16 Elaine Brody, Music in Opera (Englewood Cliffs, New Jersey: Prentice Hall, 1970), p. 18. See also Robert Donington, "Monteverdi's First Opera," The Monteverdi Companion; ed. Denis Arnold and Nigel Fortune (New York: Norton, 1968), pp. 266--270.

17 Lee R. Garrett, trans., Adriano Banchieri, Conclusions for Playing the Organ: 1609; ed. Albert Seay (Colorado Springs: Colorado College Music Press, 1982), in Colorado College Music Press Translations, p. 13. Emphasis mine.

Selected Bibliography

Banchieri, Adriano. Conclusions for Playing the Organ: 1609. Trans. Lee R. Garrett, ed. Albert Seay. Colorado College Music Press Translations. Colorado Springs: Colorado College Music Press, 1982. 60 p.

Bettley, John. "North Italian Falsobordone and Its Relevance to the Early stile recitativo." Proceedings of the Royal Music Association 103 (1976--77), 1--18.

Bradshaw, Murray C. The Falsobordone: A Study in Renaissance and Baroque Music. Stuttgart: Hänssler Verlag, 1978. 212 p.

-------. "Falsobordone." New Grove Dictionary of Music and Musicians. Ed. Stanley Sadie. London: Macmillan, 1980. Vol. 6, p. 375.

-------, ed. Francesco Severi: Salmi passaggiati, Vol. 38. Recent Researches in the Music of the Baroque Era. Madison, Wisconsin: A-R Editions, 1981. 76 p.

-------. Giovanni Luca Conforti: Salmi passaggiati 1601--1603. Stuttgart: Hänssler Verlag, 1985. 249 p.

Brody, Elaine. Music in Opera: A Historical Anthology. Englewood Cliffs, New Jersey: Prentice Hall, 1970. 604 p.

Donington, Robert. "Monteverdi's First Opera." The Monteverdi Companion. Ed. Denis Arnold and Nigel Fortune. New York: Norton, 1968. Pp. 257--276.

Fabbri, Paolo. Monteverdi. Trans. Tim Carter. Cambridge University Press, 1994. 350 p.

French, Richard F. "Psalm Tone." The New Harvard Dictionary of Music. Ed. Don M. Randel. Cambridge, Massachusetts: Belknap Press of Harvard University Press, 1986. Pp. 665--668.

Naldi, Hortensio. Psalmi omnes, qui . . . in solemnitatibus decantari solent. Venice: Ricciardo Amadino, 1606.

Weiser, Arthur. The Psalms. Trans. Herbert Hartwell. Philadelphia: Westminster Press, 1962. 841 p.

A Note on Copyright

Nonfiction writing presents information so that certain conclusions emerge. To ensure that our conclusions are valid—or as close to valid as they can possibly be—we generally try to assemble a broad database, drawing on a wide variety of sources, some contemporary, some historical. In either case, it is our obligation to indicate to the reader what sources we have consulted. An overview of the concepts of exclusive rights and fair use will provide a working understanding of the legal and ethical responsibilities assumed by writers when they turn to copyrighted sources for information.

The Copyright Law of 1976

Before authors begin writing—in fact, before they even select a topic—they should carefully consider the implications of copyright restrictions on their work. These restrictions, known commonly as exclusive rights, may limit the amount, character, and uses of the protected material that a writer may wish to use. The following discussion is intended as a basic introduction to the subject of copyright.

The copyright laws of the United States of America are regularly updated to take into account unfolding technological developments that may be used for the storage or transmission of information. The present law is contained in Title 17 of the United States Code, and it, along with Transitional and Supplementary Provisions, was signed by President Gerald R. Ford on 19 October 1976 as Public Law 94-553, 90 Statute 2541. The law allowed 1977 as a transitional year; hence, it did not became fully effective until 1 January 1978.

At some point, particularly if commercial publication is involved, it may be necessary for authors to obtain more detailed information. Information specialists at the United States Copyright Office are available weekdays from 8:30 a.m. until 5:00 p.m. Eastern Standard Time at (202)

707-5959; to access their recorded information system, phone (202) 707-3000. The Copyright Office provides at no charge a variety of circulars in which aspects of the copyright law are explained; authors should address their request for publications to the Publications Section, LM-455, Copyright Office, Library of Congress, Washington, D.C. 20559-6000.

For a paperback reprint of the chapters of Title 17 concerning copyright, contact the Superintendent of Documents, P.O. Box 371954, Pittsburgh, PA 15250-7954; the volume may also be ordered by phone at (202) 512-1800.

Subject Matter of Copyright

Copyright protection covers original works of authorship fixed in any tangible medium of expression, now known or later developed, from which they can be perceived, reproduced, or otherwise communicated. Works of authorship include the following categories:

1. literary works;
2. musical works, including any accompanying words;
3. dramatic works, including any accompanying music;
4. pantomimes and choreographic works;
5. pictorial, graphic, and sculptural works;
6. motion pictures and other audiovisual works;
7. sound recordings; and
8. architectural works.

Copyright protection *does not* extend to any idea, procedure, process, system, method of operation, concept, principle, or discovery, as distinguished from the particular arrangement in which such idea, procedure, process, system, method of operation, concept, principle, or discovery is described, explained, illustrated, or embodied. See 17 U.S.C. Section 102. Thus, while a particular idea or method set forth in a book or other medium is not covered by a copyright, the author's particular form of expressing such idea or method is covered.

Copyright protection is not available for government publications. Writers may use government publications freely; nevertheless, customary documentation of sources is appropriate.

Establishing Copyright Protection

Copyright is secured automatically when a work is fixed in some tangible form. Establishing copyright does not require publication, registration, or any other formal action with the Copyright Office. Formally registering a copyright, however, has many advantages, including the creation of a public record of copyright claim, various benefits in case of an infringement lawsuit, and protection against importation of infringing materials. Registration is made with the Copyright Office in Washington, D.C.

Exclusive Rights of Copyright Holders

The owner of a copyright has the exclusive right to

1. reproduce the copyrighted work;
2. prepare derivative works;
3. distribute copies of the work;
4. perform the work publicly; and
5. display the work publicly.

See 17 U.S.C. Section 106.

Limitations of Exclusive Rights

Notwithstanding the enumeration of exclusive rights just set forth, consumers have certain rights that allow particular uses or applications of copyrighted materials. These rights, generally considered, are referred to as fair use. Fair use may include reproduction of copyrighted materials for purposes such as criticism, comment, news reporting, teaching (including multiple copies for classroom use), scholarship, or research. In determining whether the use of a copyrighted work in any particular case is fair use, certain factors must be considered, among them:

1. the purpose and character of the use, including whether such use is of a commercial nature or is for nonprofit educational purposes;
2. the nature of the copyrighted work;
3. the amount and substantiality of the portion used in relation to the copyrighted work as a whole; and

4. the effect of the use upon the potential market for or value of the copyrighted work.

See 17 U.S.C. Section 107.

The first criterion addresses whether the reproduction or distribution of the copyrighted work has any purpose of direct or indirect commercial advantage. The realization of profit by the user or any person associated with the use of copyrighted matter would weigh against the application of fair-use rights.

Criteria 2 and 3 deal with the nature of the work and the amount used, and whether a self-contained component of a work (such as a chapter of a book, an aria in an opera or oratorio, a song in a musical, or an article in a periodical) is excerpted. If the item excerpted represents a self-contained unit, the excerpt would probably not fall under the category of fair use. When the excerpted portion is not a self-contained unit, it may be used only if it is not a considerable portion of the original copyrighted work.

The meaning of "considerable portion" becomes clear when considering criterion 4: the effect of the use upon the potential market or value of the copyrighted item. If reproduction or distribution of the copyrighted excerpt in any way diminishes the commercial value of the original, then such reproduction or distribution may well be a violation of exclusive rights.

In certain cases, such as the extraction of several lines from a poem, even the use of a very small portion of the copyrighted item may constitute a significant amount, if that amount compromises the viability of the original copyrighted material on the commercial market.

Particular limitations on exclusive rights are covered in sections 107–120 of the statute. Before using copyrighted materials, authors should consider these limitations carefully.

If your writing contains *any* copyrighted material, it may be necessary for you to obtain written permission for the reproduction and distribution of that copyrighted matter. Remember that "reproduction and distribution" in this case could include instances such as making multiple copies for distribution in a class or at a conference; making multiple copies for academic committee members who review theses and dissertations; and even providing a master copy for University Microfilms Incorporated (UMI). Since UMI is an organization that reproduces and distributes dissertations to scholars, they are prohibited from reproducing or distributing any dissertations that contain copyrighted material.

Duration of Copyright

Under the law in effect prior to 1978, the copyright period lasted for twenty-eight years from the date that copyright was secured. Such works were eligible for a renewal of copyright for another twenty-eight years. This system of copyright duration was modified for works already under copyright at the time of the 1976 statute; specifically, the renewal period was extended from twenty-eight years by an additional period of nineteen years for a total of forty-seven years. As a consequence, the maximum duration of copyright protection was extended from fifty-six years to seventy-five years.

According to the current copyright law, any work that was created on or after 1 January 1978 is protected for the lifetime of the author plus an additional fifty years (see 17 U.S.C. Section 302). In those cases where the identity of the author cannot be determined (as will sometimes be the case with documents prepared by employees as part of their job responsibilities [i.e., works for hire], anonymous works, and some pseudonymous works), the duration of copyright protection will be seventy-five years from publication or one hundred years from creation, whichever is shorter.

Logistics of Combining Copyrighted and Original Material

If you will be using copyrighted matter in your essay, be certain that you keep the copyrighted matter separate from your own work. By so doing, you ensure that your original work may legally be reproduced. Consider placing brief excerpts of copyrighted material in an appendix. If the copyrighted matter is extensive, it might be more convenient to place it in a separate volume. A note referring the reader to the copyrighted sources from which you cite information will suffice. If the references to copyrighted items are too numerous to include in a note, a list or table of sources may be more practical.

Copyrighted items that are reproduced in your essay with permission must be clearly identified as such. The statement of copyright should use either the conventional symbol © or the word "copyright." In addition, the year of first publication should be given along with the name of the owner of the copyright. In many cases, the copyright owner will require a specific formulation, such as "used by permission," "courtesy of," or something similar. This wording should be reproduced exactly.

These four elements of copyright information may appear in various places. In book-length documents, the acknowledgments section of the front matter is often a convenient place. In shorter documents, these details might appear in either a legend beneath the copyrighted excerpt, or in a footnote or endnote.

Bibliography

Baker, Sheridan Warner. *Practical Stylist.* 3d ed. New York: T. Y. Crowell, 1973. 182 p.

Barzun, Jacques. *Simple and Direct.* Rev. ed. New York: Harper & Row, 1985. 291 p.

Bishop, Wendy, ed. *Elements of Alternate Style: Essays on Writing and Revision.* Portsmouth, New Hampshire: Boynton/Cook Publishers, 1997. 185 p.

Elbow, Peter. *Writing with Power: Techniques for Mastering the Writing Process.* New York: Oxford University Press, 1981. 384 p.

Gibaldi, Joseph. *MLA Handbook for Writers of Research Papers.* 4th ed. New York: The Modern Language Association of America, 1995. 293 p.

-------. *MLA Style Manual and Guide to Scholarly Publishing.* 2d ed. New York: The Modern Language Association of America, 1998. 343 p.

Grossman, John, ed. *Chicago Manual of Style: The Essential Guide for Writers, Editors, and Publishers.* 14th ed. University of Chicago Press, 1993. 921 p.

Helm, Eugene, and Albert T. Luper. *Words and Music: Form and Procedure in Theses, Dissertations, Research Papers, Book Reports, Programs, Theses in Composition.* Rev. ed. Totowa, New Jersey: European American Music Corporation, 1982. 91 p.

Holoman, D. Kern. *Writing about Music: A Style Sheet from the Editors of 19th-Century Music.* Berkeley and Los Angeles: University of California Press, 1988. 61 p.

Irvine, Demar. *Writing about Music.* 2d ed. Seattle, Washington: University of Washington Press, 1968. 211 p.

New York Public Library Writer's Guide to Style and Usage. New York: HarperCollins, 1994. 838 p.

Turabian, Kate L. *Manual for Writers of Term Papers, Theses, and Dissertations.* 6th ed. University of Chicago Press, 1996. 308 p.

Wingell, Richard J. *Writing about Music: An Introductory Guide.* 2d ed. Englewood Cliffs, New Jersey: Prentice Hall, 1997. 160 p.

Index

Subheads have been kept to a minimum here since particular aspects of broader topics—such as "bibliography" and "notes"—have been enumerated in the table of contents (cf.). Pages given in italics contain illustrations.

Web sites
  in bibliography, 95–96
  in notes, 67–68
words
  as music, 197–206
  as words, 29–30, 39–40, 125, 135, 139

years, 32, 43, 47, 146
  in bibliographic imprint
    information, 74, 78–79
  in note imprint information, 54, 63
  See also dates

About the Author and Editor

Demar Irvine, an eminent and experienced researcher, writer, composer, and musician, earned his Ph.D. in music esthetics at Harvard University; in 1937 he joined the faculty of the University of Washington School of Music, where he became professor emeritus in 1978. He died in 1995, shortly after Amadeus Press published his definitive biography of Jules Massenet.

Mark A. Radice, a musicologist and composer, completed his Ph.D. at the Eastman School of the University of Rochester in 1984. He edited *Opera in Context* (Amadeus Press, 1998), a collection of essays; other publications include *Plainchant Christmas Melodies for Organ* (Warner Bros., 1998) and the forthcoming *A Concise History of Chamber Music*, also from Amadeus Press. He is on the faculty of the Ithaca College School of Music in Ithaca, New York, where he resides.